Globalizing People Through International Assignments

Globalizing People Through International Assignments

J. Stewart Black
Center for Global Assignments

Hal B. Gregersen
Brigham Young University

Mark E. Mendenhall
The University of Tennessee at Chattanooga

Linda K. Stroh
Loyola University Chicago

 **ADDISON-WESLEY**

An imprint of Addison Wesley Longman, Inc.

Reading, Massachusetts • Menlo Park, California • New York • Harlow, England
Don Mills, Ontario • Sydney • Mexico City • Madrid • Amsterdam

Executive Editor: Michael Roche
Associate Editor: Ruth Berry
Editorial Assistant: Adam Hamel
Production Supervisor: Louis C. Bruno, Jr.
Senior Marketing Manager: Julia Downs
Senior Marketing Coordinator: Joyce Cosentino
Cover Designer: Regina Hagen
Cover Illustration: © PhotoSphere Images Ltd.
Print Buyer: Sheila Spinney
Composition and Prepress Services: Pre-Press Company, Inc.
Printer and Binder: Banta Book Group
Cover Printer: Coral Graphics

This book is in the Addison-Wesley Series on Human Resource
Management.
Consulting Editor: John Parcher Wanous

Library of Congress Cataloging-in-Publication Data

Globalizing people through international assignments / J. Stewart
Black . . . [et al.].
    p. cm. — (Addison-Wesley series on managing human
resources)
    Includes bibliographical references and index.
    ISBN 0-201-43389-3 (pbk.)
    1. International business enterprises—Personnel management.
    2. Employment in foreign countries.   3. Cross-cultural orientation.
    I. Black, J. Stewart, 1959- II. Series.
HF5549. 5. E45 G635 1998
658.3—ddc21
                                                    98-45109
                                                         CIP

1 2 3 4 5 6 7 8 9 10—BAM—0201009998

Series Foreword

I am very pleased to welcome *Globalizing People Through International Assignments*, by Black, Gregersen, Mendenhall, and Stroh, to the Addison-Wesley Human Resource Management Series. With its focus on applying human resources knowledge to multinational organizations, this book is a perfect fit for the series.

The HRM Series has recently entered a new phase of productivity. Earlier this year, Tim Cline's new book, entitled *Program Assessment*, was added to the series, and several current editions will be revised as we approach the 21st century. Arvey and Faley's *Fairness in Selecting Employees* (1988) will soon appear in its third edition; this is ample testimony to the quality and popularity of this work, which was originally written by Arvey in 1979 as the first title in the HRM series. Wexley and Latham's *Developing and Training Human Resources*, published in its second edition, is currently being revised for the series, and I expect to revise my own work, *Organizational Entry* (1980, 1992), in time for the next millennium. Still available are the classic works by Heneman (*Merit Pay*, 1992), Thornton (*Assessment Centers in Human Resource Management*, 1992), and Latham/Wexley (*Increasing Productivity Through Performance Appraisal*, 1994).

As always, this series is dedicated to the articulation of new solutions to human resource problems. My charge to the authors continues to be twofold. First, present your topic so that it will be recognized for its intellectual leadership among your peers at universities around the world. Second, make sure your presentation is sufficiently readable for both college students and human resource professionals. These are challenging standards, but necessary if the best academic knowledge is to be translated into human resources practice.

John Parcher Wanous
Series Editor

Other Titles in the Addison-Wesley Series on Managing Human Resources

Program Assessment
Timothy R. Cline
(1999) 0-201-32259-5

Increasing Productivity Through Performance Appraisal, 2nd Edition
Gary P. Latham and Kenneth N. Wexley
(1994) 0-201-51400-1

Merit Pay: Linking Pay Increases to Performance Ratings
Robert L. Heneman
(1992) 0-201-52504-6

Assessment Centers in Human Resource Management
George C. Thornton III
(1992) 0-201-55403-8

Organizational Entry: Recruitment, Selection, and Socialization of Newcomers
John P. Wanous
(1992) 0-201-51480-X

Developing and Training Human Resources, 2nd Edition
Kenneth N. Wexley and Gary P. Latham
(1991) 0-673-46160-2

Fairness in Selecting Employees, Second Edition
Richard D. Arvey and Robert H. Faley
(1988) 0-201-00078-4

Table of Contents

Preface   xi
About the Authors   xv

PART I: Introduction
Chapter 1: The Strategic Roles of Global Assignments   1
Chapter 2: The Process of Making Cross-Cultural Adjustments   32

PART II: Before the Assignment
Chapter 3: Selecting: Finding the Right People   52
Chapter 4: Training: Helping People Learn to Do the Right Things   87

PART III: During the Assignment
Chapter 5: Adjusting: Developing New Mental Maps and Behaviors   107
Chapter 6: Integrating: Balancing Dual Allegiance   130
Chapter 7: Appraising: Determining If People Are Doing the Right Things   156
Chapter 8: Rewarding: Recognizing People When They Do Things Right   175

PART IV: After the Assignment
Chapter 9: Repatriating: Helping People Readjust and Perform   202
Chapter 10: Retaining: Utilizing the Experienced Global Manager   236
Chapter 11: Managing the Entire Global Assignment Cycle: Establishing Best Practices   256

References   278
Index   293

To develop a truly global perspective, you must experience the globe. *Globalizing People Through International Assignments* helps companies send people around the world to achieve strategic success!

Lorence Harmer
Executive Counsel, Global Resourcing
Nortel Networks

As companies expand into the global marketplace, international assignments play an increasingly critical role in the development of global leaders. From leadership development philosophy to practical how-to's, *Globalizing People Through International Assignments* is loaded with the facts and follies of international assignments and how to make them a success—for the company and the family.

Marion Shumway
Organization Capability Consultant
Amoco Energy International

Globalizing People Through International Assignments is useful to both managers and HR professionals. It is well-written and shows the authors' deep understanding of the many issues involved in successfully managing international assignments.

Jean M. Broom
Vice President Human Resources
Estée Lauder International, Inc.

With the rise of the information age, there is a plethora of literature out there about international assignments—but it's not easy to know what is reliable, accurate, and worthwhile. *Globalizing People Through International Assignments* is one of the best resources I have found anywhere on the subject. It is comprehensive, practical, and, most importantly, useful for those leaving on assignments or those overseeing expatriate programs. It is a very rich resource.

Mark Hamberlin
Human Resource and Organizational
Development Manager
Hallmark International

As we speed toward the end of the century, the global tumult is accelerating. Companies cannot weather this hurricane without experienced executives who understand the turmoil and interrelationships of a global economy and the concerns of the individuals and their families who will be required to guide them forward. Kudos to Black, Gregersen, Mendenhall, and Stroh for their objective analysis of the strategic decisions surrounding development and management of global leaders in light of economic, political, career, and family risks. They have identified and addressed all the questions raised by our clients today.

Nancy Carter
Global Human Resources Consulting
KPMG

Globalizing People Through International Assignments masterfully peels back the institutional myths of international assignments by providing valuable insight into the people component—both for those doing the selection and those being selected. This book should be read by all managers involved in the global marketplace.

David Barlow
Manager, Relocation
Chevron Corporation

This book speaks to future global leaders. To develop and implement business plans overseas, we must build better global human resources strategies for expatriate recruitment, training, and performance management. This book addresses these issues and more with up-to-date best practices that empower us to accomplish global business strategies.

Takashi Wada
Manager, International Human Resources
Universal Studios

In today's global environment, assignments outside of one's own country are critical to grow management talent and further meet the globalizing demands of the business. *Globalizing People Through International Assignments* not only shares the strategic value of global assignments, but also presents in a pragmatic fashion how each business should approach and manage international assignments from beginning to end.

Ben Foulk
International HR Manager
GE Capital

Globalizing People Through International Assignments establishes the benchmark framework for successfully using international assignments as a strategic developmental tool. The book introduces the global assignment success cycle and walks managers through each critical phase using lively case studies, solid empirical evidence, and practical answers to key questions that will enable companies to manage international assignments more effectively. Any firm seriously concerned with its future leaders in the new global arena will benefit dramatically from this book.

Tim S. Simmons
People AdvantEDGE, Management Consulting
Ernst & Young, LLP

Preface

The rapid globalization of business and its impact on firms is beyond dispute. The debate in corporate boardrooms now focuses on how to respond to the demand to be globally integrated while also being responsive to various local market needs. If multinational firms are to prosper now and in the future, they must develop people who can successfully function in a global context—formulating and implementing strategies, inventing and utilizing technologies, and creating and coordinating information. International assignments are the single most powerful means for developing future global leaders.

Unfortunately, the power of international assignments is not being captured. Neither the short-term business benefits nor the long-term development objectives are being fully realized. In short, firms are not getting a good return on the time and expense they invest in international assignments. Failures such as premature returns, poor performers, and repatriation turnover are common and are costing even moderately-sized multinational corporations tens of millions of dollars per year. Additionally, individuals are not getting a good return on their investment in these assignments. Seven out of ten returned expatriates believe the international assignment had a negative impact on their career. The reality is that international assignments are stressful, and that stress shows up in substance abuse, strained and broken marriages, and other family problems.

We authors have all lived overseas with our families at some time. We have experienced and seen first-hand the significant losses and profits to organizations and to individuals that result from poorly- or well-designed international assignment systems. These experiences have given us an understanding of the issues, as well as an intense motivation to provide a systematic guide for constructing effective international assignment systems—systems that achieve critical competitive results today and develop the global leaders of tomorrow.

Although firms have been utilizing international assignments for years, a systematic understanding—of what people to select; how to train them; what factors affect their adjustment, performance, or commitment; how to keep and utilize them once they return home—has not been widely disseminated across most firms. While there has been increased scholarly research on the topic recently, much of it is tucked away in academic journals and is unknown to executives who would most practically benefit from that knowledge. We saw the need to bring together best practices and solid science in an effort to improve the results of international assignments for organizations and individuals.

Audience

This book, therefore, is written primarily for the executive who must deal with the global economy and the strategic role of people in achieving international competitiveness. This includes CEOs, line managers, and especially human resource management executives. The contents of this book are designed to give executives a sophisticated but practical understanding of the strategic roles of international assignments, as well as the dynamics of the full cycle of these assignments. Each chapter has four objectives: (1) to examine a specific problem concerning international assignments, (2) to explain the underlying principles for understanding the problem, (3) to provide a framework for analyzing the issue, and (4) to present recommendations for executives to follow in redesigning or enhancing their current systems.

Overview of Contents

The book covers every major aspect of international assignments. Chapter 1 defines the strategic roles that international assignments can play and discusses how these roles need to be adjusted, depending upon the firm's particular stage of internationalization. Chapter 2 generally explains the process of cross-cultural adjustment, which is critical for effectively working and living in foreign cultures. Chapter 3 examines the issue of selecting people for international assignments, addressing both who should be selected and how they should be chosen. Chapter 4 focuses on the challenge of training people so that they perform effectively while overseas. Specifically, the chapter provides a framework for firms so that they do not over- or under-invest in the training needs of people sent on foreign assignments. Chapter 5 focuses on the factors that affect successful cross-cultural adjustment and describes ways firms can facilitate the adjustment process. Chapter 6 provides pioneering insights into the dynamics of the dual allegiance (to the parent firm and the local foreign operation) that international assignees possess and discusses how firms can foster "dual citizens" or employees with high dual allegiance to both organizations. Chapter 7 examines the difficulties of appraising employees while they are on foreign assignments and provides a model of how this can be done effectively. Chapter 8 explores the problems that most firms face regarding the high compensation costs of expatriate employees and outlines a means of significantly reducing those costs while improving the motivation of employees to accept and perform well in international assignments. Chapter 9 unravels the process of coming home, exploring the factors that affect repatriation adjustment and job performance. It points to specific steps firms can take to facilitate repatriation adjustment and performance. Chapter 10 explains the factors that determine whether high-performing repatriated managers will stay with the firm or leave. In particular, this chapter provides recommendations for retaining and utilizing high-performing managers and executives after international assignments. Finally, Chapter 11 summarizes and integrates the critical elements from the stages of the full international assignment cycle. It also describes firms that represent some of the best practices in selection, training, appraisal, compensation, and repatriation.

Acknowledgments

To the extent that this book helps firms or individuals, we owe thanks to many. First we acknowledge the support and understanding of our families for their willingness to live in such places as Japan, Finland, Switzerland, and Canada. We are also grateful to the many men and women who have shared their experiences of working and living in foreign countries. Finally, we are grateful to colleagues at the schools of business at Brigham Young University; University of California,

Irvine; University of Tennessee, Chattanooga; and Loyola University Chicago (particularly Erica Fox, Dave Murphy, and Stacey Valy), as well as others who have collaborated with us and supported our work over the years.

J. Stewart Black
San Diego, California

Hal B. Gregersen
Provo, Utah

Mark E. Mendenhall
Chattanooga, Tennessee

Linda K. Stroh
Chicago, Illinois

About the Authors

J. Stewart Black is Managing Director of the Center for Global Assignments, which produces research and publications and provides consulting services related to international assignments. Dr. Black received his Ph.D. in Business Administration from the University of California, Irvine, and was formerly an associate professor at the Amos Tuck School of Business Administration, Dartmouth College. He has received a number of academic and teaching awards and has made more than fifty presentations at professional meetings in the United States and throughout the world.

Dr. Black's research and consulting focus on the areas of global leadership, strategic human resource management, international assignments, and cross-cultural management. He has consulted and presented seminars in the areas of global leadership and international human resource management for a variety of international firms including American Express, Black & Decker, The Boeing Company, Brunswick, Exxon, General Motors, IBM, The Kellogg Company, Kodak, Motorola, NASA, Honda Motors, and Kawasaki Steel.

Dr. Black has authored more than 100 articles, chapters, and cases that have appeared in both managerial and academic publications such as *Business Week,* the *Wall Street Journal, Fortune, Harvard Business Review, Workforce, Academy of Management Review, Academy of Management Journal, Human Resource Management, Journal of International Business Studies,* and *Human Relations.* He is co-author of eight books, including *So You're Going Overseas: A Handbook for Personal and Professional Success* and *So You're Coming Home*—books written for individual expatriates and their families. He is also co-author of a new book, *Global Explorers: The Next Generation of Leaders.*

Dr. Black has traveled throughout Europe and Asia, has lived and worked in Japan, and speaks Japanese fluently. On three occasions, he has been a visiting professor at International University of Japan.

Hal B. Gregersen is Associate Professor of International Management at the Marriott School of Management, Brigham Young University. Dr. Gregersen taught previously at the Amos Tuck School of
Business Administration at Dartmouth College and at Penn State and
Thunderbird. He received an M.A. degree from Brigham Young University and a Ph.D. from the University of California, Irvine. Dr.
Gregersen speaks and writes Finnish, a result of working in Finland
for three years and completing a Fulbright Fellowship at the Turku
School of Economics and Business Administration.

Dr. Gregersen's primary research focuses on managing international assignments strategically, building global leaders, and implementing international strategy. He has authored over seventy articles,
book chapters, and cases on these subjects and published in top journals such as *Academy of Management Journal, Harvard Business
Review, Journal of Applied Psychology, Journal of International
Business Studies, Personnel Psychology,* and *Sloan Management Review.* Dr. Gregersen is a co-author of *So You're Going Overseas* and
So You're Coming Home (1998, with Stewart Black)—a series of
handbooks and workbooks designed to help expatriates and their families succeed during and after international assignments. His work on
international assignments and global leadership is cited regularly in
the business press, including *Across the Board, Business Week, Executive Excellence, Fortune, Industry Week, Los Angeles Times, U.S.
News and World Report,* and the *Wall Street Journal.*

As a senior partner at the Center for Global Assignments, Dr.
Gregersen consults with a variety of North American, European, and
Asian firms to develop effective links between global strategy and international human resource practices. He teaches regularly in executive education programs for companies such as IBM and Marriott and
speaks for organizations such as the Conference Board, Employee
Relocation Council, Human Resource Planning Society, International
Personnel Administrators, Organization Resource Counselors, and
the Institute for International Research.

Mark E. Mendenhall holds the J. Burton Frierson Chair of Excellence in Business Leadership at the University of Tennessee at Chattanooga. He received his B.S. degree from Brigham Young University in Psychology and his Ph.D. degree from Brigham Young University in Social Psychology.

Dr. Mendenhall's main research activities have been in the area of human resource management, especially the cross-cultural adjustment of expatriate managers and Japanese organizational behavior. His research interests stem from his childhood experience growing up in a multicultural community outside of Hamilton, New Zealand. That town's residents included Maoris, Pakehas (Caucasian New Zealanders), and expatriates from America, Tonga, Samoa, and Australia. On a two-year assignment in Japan, he saw expatriates face the same cross-cultural challenges as those in New Zealand faced. Dr. Mendenhall has authored many journal articles, and his books include *Readings and Cases in International Human Resource Management* (1991, with Gary Oddou), and *International Management* (a forthcoming textbook with David Ricks and B. J. Punnett). Additionally, Dr. Mendenhall is a weekly columnist for *The Chattanooga Times,* a large daily newspaper where his columns deal with issues of management and leadership effectiveness.

Dr. Mendenhall is an active consultant, conducting workshops and seminars in the areas of cross-cultural adjustment, Japanese management systems, and leadership development. He is active in the Academy of Management and has been on the executive board of the International Division, as well as the president of the division in 1993. He also has served on the Academy of Management Internationalization Committee, on the doctoral consortia for the International Division, and currently on the editorial board of *Journal of International Business Studies and of Human Resource Planning.*

Dr. Mendenhall has traveled widely, and he has lived overseas for almost one-fourth of his life—in New Zealand, Japan, and Switzerland.

Linda K. Stroh is Director of Workplace Studies and a professor at the Institute of Human Resources & Industrial Relations, Loyola University, Chicago. She received her Ph.D. from Northwestern University, her M.A. from Concordia University in Montreal, and her B.A. in Industrial Sociology from McGill University, also in Montreal.

Dr. Stroh's research focuses primarily on organizational policy impacting managers' careers, attitudes, and commitment to the organization, both domestically and internationally. Her work can be found in journals such as *Journal of Applied Psychology, Personnel Psychology, Academy of Management Journal, International Journal of Human Resource Management, Strategic Management Journal, Journal of Organizational Behavior, Journal of Management Education, Sloan Management Review, Human Resource Management Journal,* and various other journals. Dr. Stroh's work has also been cited on the front page of the *Wall Street Journal, New York Times, Washington Post, Chicago Tribune,* and in *Fortune* magazine, *Newsweek, U.S. News and World Report,* and *Business Week,* as well as various other news and popular press outlets. Dr. Stroh's work/family research has often been featured on Tom Brokaw's *Nightly News.*

In addition to her teaching and research, Dr. Stroh has served as chair of the Careers Division for the Academy of Management. She currently serves on the editorial board for the *Journal of Vocational Behavior, International Journal of Organizational Analysis,* and the *Journal of Applied Business Research.* She is also the Academic Adviser for the International Personnel Association (an association of 60 of the top 100 multinational companies in the U.S. and Canada). Dr. Stroh has consulted with over 30 organizations on such issues as motivation, leadership, change management, problem solving, and global management issues.

1

The Strategic Roles of Global Assignments

Why do some firms compete successfully in the world marketplace and others lose or fail to gain global competitive advantage? Some analysts argue that strategy is the key: the winners are the ones with the right game plans. Others contend that structure is the trick. Still others claim that technological innovation is the answer to successfully meeting today's global business challenges.

We think people are the key. People formulate and implement strategy; people design and build organizational structures; people invent and utilize technology. A 1997 study by the International Personnel Association supports our conclusion. This study shows a positive relationship between a multinational organization's ability to develop global leaders and the bottom-line success of the organization. Another study conducted by the Global Leadership Institute shows a positive relationship between the level of employee internationalization and the organization's ROA (Return on Assets). The findings from these studies suggest that globalization of people is the key to competitive international business success.[1]

Jack Welch, CEO of General Electric, put it quite well:

> The Jack Welch of the future cannot be like me. I spent my entire career in the U.S. The next head of General Electric will be somebody who spent time in Bombay, in Hong Kong, in Buenos Aires. We have to send our best and brightest overseas and make sure they have the training that will allow them to be the global leaders who will make GE flourish in the future.

When you think about it, only people can be the key to success. After all, the strategy of a company is a function of its strategy makers. For example, whether those strategists recognize or miss global threats or opportunities is a function of their experience and

1

perspective. How they structure an organization for global reach and results depends on how they see the world of organizations, markets, competitors, and so on around them. What enables these people to have an effective global mindset and perspective? In a three-year study of over 150 executives in 50 different companies across Europe, North America, and Asia,[2] the answer was: *An international assignment is the single most powerful experience in shaping the perspective and capabilities of effective global leaders.* It also happens to be the single most expensive per-person investment that a company makes in globalizing their people. It is unfortunate that most firms are getting anemic returns on this substantial investment. It is important to understand the best practices, thinking, and scientific research that can offer a sophisticated yet practical guide for maximizing the return on international assignments and effectively globalizing people.

Strategic Value of Global Assignments

In the past, U.S. firms tended not to use global assignments for strategic purposes. In general, people were sent overseas to carry out specific tasks because management felt that the local talent was in some way not up to the challenge. This tactical approach often meant that the strategic implications of the assignment, for the company and the individual, were neglected.

In contrast, leading companies today take a more strategic approach. For them, global assignments play important roles in succession planning and leadership development; in coordination and control; and in technology, innovation, and information exchange and dissemination.

Leadership Development and Global Assignments

As Jack Welch's earlier statement indicates, one of the key concerns and responsibilities of current CEOs is the development of future executives and CEOs.[3] The current CEOs know that their company's future strategy will be no better than the quality of people in the organization. For example, a Beethoven concerto may be beautiful and powerful, but you wouldn't place it in the hands of a beginning piano student. A Bill Walsh passing offense may be brilliant, but you wouldn't put it in the hands of anyone less than a Joe Montana or Steve Young. In today's business environment, it's also madness to think of trying to formulate or implement a strategy without carefully considering the global business environment in which it is expected to function.

The development of globally capable leaders should be a top priority in all companies. In fact, one report concluded that executives who fail to see the importance of international assignments in developing global leaders are unsuited for the CEO job.[4] Fortunately, most human resource executives do recognize these needs. A report from the International Personnel Association found that attracting and developing the next generation of global leaders was a top priority of human resource executives.[5] Jack Reichert, recently retired CEO of Brunswick Corporation, captured the importance of developing future global leaders:

> Financial resources are *not* the problem. We have the money, products, and position to be a dominant global player. What we lack are the *human* resources. We just don't have enough people with the needed global leadership capabilities.

To reinforce the importance of developing a new generation of global leaders, we only need to consider a few recent and significant developments in the global marketplace. Even a superficial review shows them to present both breathtaking opportunities and threats to leaders in the 21st century. Consider the following:

- The Asian financial and debt crisis
- The return of Hong Kong to China
- Liberalization of financial markets (The "Big Bang" in Great Britain, and now in Japan)
- The democratization of Eastern Europe
- The unification of Germany
- Emerging trading blocs (NAFTA, EC, etc.)
- Invasion of foreign firms into domestic markets
- The resignation of Suharto in Indonesia
- Emerging economies (China, India, Latin America)

To formulate or implement strategic plans for the 21st century effectively, managers and executives must be able to to focus on the unique needs of local foreign customers, suppliers, labor pools, government policies, and technology and, at the same time, on general trends in the world marketplace. For an individual, this requires tremendous environmental-scanning abilities, just to pick up the information. It requires vast knowledge and processing abilities, to categorize and interpret raw data effectively. It requires being able to understand and work effectively with people from different cultural, religious, and ethnic backgrounds, as well as the ability to manage teams composed of such cross-cultural members. Managers who fail to develop these skills, and organizations that fail to develop these managers, risk being irrelevant in the twenty-first century.

An international assignment is the most powerful means of developing the skills and knowledge that future leaders will need. An increasing number of companies recognize this. Greg Geiger, Director of Finance for the International Ford Motor Company, comments from his own experience:

> Let me illustrate the impact of an international assignment with the following example. Early in my career I had the opportunity to work in a manufacturing plant. After that I left the plant and worked with people who did analysis of the plants. The difference was very clear between those who had worked in a plant and those who had visited a plant. The ability to add value between those two sets is distinctly different. There is no substitute in your ability to understand manufacturing and contribute to it than to work in a plant. I believe the situation is *exactly* the same with respect to understanding foreign operations, foreign markets, and foreign cultures.

According to Geiger, there is no substitute for the learning that occurs on an international assignment. He recognizes the value of developing global leaders through global assignments. Another example is Philip Morris Companies Inc. Philip Morris claims that a key to their recent and continued growth is that they know their global "benchstrength" and they view their people as competitive "weapons." Philip Morris has 170,000 employees in 180 countries worldwide. By the year 2000, they expect that 75 percent of their staff will live outside of the U.S. Spending time on an international assignment is a common leadership-development technique at Philip Morris.

General Electric also understands the critical nature of international experience. GE estimates that 25 percent of its managers will need global assignments to gain the knowledge and experience necessary to understand the global markets, customers, suppliers, and competitors the company will face by the turn of the century.

At Gillette, they do more than just send people out from headquarters on international assignments. Beginning in the mid 1980s, Gillette started a program to send the best and brightest from throughout its worldwide organization out on international assignments. They did this to achieve a global organization with managers at all levels and in all locations who can work in a variety of local markets and who are thoroughly familiar with Gillette's corporate and strategic expectations.[6]

In response to the difficulty in finding high-quality people for international assignments, Colgate-Palmolive, in the mid-1980s, began a program of systematically providing opportunities for high-potential managers to work in a variety of global markets. Their goal was to develop the leadership skills required for top international and corporate positions. Colgate-Palmolive recently received over 20,000 applications for twenty entry-level international marketing jobs. These entry-level marketing positions allow new Colgate-Palmolive employees the opportunity to receive international experience first-hand and to be on the fast track from the beginning of their career with Colgate-Palmolive.

These are just a few examples of the increasing number of companies where people are seen as the key to effectively formulating and implementing corporate strategy in today's global marketplace, and where global assignments play a strategic role in the successful development and globalization of people.

Coordination, Control, and Global Assignments

Global assignments can also play a strategic role in the coordination and control of international corporations. In today's global business environment, the effective coordination and control of units throughout the world is complicated by three factors.

Transportation and Communication Technology. Although people say that the world is getting smaller, it is actually getting bigger. Because of advances in transportation and communication technology, companies are expanding into countries where they've never been and globalizing faster than ever. We can now phone or e-mail virtually anyplace in the world in a matter of minutes or seconds, and we can go anywhere in the world in a matter of hours. Because communication and transportation were more difficult and time-consuming in the past, not every place in the world was a part of normal business operations; the whole world has always been out there, but it has not always been relevant or accessible. Today it is. Consider Flour Corporation, headquartered in Irvine, California, a $7.4 billion engineering and construction firm with more than 22,000 employees around the globe. Flour's primary subsidiary, Flour Daniel, Inc., is usually operating in eighty or more countries at any time.[7] The coordination and control of this worldwide network are staggering. International operations have gone from the periphery to center stage.

Cultural Diversity. The second factor—the breadth and depth of cultural diversity—has implications for customers, suppliers, workers, and government relations. For example, what might be construed as a bribe in one country or culture is considered normal business practice in another;[8] low costs may be a key in one market, whereas technology and quality may be essential to another. Consider Vacuum General, Inc., a medium-sized manufacturer of pressure-control devices. Vacuum General bought Tylan Corp., a manufacturer of mass gas-flow systems, because of its subsidiaries in Germany, France, and the United Kingdom. This acquisition gave Vacuum General a new name (Tylan General) and access to the European semiconductor-equipment market. Before the merger, each European unit had been run autonomously, and each had its own focus. Top management found it extremely difficult to coordinate many aspects of purchasing, marketing, and manufacturing across its U.S. and new European units. David Ferran, CEO of Tylan General, commented, "Sometimes we talk with the manager [of the foreign subsidiary] and think that they bought in. Then we learn later that it isn't happening. Maybe it is poor communication, or maybe they don't want to understand."[9]

Geographic Dispersion. The third factor in coordination and control of geographically dispersed operations is the resulting potential for conflicting demands from governments of the countries involved. For example, one country may demand the transfer of a particular technology that the home-country government restricts; technical specialists produced by the subsidiary in one country may be needed in a subsidiary in another country whose immigration policies prohibit their transfer because of their nationality. Such was the case for Nike in China.

Recently, when Nike set up a production agreement with a Chinese manufacturing operation to produce running shoes primarily for export sales, the company discovered it needed certain technical expertise in the Chinese contractor's operations. Although China offered substantial savings in labor expenses, local Chinese management and workers lacked the technological know-how to produce the quantity and quality of shoes Nike desired. Nike's most efficient and advanced operations were in Korea, but when Nike tried to send Korean technical specialists in to help the Chinese operation improve its production methods, the Korean workers were denied even temporary visas. This action was primarily because of the supportive political relationship between North Korea and China and the political tension between North Korea and South Korea. Eventually, to transfer technological know-how to the Chinese operation, Nike officials made tapes of the training and instruction that the Korean workers could not provide in person.

Geographical distance, cultural diversity, and conflicting government demands push firms toward fragmented strategy and operations even while they increase the importance and difficulty of effective coordination and control. Policies and manuals can sometimes facilitate coordination and control, but they are subject to translation, interpretation, and differences in execution often caused by local conditions (culture, government policies, economy, and so on). Furthermore, as subsidiaries grow and mature, resources such as capital, technology, and expertise may not provide sufficient leverage for home-office control.[10] A senior line executive from the Ford Motor Company noted that this coordination and control may be achieved best by using talent from around the world:

> Prior to Ford 2000 we were a collection of regional companies and 99 percent of the people could advance a very long way in a single region. Two years ago Ford 2000 flipped the light switch on for global leaders. The need to grow in markets where we didn't have operations suddenly demanded a portfolio of skills in key people that were not what we had developed in a regional setting. Now I have the responsibility to find people for positions around the globe. Guess what? None of these people come from North America or Europe. They're from South Africa, Australia, Taiwan, New Zealand, where they gained the unique skills required to start up overseas operations.

Like maturing children, subsidiaries may want more freedom, and they may resist direction and control from the parent company. Global assignments are an effective means of placing individuals with shared objectives and interpretations in key positions around the world, to serve as critical sources as well as means of coordination and control.

Technology, Innovation, Information Transfers, and Global Assignments

Geographical distance, cultural diversity, complex local and global demand or supply conditions, dispersed innovations, and so on, create a tremendous need for the various units of an international firm to share and exchange information. Exhibit 1.1 shows that information can flow to or from the parent organization, in or out of a foreign subsidiary, across foreign subsidiaries, or in none of these directions.[11]

	Low Flow In	High Flow In
Low Flow Out	Island	Implementor
High Flow Out	Innovator	Integrator

Exhibit 1.1
Information Flow

Although each cell in Exhibit 1.1 is fairly self-explanatory, all may benefit from a brief description. While the analysis and descriptions could be applied to any organizational unit within a company (e.g., headquarters, foreign subsidiary, division, or even department), we will use a foreign subsidiary as the example.

An *island* foreign subsidiary is one in which little information (e.g., competitive intelligence, product technology, strategic direction) flows **in** from the parent company or other foreign subsidiaries or **out** to these same units. In essence the subsidiary does "its own thing" in its domestic market.

An *implementor* foreign subsidiary is one in which a lot of information flows **in** from the parent company or other foreign subsidiaries but little flows **out** to these same units. In essence, the subsidiary does what it is told to do (i.e., implements) in its domestic market.

An *innovator* foreign subsidiary is one in which little information flows **in** from the parent company or other foreign subsidiaries but a significant amount of information flows **out** to these same units. The subsidiary is a source of ideas, direction, etc., for other units.

An *integrator* foreign subsidiary is one in which significant amounts of information flow **in** from the parent company or other foreign subsidiaries *and* **out** to these same units. The heavy two-direction flow of information is what creates the need for significant levels of integration and coordination.

None of these four descriptors is inherently good or bad. Each could be appropriate in a given business environment. The critical point is that, except in a totally insulated and isolated subsidiary, the flow of information is an important strategic function. It provides the basis for making strategic and competitive decisions. Mechanisms such as newsletters and intracompany conferences are ways of facilitating information sharing and exchange. Although the Internet and e-mail are still limited by hardware compatibility and language standards, they are also becoming widely used for this purpose. Nevertheless, the most valuable information tends to be rich in texture, nuance, and subtleties. As a consequence, it is not easy to digitize. The effective exchange of this kind of information requires a relationship and trust between the parties. Global assignments provide the opportunity for people to work together, side by side, over an extended period of time, thereby developing the level of trust and understanding necessary for exchanging rich information.

We need to keep in mind, however, that this exchange of information takes place both *during* and *after* the assignment. For example, recently Lucent and Philips formed a large joint venture to focus on personal communication products (pagers, cellular phones, etc.). To transfer manufacturing process technology, the joint venture transferred operations personnel from Asia to the U.S. To ensure the maximal exchange of semiconductor information and technology, the joint venture transferred leading scientists from throughout its worldwide operations to Silicon Valley. Although expensive, these transfers were necessary. The benefits from relationships developed among the various individuals did not stop after each returned home or went on to the next international assignment; they continued. Individuals continued to exchange competitive, market, and technological information to an extent that had never existed before because of the personal relationships developed during the international assignments. As a consequence, the joint venture was able to respond much more quickly to competitors such as Nokia, because more people had more information sooner.

While global assignments can play tactical roles, leading companies also use them to achieve strategic roles. International assignments are vital to the development of the global leaders. They are extremely valuable in the coordination and control of a firm's worldwide operations, and they are effective in the exchange and enhancement of technology, innovation, and information transfer—both during and after the time abroad.

Rethinking Our Views of Global Assignments

Despite the strategic role that international transfers can play, many executives have a rather narrow and myopic view of how they can be used and who should be involved in them. Most U.S. firms make global assignments primarily on the basis of the needs of a given position and their inability to fill it with a host-country employee.[12] In the day-to-day reality of the decision makers responsible for global assignments, succession planning and managerial development are often irrelevant. Succession planning becomes replacement planning, and what is urgent drives out what is important.[13]

Even when executives do begin to focus on the strategic role that global assignments can play, that focus is typically directed toward the assignment of parent-country nationals to foreign subsidiaries. Two factors combine to create this focus on the strategic role that global assignments can play for host-country managers.

First, many foreign governments are pressuring multinational firms that operate within their borders to "localize" management—that is, to develop and promote local managers to positions of responsibility and get expatriates out. Second, many firms have discovered that local managers with no international experience have a tendency to be oversensitive to local conditions, to view nonlocals as alien, and to misunderstand or even fight corporate directives, plans, and strategy. Host-country managers often become liabilities rather than assets when they do not understand the parent firm, its global strategy, or how other foreign subsidiaries are related to one another. As a consequence it may not be a good move to simply move a local manager into an expatriate's position to lower costs and/or to meet localization pressures. For this reason, firms have begun to think about and utilize international assignments to globalize people throughout their worldwide operations. For example, Kodak has a program whereby high-potential host-country managers are identified and then sent on global assignments to important operations in the United States. Such assignments are designed to serve all three strategic purposes described earlier. The overseas assignments facilitate strategic succession planning and managerial development because they provide these managers with experience outside their home country, broaden their perspective, enhance their knowledge base, heighten their interpersonal and communication skills, and improve their ability to assume higher positions back home. The assignments enhance the coordination and control functions of the corporation by socializing the individuals into the Kodak culture and philosophy. They also facilitate information sharing between the foreign managers and domestic U.S. managers.

It is not necessary, however, for a host-country national to be sent on a global assignment only to the parent-firm's country. Ford

Motor Company increasingly transfers foreign nationals to "third countries"—that is, countries that are foreign to the individual and to the parent firm. Officials at Ford believe that such assignments develop managers with the necessary leadership skills for the future, facilitate coordination and control functions between the parent and subsidiaries and among subsidiaries, and enhance the sharing and exchange of information throughout Ford's worldwide network.

In short, although global assignments are most often utilized to "fight fires," they can also be utilized to meet strategic objectives. Although utilizing global assignments for strategic roles is clearly important for parent-country employees, it is equally powerful for globalizing key people throughout the firm's worldwide operations.

Costs of Poorly Managed Global Assignments

At this point, some readers may be convinced of the strategic role of global assignments, while others may not be. Whether global assignments are used to "fight fires" or to develop future leaders, it is important to describe the wide-ranging and severe costs that the improper design and execution of global assignments can create. These costs can be roughly divided into five categories: failed assignments, "brownouts," turnover after repatriation, downward-spiraling vicious cycles, and gutting of executive capability at headquarters.

Failed Assignments

The proportion of U.S. expatriates who fail in their global assignments (that is, return prematurely) ranges from 10 percent to 45 percent, with the higher rates associated with assignments in underdeveloped or developing countries.[14] This means that from one in ten to half of all U.S. expatriates sent overseas fail. The failure rates for European and Japanese firms is less than half this rate. (The factors that explain U.S. failure rates, as well as the difference between the failure rates of U.S. and European or Japanese firms, are examined in more detail in Chapter 5.)

Direct Moving Costs.
The first and most direct costs of failed assignments are those associated with physical displacement. It is very expensive to ship an expatriate and his or her family and belongings overseas (85 percent of U.S. expatriates are married[15]). For example, a typical transfer to Tokyo from the United States might cost $75,000 ($8,333 relocation allowance, $19,000 temporary living

costs, $14,000 brokers' commission, $11,000 one-way travel to Japan, $20,000 moving costs, $3,000 property management).[16] It would cost approximately another $60–70,000 to bring the expatriate and family home, plus another $75,000 to send a replacement. The relocation costs alone can be more than $220,000 for a failed assignment.

Downtime Costs. During the expatriate's predeparture preparations, there is a period when the individual is receiving a full salary but is not capable of fully performing duties. There is also a time, during the first few months of the global assignment, when the expatriate is adjusting to the new culture, the environment, and the job. This is natural. In the case of failed assignments, the problem is twofold. Unlike expatriates who recover, adjust to, and perform well in overseas positions, those who fail provide no long-term return on the downtime. Also, once an expatriate is overseas, the base salary, foreign-service premium, housing allowance, education allowance, cost-of-living differential, tax-adjustment allowance, and so on, usually at least double the total compensation package; and this doubles the cost of the adjustment downtime, for which there is no long-term return in the case of a failed assignment.

Indirect Costs. In addition to these measurable economic costs, there are significant indirect, difficult-to-measure costs to both the organization and the individual. In the case of the organization, a failed global assignment can result in damage to several important constituencies, including local national employees, host-government officials, and local suppliers, customers, and community members. If these damages occur, the replacement person, even the most capable one, may find it hard to repair them and effectively carry out other duties and tasks. Despite the difficulty of quantifying these costs, they are sometimes the most significant. For the individual, a failed global assignment will likely hurt his or her career and self-esteem. In fact, many expatriates we have interviewed over the years said that they stayed in their global assignments only because they feared the negative consequences of leaving early. For the firm, lost business opportunities, lower employee morale, upset government officials, and disappointed customers can all negatively affect financial performance.

Brownouts
"Brownouts" are managers who do not return prematurely but are nevertheless ineffective in performing and executing their responsi-

bilities. Estimates are that between 30 percent and 50 percent of all U.S. expatriates fall into this category.[17]

A 1995 survey by the National Foreign Trade Council showed that the costs associated with expatriate failure ranged from $200,000 to $1.2 million per assignment.[18] These costs reflect only directly identifiable expenses, such as compensation, training, orientation, development, and termination. The figures could easily be twice as high if they included hidden costs associated with failure, such as damaged relationships, decreases in productivity, resignations by host-country nationals, missed business opportunities and so on. Perhaps the best way to illustrate some of the costs associated with poor performance during the international assignment is through an experience at General Electric.[19]

Case 1: General Electric–Cie Générale de Radiologie

In the mid-1980s, GE went through a massive strategic restructuring, during which medical technology became one of GE's core business areas. GE's stated goal was for all strategic business units (SBUs) to be in first or second place among their worldwide competitors.

In an effort to increase its global strategic position in medical technology (especially imaging technology), GE took control of Cie Générale de Radiologie (CGR) in 1988. CGR was a French medical equipment manufacturer that was owned by the state and run much like a government ministry. GE got CGR and $800 million in cash from state-controlled Thomson S.A. in return for GE's RCA consumer-electronics business. The acquisition of CGR was viewed by many as a brilliant strategic move, and GE projected a $25 million profit for the first full year of operations. Things did not go as the strategic planners had projected, however.

One of the first things GE did was to organize a training seminar for the French managers. GE left T-shirts with the slogan "Go for One" for each of the participants. Although the French managers wore them, many were not happy about it. One manager stated, "It was like Hitler was back, forcing us to wear uniforms. It was humiliating."

Soon after the takeover, GE also sent U.S. specialists to France to fix CGR's accounting system. Unfortunately, these specialists knew very little about French accounting or reporting requirements, and they tried to impose a GE system that was inappropriate for French reporting requirements and for the way CGR had traditionally kept records. This problem (and the working out of an agreement) took several months and resulted in substantial direct and indirect costs.

GE then tried to coordinate and integrate CGR into its Milwaukee-based medical equipment unit. Because CGR had racked up a $25 million loss instead of the projected $25 million profit, an executive from Milwaukee was sent to fix things at CGR. Several cost-cutting measures, including massive layoffs and the closing of roughly half of the twelve CGR plants, shocked the French workforce. The profit-hungry culture of GE continued to clash with the state-run uncompetitive culture of CGR.

GE's efforts to integrate CGR into the GE culture, by putting up English-language posters everywhere and flying GE flags, met with considerable resistance from the French employees. One union leader commented, "They come in here bragging, 'We are GE; we're the best and we've got the methods.'" The reaction was so strong that a significant number of French managers and engineers left GE-CGR, and the total workforce shrank from 6,500 to 5,000. GE officials had estimated GE-CGR would produce a profit in 1990; instead they lost another $25 million.

In this case example, we do not mean to point an accusing finger at GE; most experts view GE as a well-run multinational corporation. The example does illustrate the costs of poorly designed or poorly executed global assignments, however. Managers who do not perform well on global assignments often do not provide an adequate return on investment; they may initiate programs or projects that cost time and money, and they may damage relationships that are difficult to repair. They may even drive out high-potential local managers who will be needed in the future.

Turnover After Repatriation

Repatriation is perhaps the least carefully considered aspect of global assignments and potentially the most costly. Unfortunately for U.S. firms, the proportion of managers who quit and leave within one year after repatriation is approximately 20 percent.[20] On average, firms spend $150,000 to $250,000 on all expenses (salary, allowances, and so on) for each overseas manager each year.[21] For example, maintaining an American expatriate who earns a base salary of $100,000 and has two children costs at least $220,370 in Tokyo, $180,312 in Singapore, and $157,762 in Beijing per year.[22] Philip Morris claims their company spends $816,000 per year to maintain a $100,000 salaried expatriate in Tokyo ($25,000 targeted bonus, $86,000 commodities/services allowance, $5,000 hardship pay, $171,000 housing costs, $31,000 home leave, $90,000 education for two children,

$75,000 relocation costs; plus $125,000 salary equals $816,000). For the average four-year assignment, the firm invests from $1 million to nearly $3.5 million per manager. This investment is especially important if the assignment is part of succession planning and the managerial development agenda. On average, U.S. firms face a 20 percent chance that they will receive no long-term return on this substantial investment. They may even have to duplicate these investments to develop replacements. Furthermore, because these employees often leave to join competitors, the firm has *de facto* financed the development of global leaders for its rivals. The factors that contribute to repatriation adjustment and turnover problems are explored in detail in Chapter 9; the important point here is the tremendous expense that the poor repatriation management can produce.

Downward-Spiraling Vicious Cycles

All these costs can combine to create circumstances that set off a downward-spiraling cycle, which may erode or destroy a firm's global competitive advantage. Failed global assignments, rumors of "brownouts," and turnover problems among repatriates can lead the best and brightest in an organization's worldwide operations to view global assignments as the kiss of death for their careers. This reputation makes it difficult to recruit and send top-quality candidates on global assignments, which in turn increases the likelihood of more failures. This downward-spiraling quality of candidates and performance can feed on itself, gaining momentum with every turn. The firm may stop sending anyone on assignment outside the home country, which in turn can lead to more difficult coordination and control, as well as to problems with information exchange. Like a plane falling from the sky in a tailspin, it's difficult to regain control once this spiral starts. Recovery is possible, however. GE Medical, for example, learned from its experience in France, dramatically changed its policies and practices, and is now one of the leading companies in terms of international assignment policies and practices.

Gutting of Executive Capability at Headquarters

Perhaps most important, this vicious cycle may lead to a shortage of leaders who have vital understanding and experience in the global arena, which can result in poor strategic planning and implementation and an ever-worsening competitive position globally. Mismanagement ultimately leads to a loss of managerial resources—a fatal flaw for globalization—because without international experience, executives are unable to formulate and implement global strategy accurately. A recent study by the Korn/Ferry International shows that international assignment experience will be increasingly necessary for CEOs of the future.[23]

Many managers and executives may feel that such a scenario is unlikely; but this cycle is easier to start than might be expected, and it is much more difficult to stop or reverse than might be estimated. To fulfill the strategic roles that global assignments can play, or simply to avoid the staggering costs that poorly managed assignments can produce, organizations must provide a framework for effective people management and international assignments.

Framework for People Management and Global Assignments

Before we explore how to manage global assignments and the people in them successfully, it is essential to develop a basic framework for our discussions and recommendations. From our perspective, the effective movement and management of people in global assignments is most logically framed in terms of the generic issue of people management. The term *people management* is often used as if everyone had the same idea of what it means, but we all have very different ideas of what is involved. Exhibit 1.2 illustrates conceptualization of the term through the Global Assignment Success Cycle.

Five Dimensions of People Management

We view people management, not as a function of a specific department (such as personnel or human resources), but as a set of activities that any manager in any functional area of a firm must master. Each activity builds upon the others as the process becomes an integrated package. Simplified, there are five generic functions of managing people.[24]

Getting the Right People (Recruiting/Selecting). First, a manager must identify, recruit, and then place individuals in appropriate positions within the organization. Sometimes this process involves people who are already in the company, and sometimes it involves hiring individuals from outside. This first aspect of people management also includes determining the types and numbers of individuals who will be needed in the future for certain positions and examining the existing pool for people who could meet those needs. At the corporate level, this raises such questions as "Are managers with the necessary skills and experience placed in strategic positions throughout the firm's global operations?"

Exhibit 1.2
Global Assignment Success Cycle

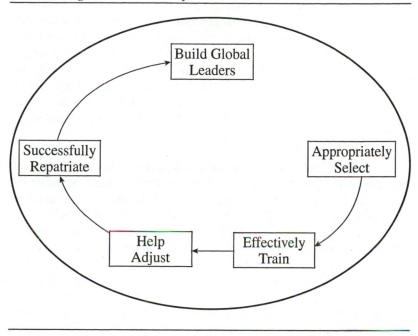

Most U.S. multinationals select individuals for overseas assignments on the basis of their domestic track records. Although this is one important criterion, it does not guarantee success overseas. Research has demonstrated that it is important to examine several other factors in selecting individuals for international work.[25] Chapter 3 details the problems that firms face in selecting candidates for global assignments and discusses common practices, their consequences, and the principles that explain why some practices are more effective than others; it also describes how firms can successfully structure staffing and selection practices for global assignments.

Helping People Do the Right Thing (Training). The jobs that managers are expected to do and the standards by which performance will be judged must be determined, and the necessary training must be provided. This necessity begs the question of whether a firm's managers—who must deal with employees, customers, suppliers, or competitors from different cultures and countries—are adequately trained to understand and work successfully with these groups. The vast majority of U.S. multinational firms fail to prepare individuals adequately to work with individuals from other cultures. While a 1995 survey conducted by Windham International and the National Foreign Trade Council said 62 percent of companies provide some type of cross-cultural preparation,[26] approximately 70 percent of Americans who must work overseas receive *inadequate* training or preparation for their international work.[27] Chapter 4 details common practices and consequences in corporations, the dynamics that explain why training is or is not effective; it also describes how effective training programs for global assignments can be designed and implemented.

Determining How People Are Doing (Appraising). Once an employee has been trained, his or her performance must be measured. However, measuring the job performance of managers who have been sent overseas is tricky. For example, if traditional U.S. variables such as profit, sales, and market share are utilized as quantitative measures, should factors that apply to the local business environment (such as movements in exchange rates) be incorporated into the performance evaluation as well? Most firms have little idea about which factors facilitate or inhibit cross-cultural adjustment, organizational commitment, or job performance during an overseas assignment. Chapters 5, 6, and 7 detail the important factors and the underlying processes that affect these outcomes; these chapters also describe effective means of enhancing and measuring adjustment, commitment, and job performance.

Encouraging the Right Things That People Do (Rewarding). In addition to measuring an individual's job performance, the organization must provide rewards for specific performance behavior, as well as general compensation and benefits. This aspect of people management raises such questions as "Should all managers receive equal benefits and bonuses, regardless of the country in which they are working?" Most firms complain about the high costs of global assignments, and many firms have cut the total number of expatriates to reduce costs. In the absence of understanding or analysis of the reward systems for global managers, this is unlikely to reduce costs per expatriate or to improve the performance of individual managers. Chapter 8 details common practices and consequences in the area of compensation and rewards and discusses the dynamics that motivate global managers; it also describes how rewards can be structured to enhance motivation and performance during global assignments.

Doing Things Right for People (Developing). Over the long term, a sequence of positions, opportunities, responsibilities, and so forth will be needed to develop the maximum potential of managers. This aspect of management raises such questions as "How should managers sent on international assignments be utilized once they return?" There is strong evidence that most U.S. firms do very little planning for the systematic development of global managers.[28] Specifically, most U.S. firms do little planning for the return and integration of global managers who have been overseas for some time. Many of these managers are dissatisfied with their jobs and responsibilities after returning to the United States; one in five leaves the firm within a year after repatriation. Chapters 9 and 10 detail the factors and processes that affect repatriation adjustment, commitment, and turnover; they also describe how firms can more effectively manage this aspect of global assignments. Chapter 11 combines the separate aspects of successfully managing people and global assignments into a comprehensive system and places it in the context of the likely business environment of the year 2000 and beyond.

Exhibit 1.3 provides a list of common questions about the five aspects of people management and international assignments that most companies have to face and answer.

Exhibit 1.3
Basic Questions of People Management and
International Assignments

Staffing	• What characteristics should be utilized in selecting expatriates?
	• Why are expatriates likely to accept/reject international assignments?
	• How can a larger pool of potential international assignees be identified and developed?
	• Can questionnaires and interviews be used effectively to screen and select candidates who are more likely to be successful overseas?

Exhibit continues

Training	• Should all expatriates receive training?
	• What are the most effective training methods for international assignments?
	• What should be the relative mix and content of predeparture and postarrival training?
	• How can the cost effectiveness of training be calculated?
Appraising	• How can expatriate performance be monitored in light of exogenous factors, such as foreign exchange rates, that can dramatically affect business performance?
	• What is the appropriate mix of quantitative and qualitative measures of expatriate job performance?
	• To what extent should local nationals be involved in evaluating expatriates?
Rewarding	• To what extent should an expatriate compensation package be utilized to entice employees to accept overseas assignments versus simply equalizing cost-of-living expenses?
	• How should different tax laws for expatriates from different home countries be factored into compensation?
	• How should compensation inequities be handled that arise when expatriates of similar level but from different home countries work in the same assignment country?
Developing	• To what extent should shorter assignments be used to develop young managers early in their careers?
	• How can the immediate task needs in the assignment and the development needs in the individual be effectively balanced?
	• How can employees with successful international experience be effectively repatriated into other organizational units?

People Management in the Global Context

While most of the principles and best practices are relevant to all firms independent of their size or industry, some important nuances are beneficial to explore. These nuances are perhaps most apparent when we look at a firm's current and future globalization plans.

Patterns of Globalization

Although the five aspects of people management apply to all firms engaged in transferring people across national borders, slightly different issues emerge as a function of the stage or pattern of a firm's globalization.[29] When we use the term *globalization,* we have in mind not one fixed point at which a firm is globalized but rather a series of patterns of globalization. In the next five sections, we briefly describe each general pattern of globalization and some of the specific international assignment challenges and issues associated with each.

Export Firms. Export-oriented firms have most of their value-chain activities in one or a few countries and have little coordination among global organizational units.[30] Firms of this type, such as L.L. Bean, are primarily concerned with exporting products and then marketing, selling, and distributing them in several countries. From a strategic perspective, export sales are an "add on" to domestic sales. The best evidence of this can be seen when demand exceeds supply. In this situation, the demands of domestic customers are given priority over those of international customers. Consequently, the focus of international people-management activities is often staffing, training, appraising, rewarding, and developing local nationals involved in these downstream activities. There is a generally low use of expatriate managers in export-oriented firms; instead, home-based managers with geographical or product responsibilities visit various international countries and sites. When international managers are used at all, they are usually placed in positions of general management and have rather broad geographical responsibilities. Most expatriates are sent out from the country of the parent firm, and very few if any managers are transferred from foreign countries into the parent organization or between foreign operations.

In firms whose international operations are export oriented, international assignments and assignees are often not top priorities. Careful attention to best practices, policies, and top international candidates is lacking. In one sense, this is both understandable and logical. However, problems arise when the firm begins to make international activities a stronger priority. At this point the firm may want to send its best and brightest out to its now-more-strategically important international operations. Unfortunately, the minimal past attention on international assignments and assignees makes this action a difficult transition. Because the firm has not valued international assignments, the best and brightest may be reluctant to go "out of sight and out of mind." Executives in export-oriented firms today must balance the needs of the moment with laying the groundwork for the future.

Multidomestic Corporations (MDCs). A multidomestic firm is one that has multiple foreign operations, but each foreign affiliate is basically focused on local markets, competitors, and so on. This situation results in multiple domestically focused operations. Such multidomestic firms as Castrol and Quaker State are most common in industries where competition in one country (or in one small group of countries) is independent of competition in others. Because competition for each geographically distinct unit within the firm is focused on the country and the market in the unit's location, a high degree of specialization and adaptation of the unit's value-chain activities is required. The culture- and country-specific knowledge that local nationals have is important for the appropriate specialization of the unit's activities. It is therefore only natural that the use of international managers, while higher than in the case of export firms, is still relatively low in MDCs. Moreover, the international managers tend to be of two types: executives or technical specialists. The executives are often from a cadre of "career internationalists"—managers who have made and spent most of their careers outside the firm's home office and home country. The technical specialists are generally on assignment for a relatively short time (one to two years) and are overseas for specific reasons (for example, to transfer a particular technology or to solve a particular problem).

The multidomestic orientation generally does not lead to systematic policies and practices formed for expatriate selection, training, or repatriation because only a small percentage of employees ever serve in overseas assignments, and these employees are generally "out of sight, out of mind" insofar as policymakers at the home office are concerned.[31] Instead, MDCs focus on international-assignment compensation practices and policies, in order to attract a sufficient number of reasonably capable international managers. However, from a strategic perspective, MDC firms should focus on all aspects of international assignments. International-strategy formulation and implementation are primarily restricted to an individual country, and for the country-centered strategic plan to be effective, key executives must incorporate the important and unique aspects of the country, culture, and market where the unit competes into their business plans. Consequently, even though only a few international managers are utilized in MDCs, great care must be taken to ensure that the right people are selected, trained, and prepared for a quick and effective adjustment, so that they can make exceptionally good decisions about *what* and *how* things should be done in the local market.

Global-Strategy Multinational Corporations (MNCs). Like multidomestic corporations, global-strategy MNCs (referred to simply as MNCs) also have geographically dispersed operations and units. In contrast to multidomestic firms, however, MNCs such as Xerox and Dow Chemical have extensive coordination between units in different geographical locations. This coordination and control is achieved through a variety of mechanisms. One particularly effective means is the establishment of a common organizational culture across its worldwide operations. MNCs tend to utilize more international managers, utilize both home-country and third-country international managers, and place international managers in a variety of organizational levels within foreign operations.[32]

In addition to engaging in the common practice of sending home- or parent-country nationals on overseas assignments in foreign countries, MNCs often also have foreign nationals serving in overseas assignments at the home or parent office. Bringing foreign nationals into the home or parent country (sometimes called "inpatriation") can help socialize foreign nationals to the philosophy or culture of the parent firm, as well as cross-fertilize the home operation with the ideas of foreign nationals and their own home-country operations. Because the international movement of employees provides a powerful informal means of controlling and coordinating activities across countries, MNCs with this orientation are more likely to have developed, over time, systematic policies and practices for expatriate selection, training, and repatriation.

The two-way directionality of informal coordination raises some very important issues with respect to repatriation. Because expatriate employees gain important experience that prepares them to understand various international markets, competitors, and operations, they are in a unique position to contribute effectively to international-strategy formulation and implementation at corporate and regional headquarters. Therefore, in addition to a need for excellent selection, training, and international-assignment support policies and practices, MNCs also need effective repatriation policies. Without them, the typical high post-repatriation turnover would significantly and negatively impact the firm's ability to populate its management ranks with the requisite international knowledge and experience it needs to compete effectively.[33]

Multifocal Corporations. Firms at the multifocal stage of internationalization, such as Coca-Cola and Airbus, are generally within industries where a firm's position in one country is substantially influenced by its competitive position in another. The objective for a firm with a global orientation (what Bartlett and Ghoshal have called a "transnational" firm[34]) is to coordinate value-chain activities on a global scale and thereby capture comparative advantages and links among countries. If transnational or global corporations were free from government restrictions, they would tend not to think of employees as home-country managers or local nationals; they would simply try to place individuals with comparative advantages and needed skills in appropriate locales much the way a firm moves people within domestic borders. These value-chain activities in turn could be concentrated in specific countries with comparative advantages relative to other countries. For example, if research and development (R&D) were in France, scientists and related people who had the knowledge and skills to contribute to R&D would be moved to France, regardless of nationality. The reality is that a "borderless world," in terms of the movement of people, does not yet exist. Nations have visa laws, domestic employment policies, tax structures, and other restrictions that prohibit the free and uninhibited movement of people across borders. In practice, global corporations are restricted in the movement of international staff people.

Even though global companies are not completely free to move people across borders, they still must focus on developing managers and executives with global leadership capabilities independent of nationality. As a consequence, these firms must benchmark their international assignment against the best policies and practices, not just within their industry or home country, but against the best firms across the globe.

The Issue of "Fit." No matter which globalization stage a firm is in, its international assignment policies and practices must fit the environment and must be congruent with each other. The balance of international-assignment policies and practices with the marketplace creates an *external fit*. The balance and congruence among the five aspects of people management within a firm (staffing, training, appraising, rewarding, and developing) constitutes *internal fit*. Without good external and internal fit, a firm will experience significant difficulties in effectively formulating and implementing strategies. Two examples will illustrate this point.

Case 2: WestCoast Bankcorp

Recently a large West Coast bank (the name of the firm has been disguised) was trying to reduce its total expenditures on international assignments. The bank was at a coordinated MNC stage of globalization. It had operations in over twenty countries and sought to closely coordinate among its subsidiaries such value-chain activities as lending, foreign exchange, and retail banking. The bank also sought to compete by offering low interest rates and fees for the services it provided.

The bank found that its international managers were usually two to three times more expensive to employ than comparable employees in the home country and several times more expensive to employ than local nationals. These high costs for expatriates were consistent with what most other U.S. banks experienced. WestCoast Bankcorp tried to lower its costs by reducing its aggregate expatriate costs. This goal was achieved over just a few years, by reducing the total number of global managers by half. The bank also tried to reduce the average cost per expatriate by reducing or cutting various aspects of the standard expatriate package (reducing allowances, locating global managers in low-tax countries, cutting predeparture training, and so on).

*The critical implication of this particular cost-reduction program concerns the issue of **external fit**. The key question is whether the effort to lower total costs was carried out in a manner that inhibited or facilitated the firm's competitive advantage. Although cutting the total number of global managers reduced the aggregate costs, coordination and control between the parent and subsidiaries, as well as among subsidiaries, became much more difficult. The effort to lower the cost per global manager by reducing predeparture training also reduced the ability of these managers to function effectively and made it difficult to attract top quality managers to international* *assignments. Fewer global managers were now being placed in top positions within the foreign subsidiaries, and in order to facilitate effective coordination they had to understand both the home office and the local operation. Lack of resources for cross-cultural training reduced their ability to quickly understand the local situation and to facilitate coordination.*

This couldn't have happened at a worse time. WestCoast Bank found itself competing with new foreign rivals, especially from Japan, in its home market and in its key overseas markets. WestCoast Bank needed global coordination and control to fight off the coordinated attacks from foreign competitors, but its international assignments practices and policies made it difficult to do so. This poor external fit had a significant and negative affect on the bank's subsequent financial performance.

Case 3: International Hotel

International Hotel is a large U.S.-based hotel corporation that tried to maintain its competitive advantage through differentiation, by offering guest services (for example, business centers equipped with fax machines, computers, copiers, secretaries, and so on) that far exceeded those of its competitors. The exact services varied considerably from country to country, as a function of its multidomestic pattern of globalization. International managers were encouraged to formulate their own location-specific approaches to this "high-quality service" strategy and were monitored on the basis of their financial results. Reasonable levels of predeparture and postarrival training were provided, which facilitated the managers' ability to quickly gain an in-depth understanding of the values and needs of local markets and to design services to meet those needs.

*Unfortunately, much of an international manager's performance bonus in this organization was based on overall corporate results, and so while the training led managers to want to focus on understanding local markets, the appraisal and compensation policies had the opposite effect. The managers knew that if they could reduce costs (in some cases, by eliminating certain costly services), profits would increase, and so would their bonuses. In this case, the **internal fit** among training, rewarding, and appraising was poor and did not facilitate or encourage expatriate managers' ability to differentiate their hotels in the local markets where they were competing.*

Key Implication #1: Figure and Ground

As anyone who has ever seen a photograph or painting knows, what you focus on as you look at the picture depends on what is "figure" and what is "background." If a tree is front and center in the picture, you tend to focus on it and see it in detail. If the tree is part of the background, you might not even notice it. Managers in your company are astute observers of figure and ground. On many occasions, we have been called in to help a company figure out why it can't get good (let alone the best) managers to take international assignments. While a variety of factors can influence a decision to accept or reject an overseas stint (we will explore these in depth in Chapter 3), time and time again employees have said something similar to the following:

> Yeah, I hear the rhetoric about international, but talk is cheap. If international is so important, why don't any of the senior executives have any overseas experience? Why, if it matters so much, was (Fred, Sally, Juan, or whoever) left dangling in the wind? They had only a month's notice before they had to leave. They got zero training. They were out-of-sight and out-of-mind while they were gone. No one knew what to do with them when they came back. Their peers moved ahead of them during the assignment. So why won't I or others like me take an international assignment? I wonder.

Quite frankly, many companies don't know what is perceived as figure and ground by their employees when it comes to international assignments. Many firms have been surprised by the results of surveys and interviews with their people. However, the insights proved invaluable in knowing where to focus efforts at improving both the perception and reality of international assignments.

Key Implication #2: The Whole Picture

The best results are achieved by looking at a whole picture. Traditionally, compensation has been the focus for most companies. In one sense, this is understandable; after all, people have to get paid and taxes have to be taken care of. However, leading companies use a more systematic perspective. They know that all aspects of international assignments—selecting, training, rewarding, appraising, repatriating—have to be considered together. Each can have a significant impact on the others. For example, if you fail to select the right person, no amount of training can compensate for that. However, starting with the right person but ignoring training will also not guarantee success. Whether in music, sports, or business, even the most talented individual needs education, training, and coaching to excel. So, even though we will examine each of the aspects of international assignments separately, they are all interconnected and best understood by looking at the whole picture.

Key Implication #3: Looking Ahead

Even if we look at the whole picture and get the right things in figure and background, as the picture is today, we must also look ahead. Global leadership skills are not developed overnight, but the need for them can erupt with little notice. If a foreign competitor starts moving in on your home turf, or major customers expand internationally, or a new business opportunity appears in an emerging market, in short order you find your firm in desperate need of quality global leaders. In fact, in a recent survey of *Fortune 500* firms, we found that the strong majority had neither the quantity nor quality of global leaders they needed. The major reason is that in most companies the international-assignment policies and practices lag behind the strategic needs of the business. Because it takes some time to develop global leaders, these policies and practices need to **lead** rather than lag behind the business. Executives need to look five or ten years out into the future, anticipate the quantity and quality of global leaders they will need, and start building today.

As we said at the outset, international assignments are not the only means of developing global leaders, but they are the most powerful. Consequently, they must be the best planned and best managed of all your firm's international activities. In too many companies, this is not the case. To gauge where your company is, ask yourself: If I asked twenty senior executives to rank the importance of the following international activities, where would international assignments fall? International strategy, organizational structure for global reach, international marketing, offshore manufacturing, cross-border alliances and joint ventures, international assignments.

If international assignments don't rank at the top, they should—not for altruistic reasons but for hard-core business reasons. For example, we found a correlation between the degree of "globalization" of a business (indicated by the percentage of international sales) and the extent to which top executives with international experience have a significant impact on financial performance (such as return on assets). Although we have already said it, it's worth repeating: Global leaders are not made overnight; if your firm will need them in the future, start developing them today. Few things could be of greater value than (1) a top-to-bottom review of your current international assignment policies and practices, especially as perceived by your people, and (2) working to ensure that your overall system has superior external and internal fit.

Summary

We began this chapter by saying that people are the key to global competitiveness and that global assignments can serve three strategic functions in the utilization of people in today's global marketplace. Global assignments can play a strategic role in succession planning and leadership development, coordination and control of international operations, and technological and information exchange between the parent and subsidiaries and among subsidiaries. We argued that, in addition to considering global assignments as more than a "firefighting" tool, firms should include both home-country nationals and foreign-country nationals in strategic global assignments. We also pointed out that, independent of the "firefighting" or strategic role of global assignments, there are significant and sometimes devastating costs associated with poor design and management of global assignments.

Next, we presented a general framework of people management, to structure later chapters on the selection, training, cross-cultural adjustment, performance, evaluation, compensation, and repatriation of people. We also suggested that these issues become increasingly important as firms move from export patterns to coordinated MNC patterns of globalization. Consequently, executives need to examine the external fit among the marketplace, the pattern of globalization, and the firm's international management policies.

The remainder of this book summarizes the best thinking, practice, and scientific evidence available on the international management of people. The remaining chapters also discuss in more detail how general recommendations may vary according to a firm's pattern of globalization. In terms of our style and approach, we try to walk the razor's edge. One the one hand, we present the latest scientific evidence and research findings. Like a practicing doctor, we believe you can serve your "patients" best when you have the latest research available to you. On the other hand, we wanted to make the information accessible and easy to read. We wanted to make this book informative but interesting. Hopefully, we succeed.

Notes

1. Stroh and Caligiuri, "Increasing Global Competitiveness Through Effective People Management." 1997 Global Leadership Institute Technical Report.
2. Black, Morrison, and Gregerson, *Global Explorers: The Next Generation of Leaders*.

3. Bowman, "Concerns of CEOs."
4. Hambrick, Korn, Frederickson, and Ferry, *21st Century Report*; Stroh and Lautzen-hiser, "Benchmarking Global Human Resources Practices and Procedures."
5. Stroh and Caligiuri, "Strategic Human Resources: A New Source for Competitive Advantage in the Global Arena."
6. Laabs,"How Gillette Grooms Global Talent."
7. Brandt, "Global HR."
8. Dennis and Stroh, "A Little Jeitinho in Brazil: A Case Study on International Management."
9. DeYoung, "The Clash of Cultures at Tylan General," p. 149.
10. Kobrin, "Expatriate Reduction and Strategic Control in American Multinational Corporations."
11. Gupta and Govindarajan, "Knowledge Flows and the Structure of Control Within Multinational Corporations."
12. Moran, Stahl, and Boyer, *International Human Resource Management.*
13. Hall, "How Top Management and the Organization Itself Can Block Effective Executive Succession."
14. Swaak, "Expatriate Failures: Too Many, Too Much Cost, Too Little Planning."
15. Harvey, "Repatriation of Corporate Executives: An Empirical Study."
16. Data provided by the Philip Morris Companies.
17. Copeland and Louis, *Going International.*
18. Swaak, "Expatriate Failures."
19. "GE Culture Turns Sour at French Unit."
20. Adler, "Re-entry: Managing Cross-Cultural Transitions"; Black and Gregersen, "When Yankee Comes Home: Factors Related to Expatriate and Spouse Repatriation Adjustment"; Stroh, "Predicting Turnover Among Repatriates: Can Organizations Affect Retention Rates."
21. Munton, Forster, Altman, and Greenbury, "Job Relocation: People on the Move."
22. Lublin and Smith, "Management: U.S. Companies Struggle with Scarcity of Executives to Run Outposts in China"; Birdseye and Hill, "Individual, Organizational/Work and Environmental Influences on Expatriate Turnover Tendencies: An Empirical Study."
23. Hambrick, Korn, Frederickson, and Ferry, *21st Century Report.*
24. Baird and Meshoulam, "Managing Two Fits of Strategic Human Resource Management"; Devanna, Fombrun, and Tichy, "A Framework for Strategic Human Resource Management"; Miller, Beechler, Bhatt, and Nath, "Relationship Between Global Strategic Planning Process and the Human Resource Management Function."
25. Mendenhall and Oddou, "The Dimensions of Expatriate Acculturation: A Review"; Miller, "The International Selection Decision: A Study of Managerial Behavior in the Selection Decision Process."
26. Windham International and the National Foreign Trade Council, *Global Relocation Trends 1995 Survey Report*, 1996.
27. Mendenhall and Oddou, "Dimensions of Expatriate Acculturation"; Black and Mendenhall, "Cross-Cultural Training Effectiveness: A Review and Theoretical Framework for Future Research"; Misa and Fabricatore, "Return on Investment of Overseas Personnel"; Moran, Stahl, and Boyer, *International Human Resource Management.*

28. Adler, "Re-entry"; Adler, *International Dimensions of Organizational Behavior;* Black and Gregersen, "When Yankee Comes Home"; Clague and Krupp, "International Personnel: The Repatriation Problem"; Harvey, "The Other Side of Foreign Assignments: Dealing with the Repatriation Problem"; Harvey, "Repatriation of Corporate Executives"; Kendall, "Repatriation: An Ending and a Beginning."
29. Ghadar and Adler, "Management Culture and Accelerated Product Life Cycle."
30. Porter, "Changing Patterns of International Competition."
31. Adler, "Re-entry"; Adler, *International Dimensions of Organizational Behavior;* Black and Gregersen, "When Yankee Comes Home"; Clague and Krupp, "International Personnel"; Harvey, "Repatriation of Corporate Executives."
32. Edstrom and Galbraith, "Transfer of Managers as a Coordination and Control Strategy in Multinational Organizations"; Jaeger, "Contrasting Control Modes in the Multinational Corporation: Theory, Practice, and Implications."
33. Black and Gregersen, "When Yankee Comes Home"; Adler, "Re-entry."
34. Bartlett and Ghoshal, "Organizing for Worldwide Effectiveness: The Transnational Solution."

2

The Process of Making Cross-Cultural Adjustments

If adjustment to life and work in other cultures were not such an elusive target for managers and their families, there would be little need for this chapter or those that follow. Most people, however, find cross-cultural adjustment difficult, and for this reason much of the first half of this book focuses on the aspects of culture that affect adjustment and important outcomes such as turnover and job performance. Before we tackle the topic of cross-cultural adjustment, we need a clear idea of what we mean by *culture.*

What Is Culture?

People usually think of culture as something a country, region, or firm has—something you can see, hear, touch, smell, or taste. They think of ceremonies, clothing, historical landmarks, art, and food as examples of a country's culture. Clearly, these things differ substantially from one country to another, and the critical question is why.

The answer lies in a view of culture that goes beyond what's visible.[1] One way to picture a culture is as a tree, with parts visible, above the surface, and parts below—including supporting roots (see Exhibit 2.1). The tangible aspects of a culture—those things one can see, hear, smell, taste, or touch—are *artifacts,* or manifestations, of underlying values and assumptions that a group of people share. The artifacts are what we can see, but what we see is only a small fraction of what is there. What we cannot see—the values and assumptions—are what support and give life to the culture.

A culture is not simply the total collection of assumptions, values, or artifacts shared by people. It also consists of the set of common assumptions and values that consistently influences people's

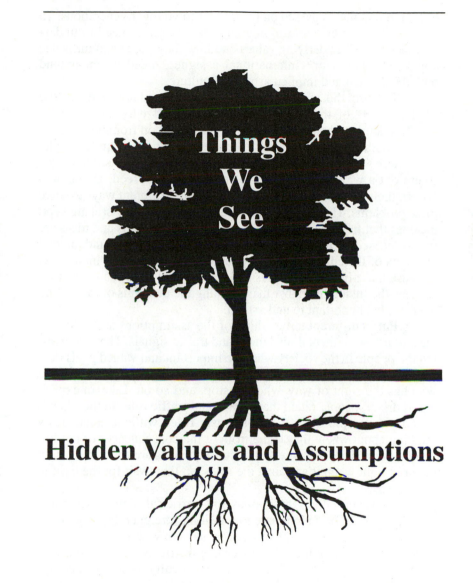

Exhibit 2.1
A View of Culture

behavior, and that is passed on from older to younger generations. To adapt well to a new culture, international assignees need to understand a culture's underlying values and how they guide and influence appropriate behavior.[2] International assignees need to understand both the explicit and implicit aspects of culture.

To begin this process, we need to understand how and why the implicit roots of the culture emerge, how and why they become widely shared, and how and why they get passed on from one generation to another.[3] The basic answer to these questions is quite simple. All societies face and must solve a limited set of problems. They must figure out a way to communicate and to educate, feed, clothe, and govern their people. Societies experiment with different ways to solve these problems. The methods and ideas that prove successful are kept; the ones that fail are discarded. The successful methods and ideas are in turn passed on to future generations. Because these fundamental elements of the culture reside in people's heads, they are intangible. Because these intangible values and beliefs guide and shape what we can see, the intangible rather than the tangible elements of the culture are the most important to understand.

Put in different terms, think of the assumptions and values of the culture as the mental road maps and traffic signals. The road maps tell the people in the society what the important and valued goals (key destinations) are and the ways to get there; the traffic signals tell them who has the right of way, when to stop, and so on. Like an experienced driver, people retain these maps and traffic rules in their heads over time. People obey the most basic rules without consciously thinking about where they came from or the consequences of not following them. They know what the consequences are for turning right on a red light when it's against the rules, so they wait for the light to turn green.

However natural these maps and traffic rules might seem to a "local," they can be a nightmare to a visiting foreigner. Imagine being put into the heart of the Tokyo freeway system with no map, no road signs, and no idea of the rules governing traffic. Suddenly, your previous road maps and traffic rules are practically useless or perhaps even deadly—after all, the Japanese, like the British, drive on the left side (Americans would say "wrong side") of the road.

A similar process occurs as people move from one culture to another on global assignments. Suddenly, previous social and interpersonal guides are useless or even deadly, and people are forced to learn new maps and rules to navigate social and interpersonal situations. The complication is that unlike actual road maps and traffic rules, the deep-rooted aspects of a culture are not explained in a convenient manual.

What happens when you violate (probably unintentionally) cultural traffic rules? Just as violations of some traffic rules entail simple warnings or small fines, while others require time in jail, not all the rules of a culture incur the same penalties for infractions. A helpful way of thinking about the importance of the cultural rules and the severity of the consequences for breaking them is to conceptualize cultural values along two dimensions—the extent to which they are widely shared among group members and the extent to which they are deeply held. This conceptualization is illustrated in Exhibit 2.2.

Those assumptions, values, or rules of the culture that are widely shared and deeply held generally result in substantial rewards or punishments. For example, a widely shared and strongly held rule in the United States is that people do not talk to themselves constantly or loudly. When we see a person doing this, we become nervous and concerned, even if the person poses no physical threat to anyone.

Exhibit 2.2
The Matrix of Culture

	Narrow	**Wide**
Deep	**Deeply Held, Narrowly Shared** These are core values within a subculture.	**Deeply Held, Widely Shared** These are the core values of the culture.
Shallow	**Shallowly Held, Narrowly Shared** These are transient values of the culture.	**Shallowly Held, Widely Shared** These are the surface values of the culture.

What happens to those who violate this rule? In many cases, they get sent to mental institutions.

What about rules that are deeply held but not widely shared? In this case, the rewards or punishments are often informal. For example, some people, but not everyone, consider burping after a meal to be a serious violation of proper behavior. You will not be put in jail for burping, but you may be cut out of particular social circles, at least in the United States. In other countries, you can offend a host by *not* burping after a meal.

In the case of rules that are widely shared but not deeply held, violations often entail uniform but rather mild punishments; infrequent violations may carry no punishment at all. For example, in the United States, people are taught not to interrupt. If people occasionally interrupt, however, it is unlikely that the punishment will be significant.

The Nature of Assumptions About the World

To understand another culture, we must understand the roots of that culture, which are found in its fundamental assumptions. From these assumptions grow the values, beliefs, and visible artifacts and behaviors of the culture. Not all cultural trees have the same root systems. Consequently, it is important to discuss briefly the nature of assumptions and how they differ from one culture to another. Fortunately, we do not have to examine 200 or more countries and cultures to get a sense of these different assumptions. Even though different societies are based on different cultural assumptions, the basic underlying assumptions can be divided into five categories.[4] Exhibit 2.3 summarizes the general nature of these assumptions and gives examples of specific forms they may take, as well as their implications for management.

Humanity's Relationship to the Environment
The first category of assumptions concerns those made about the relationship of humanity to nature. For example, in some cultures, including the United States, the assumption is that humans dominate nature and utilize it for the wealth and benefit of humankind. In other cultures, the assumption is that humans and nature should coexist harmoniously. These differing assumptions lead to significantly different implications. In the United States, this assumption is an important basis for the building of dams, the mining of minerals, and the logging of trees. The implications may reach beyond these basic activities,

Nature of Assumptions	Specific Assumptions	Managerial Implications
Environment (assumptions about the relationship between humans and the environment)	People are meant to dominate the environment. People must coexist harmoniously with the environment.	Strategic plans should be developed to enable the firm to dominate its industry. Firms should seek positions that allow them to coexist with others.
Human Nature (assumptions about human nature)	People are generally lazy. Work is as natural as play for people.	Implement systems for monitoring behavior and establish clear punishment for undesired behavior. Provide people with opportunities and responsibilities and encourage their development.
Relationships (assumptions about how humans should relate to each other)	Individuals have certain rights and freedoms. People exist because of others and owe them an obligation.	Individual performance should be measured and rewarded. Cooperation with and contributions to the group should be evaluated and rewarded.
Activity (assumptions about the property types and targets of human activity)	People create their own destinies and must plan for the future. People should react to and enjoy whatever the present provides.	People who fail to plan should plan to fail. Planning the future only gets in the way of enjoying the present.
Truth (assumptions about the nature of truth and reality)	Truth exists objectively. Truth is what is socially accepted.	Facts and statistics are how you convince and influence people. Opinion leaders are how you influence people and decisions.

Exhibit 2.3
Basic Assumptions and Their Implications

however, to strategic planning or management practices in business. Consider how most U.S. firms view the business environment and how they strategically approach it. Is the business environment viewed as something that people must accept and with which they must try to harmonize? Or is it viewed as something that must be mastered and dominated, if possible? For example, no one would accuse Microsoft of believing that it must harmonize with the software industry environment. In fact, Microsoft's confrontation with the Justice Department stems largely from its attempt to dominate its environment.

Human Nature

Different cultures also make different assumptions about the nature of people. In some cultures, the assumption is that people are fundamentally industrious; in others, the assumption is that people are inherently lazy. Douglas McGregor demonstrated the relevance of this difference in his book *The Human Side of Enterprise*. McGregor argues that every manager acts on a "theory" or set of assumptions about people. Theory X managers assume that "the average human being has an inherent dislike for work and will avoid it if he can" (p. 33). Consequently, managers who accept this view of people believe that "people must be coerced, controlled, directed, and threatened with punishment to get them to put forth adequate effort toward the achievement of organizational objectives" (p. 34). By contrast, Theory Y managers assume that "the expenditure of physical and mental effort in work is as natural as play or rest" (p. 47). Consequently, managers who accept this view believe that "external control and the threat of punishment are not the only means for bringing about effort toward organizational objectives. Man will exercise self-direction and self-control in the service of objectives to which he is committed. Commitment to objectives is a function of the rewards associated with their achievement" (p. 47).

Human Relationships

This category of assumptions concerns a variety of questions: What is the right way for people to deal with each other? How much power and authority should any one person have over another? How much of an individual's orientation should be toward meeting his or her own goals versus meeting the goals of the collective society.[6] A large-scale study of forty countries conducted by Geert Hofstede found significant differences in the answers to these questions.[7] For example, Hofstede examined the degree to which people accepted power and authority differences among people. He found that people from the Philippines, Venezuela, and Mexico had the highest levels of acceptance of power differences. In other words, individuals from these and other "high power distance" cultures thought that people with higher rank should have significantly more power, influence on decisions, and so on than people of lower rank. By contrast, people in Austria, Israel, Denmark, and other "low power distance" cultures did not think that rank entitled people to significantly more power and influence; they tended to think that everyone's voice should be heard. Hofstede also found that people from the United States, Australia, and Great Britain ranked highest for their individual orientation. To "high individualism" cultures, individual freedom and rights were the most important. In contrast, people from Venezuela, Colombia, and Pakistan ranked highest for their collective orientation. In other words, to "low individualism" or "high collectivist" cultures, the group's interests matter more than those of the individual.

Human Activity

This category of assumptions concerns what the culture considers correct behavior and expectations about whether people should be active, passive, or fatalistic. In the United States, people brag about working eighty hours a week, about having no time for vacations or to watch TV, and about doing several things at once on their computers. They believe in such phrases as "People who fail to plan should plan to fail." In other cultures, such as Vietnam and Yemen, people believe that a preoccupation with planning gets in the way of enjoying the present. In these countries, high-strung activity is not valued and may even be seen as a waste of time and energy.

Reality and Truth

People in different cultures also have different assumptions about the nature of reality and truth and about how they are verified or established. For example, the adversarial criminal justice system in the United States is based on two assumptions: truth exists and the fire generated by opposing views will ultimately *illuminate* what really happened. In other cultures, such as Japan, reality is more subjective and dependent on what people believe it to be. Consequently, opinion leaders or persuasive stories rather than "hard facts" are used to influence people and business decisions.

Our purpose in discussing these five categories of assumptions is to illustrate two key issues. As mentioned earlier, assumptions are the source of values and behavior. To understand the visible artifacts of culture, we must understand the invisible values and assumptions. Like the roots of a tree, fundamental assumptions by their very nature are not only invisible, but generally are also taken for granted. Their taken-for-granted nature makes them difficult to uncover or understand, because the people who hold them are not usually conscious of them and, therefore, cannot easily identify and explain them to foreigners. People are as unaware of how their cultural assumptions affect their behavior as they are of the oxygen they breathe in the air around them. Breathing and following cultural norms are natural and almost automatic processes. Furthermore, the taken-for-granted nature of cultural assumptions makes them difficult to change. Behavior may change, but underlying values and assumptions remain and are not changed either easily or quickly. For example, Japanese businessmen stopped wearing kimonos and started wearing Western clothes. This change in behavior might indicate that key fundamental values had changed, but they had not. The key cultural value of conformity remained unchanged. Nearly all Japanese businessmen today wear the same business attire—dark suit, white shirt, conservative tie. What you see on the outside has changed, but what goes on inside remains unchanged.

This observation brings us back to the discussion of why cross-cultural adjustment is difficult. Although each culture has visible components (artifacts and behavior) and invisible ones (values and assumptions), the *in*visible components are more important because they are the source of the visible aspects of the culture. Unfortunately, since most foreign sojourners have neither a mental road map nor a guide to the implicit traffic signals, they encounter everything from close calls to fatal cultural crashes. Consider the case of Gerald Carlson, who had been recently assigned to the Kuala Lumpur (KL) Malaysian office where he was to serve as General Manager of Pittsburgh-based PENNBANK's merchant banking operation.[8]

Case 4: PENNBANK Malaysia

Gerald Carlson

Gerald Carlson had worked in a wide variety of managerial positions for PENNBANK over a period of eight years, during which time he and his family (wife Susan, ten-year-old son Johnny, thirteen-year-old daughter Kit, and dog Tipper) had moved to four different cities within the U.S. as part of Gerald's corporate development. His most recent assignment had been as Vice

President of Corporate Affairs of PENNBANK'S Chicago Branch. Susan, had taken courses in four different colleges due to the family's moves, and had finally become qualified to work as a school social worker in the local high school system.

PENNBANK Goes Global

Two years prior, PENNBANK had expanded its operations to the international arena, with a particular emphasis on establishing a presence throughout Southeast Asia. Malaysia, a strategically located nation of slightly over 17 million people (14 million living in Peninsular Malaysia and the rest in Sabah and Sarawak on the island of Borneo), had been targeted as the first Asian site for PENNBANK. PENNBANK had also examined possible sites in Europe and North Africa, but first wanted to establish its Malaysian branch. Malaysia had attracted foreign investments because of its solid position in commodities—tin, palm oil, rubber, tropical hardwoods and, most recently, offshore petroleum. Thus far, PENNBANK had successfully established itself as a merchant bank in Kuala Lumpur, the capital city of Malaysia, by providing financing support for commercial and industrial ventures. Malaysia preferred that new foreign banks enter the economy on that level. The government generally restricted the nature of a new bank's investments, ensuring that all major investments were part of a multi-bank coalition with other established Malaysian banks. Malaysia placed particular emphasis on co-investment with Bumiputera banks.

"Bumiputera," often shortened to "Bumi" or Bumis," literally means "sons of the soil" and generally refers to the native Malay people as opposed to Chinese Malays or Tamil Indian Malays. Bumi can also include those Chinese or Tamil Indian Malays who have established a three-or-more-generation heritage in Malaysia. Additionally, Malays can become a Bumi by converting to Islam. The Bumis constitute 54–56 percent of Malaysia's population. Historically controlling only a small percentage of the economy, Bumis have been deemed by the government to need special assistance and encouragement in the economy, including the banking community. Thus, initial start-up banks such as PENNBANK were expected to hire a disproportionate share of the Bumi population (i.e., greater than the 54–56 percent present in the population) and to assist in financing Bumi–owned or controlled projects. This requirement constituted a kind of affirmative action policy on behalf of the majority group. The Malaysian government also generally kept start-up foreign banks out of full-service banking positions for several years. Expansion of PENNBANK's ability to lend and eventually take a major position in financing large-scale commercial and industrial projects depended on development of a goodwill relationship with

the Malaysian government, the Malaysian banking community, and the Bumiputeras.

As the newly assigned General Manager of its two-year-old Kuala Lumpur main branch (PENNBANK-KL), Gerald had limited experience in Southeast Asia. He had been sent to KL on several extensive trips during the period that PENNBANK was establishing itself in the local economy. During those trips, Gerald worked well with the local people. For Gerald, this assignment was a major promotion in status, responsibility, compensation, and benefits. It also represented a significant challenge and change in duties with regard to locale, type of banking and cultural diversity.

PENNBANK-KL's Need for a New GM

The previous and first General Manager of PENNBANK KL, a bachelor, had just been removed from the assignment after he was charged, by a person unknown to him, with violation of the "close proximity" law regarding Muslim women. The Muslim close proximity law in Malaysia states that if a citizen of good repute reports that any man is seen in close proximity to an unmarried Muslim woman, such as holding hands in a park or walking together on the beach in the evening, the man must immediately marry the woman or serve a jail term. While not usually enforced in KL, but often enforced in some of the more traditional States of Malaysia, such as Terengganu and Kelantan, the close proximity law is a religious law that has been used as a device to "control" foreign competitors. That is, a competitor might seek out an opportunity to observe the improper behavior and report it to the police. The result, in this case, was that PENNBANK's General Manager was hurried out of the country. The trial and charges were subsequently dropped; however, PENNBANK received considerable adverse publicity in the Malaysian newspapers. The Acting Assistant General Manager, Abd Mahmoud bin Malek, a local Bumiputera, attempted to fill the vacancy, but had only limited previous experience with PENNBANK. He did not do well, but no other local replacement of sufficient experience and ability was available to fill the job. Yet, some of PENNBANK-KL's more fundamentalist Bumi employees continued to express outrage over the past General Manager's activities and demanded a local General Manager. PENNBANK'S executives in Pittsburgh believed that the branch was not yet well enough established in the Malaysian economy to justify using a host-country national. These corporate executives felt that they had to bring in another General Manager immediately.

Gerald's Big Chance

Upon his selection as the new GM, Gerald was given a fast-track preparation course. He spent one day with several other PENNBANK officers who had previously visited KL, two days with people at the Malaysian Industrial Development Authority's Chicago office, and a day with PENNBANK's human resource department in Pittsburgh to discuss temporary living arrangements, flight schedules, allowances, compensation, benefits, deferred income, Malaysian taxes, and so on. He was also given a copy of the book **The Malay Dilemma**, by Dr. Mohatir, Prime Minister of Malaysia, to provide background information. He then had an additional week to pass on his job responsibilities to his successor at PENNBANK'S Chicago branch. No cultural, historical, language, problem-solving, skill-building, or other preparation or training was provided for Gerald or his family.

The Family

Fortunately for the children, the move occurred in the summer, so they did not encounter any unusual school problems in the U.S. However, when they arrived in KL, they found themselves in the middle of the school year, which starts in June. When the family arrived in KL, after a 32-hour trip via Tokyo and Hong Kong, they were booked into a luxury hotel until they could find permanent accommodations. It took Susan six weeks to find a house, clear the sale, and secure permits for electricity, water, telephone, and television (all separate government monopolies). Susan also found out that she now had a live-in maid/cook, because Gerald's position required such services. Due to Gerald's new status in the KL expatriate community, Susan was expected to be a member of the American Club and several country clubs, and the couple was frequently invited to U.S. Embassy receptions.

Life changed very radically for Susan and the children. Susan discovered she could not practice her newly achieved profession of school social worker, since Malaysia (like the U.S.) only issues a work permit for one of the married aliens. The family also discovered they could not get their dog Tipper out of customs' quarantine. Malaysia has strict rules against importing dogs, because they are considered unclean in the Muslim faith. Tipper was eventually "put away," much to the consternation and trauma of the entire family.

In addition, instead of relishing the freedom of summer vacation, the children found themselves in a new private school dealing with a new curriculum and a new language. The students in the school were mostly embassy offspring and came from virtually every embassy in KL—an interesting and varied assortment. The school had a decidedly British orientation. The children were not happy with their course of studies or manner of instruction. They began to object to the mandatory course in Bahasa Malaysia since, as they stated: "Everyone speaks English anyway, and besides, we're Americans, not Malay."

Problems at PENNBANK-KL

Gerald, in the meantime, was experiencing many problems, but operating on an exhilarating level of frustration and problem solving. He quickly noted that the acting general manager had hired several of his Bumi relatives, despite PENNBANK'S absolute policy against nepotism. Gerald was also disturbed that most of the locals were going to his assistant, Mahmoud, with their problems instead of directly to him. Gerald was concerned as well with the obvious difficulties the various ethnic/racial/religious groups seemed to have with each other. The Bumiputeras were claiming they should have a greater percentage of the jobs. The Chinese Malays seemed to go about their business well, but were unwilling to provide assistance to the Bumi. The few Tamil (Indian) Malays seemed to have a resigned attitude about promotion potential and defined their jobs in very limited ways. Gerald also noticed that supervisors were unwilling to accept responsibility, and his efforts at delegating were to no avail.

On the positive side however, new accounts, which had virtually dried up before Gerald had arrived, were making a steady but slow recovery. Gerald had personally participated in packaging several small project loans with Malaysian Banking Berhad. In short, the job was tough but rewarding.

The Ultimate Ultimatum

At the end of the third month many things had changed. At Susan's insistence, Gerald and Susan discussed returning to the States. The children seemed to be suffering from the move; Johnny would not leave the house, and Kit had become friends with an unruly group of embassy children. Gerald and Susan were concerned about the long-term effects of this international assignment on the children. Gerald acknowledged that the new position was not as exciting as they had been led to believe, although he felt he was making real progress. He was becoming increasingly frustrated with the energy level required to do what he had determined was a mediocre job at best, but still wanted to stick with the job and finish the assignment. Susan missed her career more than she had anticipated. Susan and the children wanted to go home, and made this clear in no uncertain terms. Family pressures had built up, and after several heated discussions, they finally agreed that Gerald should tell his boss that the new position had not worked out for either him or his family. The next day, Gerald sent a fax to his boss in the United States. The tone of the fax was quite negative. Gerald reminded his boss that he was promised there would always be a job for him in the U.S. if he agreed to go to Malaysia and help out PENNBANK-KL. Gerald reported the following problems and frustrations with the job:

1. The Malaysian government's limitations on banking itself.

2. Frustrations with a *no nepotism* rule in a country where nepotism was seen as a normal way of life, making it impossible for Gerald to dismiss some of the deadwood at PENNBANK-KL.

3. Constant infighting between himself and Mahmoud coupled with Mahmoud's popularity among the employees. How could he ever gain the legitimate power needed to run the bank as needed?

4. The incessant struggles between the various ethnic/religious groups.

Other personal reasons not noted in the fax were:

- Susan was tired of being followed around all day by the maid, who was always giving sweets to the children behind her back.

- Susan did not want to spend another hour with the vapid alcoholics at the club.

- Susan was sick and tired of being in a country that wouldn't let her use her skills to work outside the home.

- Kit had come home from school in tears because she was told she must learn to speak Bahasa Malaysia. She didn't see why she should have to do this, because she's an American. In addition, there were no age-appropriate friends in this area suited for Kit.

- Kit and Johnny were both frustrated by the requirement that everyone had to study the Bahasa Malaysia language in school, even though everyone spoke English.

- Kit and Johnny were further frustrated by the fact that the television mostly showed Bahasa Malaysia films. The American and English films were usually played later in the evening after their bedtime.

- Johnny was failing his course in the history of Victorian England and couldn't understand why he couldn't study American history instead.

- The home telephone had stopped working for the third time that week.

Cross-Cultural Adjustment: The Process

The episodes depicted in the preceding case are common. Many global managers and their families experience adjustment difficulties similar to those of the Carlsons. Most of the time, the spouse, quite often a wife, has to give up a job, a house, friends, and family to accompany her husband on his foreign assignment. Consequently, she may have even greater difficulty than her husband adapting to the foreign culture. In a later chapter, we will discuss the relationship of the family to the international assignment and, in particular, the spouse. For now, the reasons cross-cultural adjustment is so difficult should become clearer as we examine the dynamics of this process, which seriously disrupts the individual's *routines* and dramatically affects the individual's *ego* and *self-image*.

Routines

Almost no one wants total uncertainty in life. In fact, most people want a reasonably high degree of certainty and predictability. That is primarily why people establish routines. The global success of McDonald's is testimony to the general human need for a certain level of predictability in life. When we go into a McDonald's, there are a variety of items from which to choose, but we know how a Big Mac is going to taste before we order it. A Big Mac is a Big Mac. People like not only the product but also its predictability.

People's routines affect all aspects of their lives, from the mundane to the critical. For example, people establish routines for waking up in the morning: shut off the alarm, get up, take a shower, get dressed, eat, run out the door. People also establish more serious routines regarding initiating and developing relationships, dealing with conflict, and forming expectations about relationships.

Because we cannot consciously process an infinite number of issues simultaneously, we establish routines. Routines and the certainty they provide create a kind of psychological economy. Because we know how a Big Mac will taste, and because we know that once we get up we will take a shower, we do not have to devote a lot of time and energy to thinking about and processing those issues. When a routine is disrupted, however, more time and energy must be devoted to processing even mundane matters. Mental time and energy are limited; therefore, the disruption of routines decreases mental time and energy available to devote to other issues. Not all disruptions are equally severe, however. The severity is a function of three dimensions.

Scope. The greater the number (or scope) of disrupted routines in a new cultural environment, the more difficult the process of dealing with the disruptions and the greater the frustration, anger, and anxiety that are likely to follow. Having the morning-shower routine disrupted, is one thing but having the eating, sleeping, commuting, and working routines disrupted is quite another. It may be inconvenient to have to give up a handshake for a bow when greeting someone, but it can be truly upsetting to have to alter most of the dimensions of how one delegates authority, makes decisions, influences people, plans and organizes the workday, and motivates subordinates.

Magnitude. The continuum of disruption for any given routine ranges from slight alteration to total destruction. The greater the magnitude of the disruption, the greater the time and energy required to deal with it and the greater the frustration, anger, and anxiety that are likely to follow. If a shower was previously the first task of the day, having to take a bath would be somewhat less of a disruption than not being able to do either without going to a public bathhouse. It may be somewhat irritating to have to switch from cash bonuses to days off as motivation incentives, but it can be totally frustrating to have the ability to use incentives completely removed and placed in the hands of a labor ministry.

Criticality. Some routines are critical and others are trivial. The greater the criticality of the routine that is disrupted, the greater the time and energy required to deal with it and the greater the frustration, anger, and anxiety that are likely to follow. Not having a reserved parking spot is probably less frustrating than having to change from a tell-and-sell style of leadership to one that entails consultation and consensus decisions.

Culture Shock

Culture shock is the set of psychological and emotional responses people experience when they are overwhelmed by their lack of knowledge and understanding of the new, foreign culture and the negative consequences that follow. The psychological and emotional symptoms of culture shock include frustration, anxiety, anger, and depression. So far, the primary explanation for culture shock we have offered is that (1) living and working in new and unfamiliar cultural environments disrupts routines; and (2) the more routines are disrupted, the more severely any given routine is altered; the more critical the disrupted routines are, the greater the time and mental energy required and the greater the frustration, anger, and anxiety. While all these statements are true, they don't produce the severity of culture shock that people often experience. Having important routines disrupted, even severely, doesn't explain the level of depression, anxiety, and even anger that people experience.

To fully understand the forces behind culture shock, let's go back to the beginning. Most people do not experience culture shock initially. Typically, during the first few weeks or months of an international assignment, most people experience a "honeymoon" period. During this phase, even though the assignee and family members may be violating cultural traffic rules, they do not realize they are receiving negative feedback. They don't know enough about the culture to know what cultural mistakes they are making, so they might also miss the negative signals from host nationals that they are making mistakes.

In addition, an even more powerful explanation exists for this honeymoon period and the culture shock phase that usually follows. This explanation lies in something that for most of us is quite delicate and fragile and that we often go to great lengths to protect—our ego. Most of us have positive self-images that we want to maintain and protect. Few of us want to look like a fool if we can avoid it. Early in an international assignment, we tend to ignore or downplay the negative signals that we pick up; however, after a while, the sheer number of negative signals becomes overwhelming, and we can't deny or ignore them any longer. Culture shock sets in.[9]

If it is true that for every action there is an equal and opposite reaction, would the reverse also be true? For every reaction is there an equal and opposite cause? One would expect this to be true in the case of culture shock.

It may not seem obvious, but routines are a great source of self-image. In a sense, a routine demonstrates a level of proficiency, which is usually taken for granted. Living in a foreign culture, however, challenges these basic proficiencies and raises them from a taken-for-granted level to a very conscious one. In fact, the more the proficiency is taken for granted, the more severe the reaction to its loss often is.

A closer examination of Gerald Carlson's case should make the close interconnection between these components of cross-cultural adjustment much clearer. A few months into his assignment in Kuala Lumpur, Gerald found himself frequently so angry that he sometimes had to struggle not to vent his anger by striking someone. At other times, he found himself so depressed he could find very little reason to get out of bed in the morning. The extent of these emotions was not visible on the outside, and Gerald worked hard to keep it that way. In

Gerald's case, and in other severe cases like his, there has to be more than a disruption of routines to explain why Gerald and his family would pack up and head home, or why one in five Americans leaves a foreign assignment prematurely.

For Gerald—someone who had been to countless important dinners with clients and had developed a rather impressive ability to deal with these situations smoothly—the interpersonal problems with his assistant, Mahmoud, and his employees was a significant blow to his self-confidence and ego. These assaults on his self-esteem, and not just the disruption of routines, led to Gerald's severe level of culture shock.

The more basic the routine that is disrupted because of cultural ineptitude, the more severe the blow to the ego, and the more severe the resulting culture shock. For example, getting around in the city in which one lives is a skill that is often taken for granted. For Susan Carlson, driving around Pittsburgh, despite heavy traffic, was something she did without even thinking about it. Getting lost in Kuala Lumpur, and not even being able to go from her house to a friend's house, was a severe shock to her self-image as an independent, capable person. For others like Susan and Gerald, foreign assignments involve a steady stream of such incidents, from the simple to the complex, that challenge self-image. Expatriates and family members are constantly confronted with situations that send certain messages: "You don't understand this," "You can't do that," "Even six-year-olds in this country know that," "You're an idiot."

These incidents build over time in number and magnitude, and people get worn down and can no longer ignore them. Although the specific symptoms vary among individuals, and even within individuals from week to week, anger and frustration are common. Anxiety and depression are also prevalent as their positive self-image gets battered and their confidence crumbles. Quite often, the inherent mechanisms by which people defend and maintain their egos cause them to direct their frustration toward others. This is a primary reason behind the common symptom of blaming others. In any gathering spot for Americans, one is likely to find conversations peppered with statements like these:

- I can't believe how stupid these locals are. Their street addresses make absolutely no sense.
- These people think they're so superior to the rest of us. I think locals really resent foreigners.

- The locals are just plain lazy. It's impossible to motivate them, and they feel no loyalty to the company.
- This whole thing is my spouse's fault. He has no appreciation for what I'm going through. He has his comfortable little cocoon at the office.

Unfortunately, many people never recover from culture shock. Some return home early, but not all. Many of those who never recover stay for the duration of their overseas assignments, usually fearing the consequences of returning early or sometimes hoping that their situation will improve with time.

Most of those who stay eventually work their way through culture shock and gradually adjust to living and working overseas. The pain of making mistakes is the primary cause of culture shock, but it can also be a source of adjustment. Once a cultural mistake is made and, more importantly recognized, it is less likely to be repeated or to become an ongoing source of frustration or embarrassment to the expatriate. Gradually, by making mistakes, recognizing them, and observing how others in the culture behave, people learn what to do and what not to do.[10]

Summary

This chapter has elaborated on several general statements about cross-cultural adjustment. People establish routines to obtain predictability in life and to achieve psychological economy. Routines also provide an important means of preserving and maintaining ego and self-image. Living and working in new cultures generally disrupts established routines. The more routines are disrupted, the more severely a given routine is altered; the more a disrupted routine is critical, the greater the time and mental energy required to cope and the greater the frustration, anger, and anxiety associated with culture shock. Most importantly, however, disrupted routines are generally accompanied by situations that challenge an individual's confidence, ego, and self-esteem. Threats to these sensitive areas cause the strongest reactions associated with culture shock—depression, anger, denial, and even hatred. In principle, circumstances that increase disruption and uncertainty tend to inhibit cross-cultural adjustment, while circumstances that reduce disruption and uncertainty tend to facilitate cross-cultural adjustment. Having outlined the basic process of culture shock and adjustment, we can now focus on the specific processes of effectively selecting and training managers for international assignments.

Notes

1. Schein, "Coming to a New Awareness of Organizational Culture."
2. Dowling , Schuler and Welch, 1998; Hoecklin, *Managing Cultural Differences: Strategies for Competitive Advantage*; Hofstede, "Cultural constraints in management theories"; Linton, "The Tree of Culture"; Marquardt and Engel, "Global Human Resource Development"; Nemetz & Christensen, "The challenge of cultural diversity: Harnessing a diversity of views to understand multiculturalism"; Trompenaars, "Riding the Waves of Culture"; Welch, "International human resources management approaches and activities: A suggested framework."
3. Kroeber and Kluckhohn, *Culture: A Critical Review of Concepts and Definitions;* Linton, "The Tree of Culture."
4. Schein, "Coming to a New Awareness."
5. McGregor, *The Human Side of Enterprise.*
6. Triandis and Bhawuk, "Culture Theory and the Meaning of Relatedness."
7. Hofstede, *Culture's Consequences: International Differences in Work-Related Values.*
8. Dennis and Stroh, "Take this job and . . ."
9. Janssens, "Intercultural Interaction: A Burden on International Managers?"
10. Ward and Kennedy, "Where's the 'Culture' in Cross-Cultural Transition?"

3

Selecting: Finding the
Right People

Sue Harris, director of Emanon's environmental systems division, was on the phone. "Only five-and-a-half weeks before I have to send somebody to Sweden . . . but who?"

Bill Webster responded curtly from corporate headquarters in New York. "You know your people better than I do, Sue. Just get somebody over there fast, and make sure they put a stop to the problems!"

During the previous year, Emanon's Stockholm subsidiary, which was primarily responsible for product engineering, had missed several critical deadlines in an attempt to complete necessary redesign of a market-leading pollution-control system. These delays had been costly, since the redesign was essential to Emanon's globally integrated production process. Corporate headquarters wanted an immediate management change in Stockholm to ensure that the current redesign would be finished within three months and to set the Stockholm subsidiary on a straight course so that future engineering projects would stay ahead of production needs instead of behind them.

Sue spent the rest of the morning reflecting on who had the right technical background to effectively manage the design process for pollution-control systems. After mentally reviewing the best engineers in her division, she came up with a short list of three good candidates for the Stockholm job.

As Sue looked over the list, her mind turned again and again to Max Eisenhardt. Max was one of the best engineers she had in the United States. Perhaps more importantly, he also fully understood the pollution-control systems being redesigned in Stockholm. Besides, Max was a no-nonsense manager who had done a terrific job of fixing a product-engineering problem in the New Jersey plant over the previous two years. Without much more deliberation, Sue decided that Max was the right choice and called him to set up an interview.

Two days later, Max flew from New Jersey to Sue's office in Chicago. During the interview, Sue explained that the job in Sweden would not be easy. The Stockholm subsidiary had been consistently behind with product designs, and its new manager would have to turn the situation around. Max responded confidently: if he could do it in New Jersey, he could do it just as well in Stockholm. Sue also said that the position was a high-visibility opportunity in the firm, since corporate headquarters knew about the problems in Stockholm. Whoever turned the operation around could expect a hero's welcome upon returning. Max decided that the international assignment would be a fantastic career move. He couldn't wait to get home and convince his wife and family that the job in Sweden would be the opportunity of a lifetime.

The Technical Approach to Global Assignments: Destined to Fail

Emanon's response to the staffing problem in Sweden reflects the approach many multinationals use to select candidates for global assignments and why this approach is often destined to fail.[1] Basically, a crisis had arisen in a foreign operation and there was little time to assess the situation strategically and systematically. A strong desire to put the foreign "fire" out resulted in an obsession with the technical and managerial qualifications of the candidates and their presumed ability to solve the short-term problem. With little time to make her choice, Sue Harris ignored how the human resource department might have been able to help and considered a narrow range of potential candidates: the people she knew. She failed to consider the ability of the candidates and their families to adjust to and function effectively in a new cultural environment. Such a technically oriented selection process can easily result in costly premature returns or ineffective performance throughout an assignment—just what Sue wanted to avoid. In retrospect, Sue should have used every available resource, from people in the human resource department to other managers, in generating a complete set of candidates. In fact, according to a recent survey by Windham International and the National Foreign Trade Commission, finding suitable candidates for international assignments is a major challenge in most multinational firms today.[2]

Premature returns or ineffective performance are often direct results of firms rapidly selecting technically qualified candidates who lack the cross-cultural communication or adjustment skills to perform well in a foreign assignment. Managers of the Walt Disney Company claim this unsystematic selection process accounted, in part, for its early problems incurred at EuroDisney.[3] Furthermore, the general practice of not carefully considering the spouses' and families' situations often results in disaster when spouses and family members encounter severe cross-cultural difficulties. As one U.S. human resource executive told us, "For twenty-four years I have seen expatriate families come and go; many fail because the family can't adjust." Some failures could be avoided, however, if multinational firms would reengineer their candidate selection practices.

Common Selection Practices

Sue Harris of Emanon felt pressured by corporate headquarters to quickly find and select a candidate who would definitely change the Stockholm subsidiary's performance. Sue knew that her success as division director would seriously depend on the success of her selection for this assignment. She undoubtedly wanted to minimize any risk that her chosen candidate would fail, since failure would ultimately reflect on her own performance.[4] This approach is not inherently wrong; everyone wants to succeed. What was wrong was the inadequacy of the process she used to make her selection. Unfortunately, Sue's attempt to minimize the risk of failure probably maximized that risk.

The people with the best technical skills are not necessarily those with the best cross-cultural adjustment skills. In fact, failure in a global assignment (poor performance or premature return) generally occurs as the result of ineffective cross-cultural adjustment by expatriates and their families, rather than as an outcome of inadequate technical or professional skills. Our research has found that the successful completion of a global assignment is linked more closely to the expatriate's and the spouse's cross-cultural adjustment. Moreover, the exorbitant cost of failures on global assignments can return to hurt the parent company, the foreign operation, the expatriate, and the decision maker who selected the failed expatriate. Nevertheless, firms still rely first and foremost on technical, job-related skills when assessing candidates for global assignments. This narrow focus usually overshadows more critical criteria.[6] The reality in today's business environment is that almost 95 percent of all expatriates are selected by line managers for assignments based on their technical skills.[7] In 47 percent of these cases, the decisions are validated with input from the company's human resource department.[8]

Focusing on technical skills as the only selection criterion can also result in short-circuited selection processes. Decision makers who rapidly locate technically qualified candidates are less likely to scour the organization for candidates with similar technical qualifications but better cross-cultural skills. In a very important study of global assignment selection processes, Edwin Miller of the University of Michigan examined the activities that managers engaged in before making selection decisions.[9] He found that when decision makers did not quickly identify candidates with high qualifications (technical, job-related competence), they were more likely to carefully define the range of skills required, to determine more precisely how to measure performance during the assignment, to search more aggressively for potential candidates throughout domestic and international divisions (by seeking references from fellow managers or reviewing personnel files), and to request more assistance from human resource departments. Essentially, a paradox is inherent in the selection process of many U.S. firms. When no candidates with high technical and job-related qualifications are immediately accessible, line managers extend the search throughout the corporation, locating individuals with superior cross-cultural adaptation and communication skills as well as strong professional qualifications; but, when *one or several* technically qualified candidates quickly come to decision makers' attention, they terminate their search and *often miss candidates with equal technical abilities but superior cross-cultural skills.*

Common Selection Practices in Japan, Europe, and Scandinavia

Selection processes used by U.S. firms are similar to those found in Japan, Western Europe, and Scandinavia. Rosalie Tung's study of the selection process in the United States, Japan, and Western Europe found that "managerial talent" was one of the top selection criteria in all three geographic areas for the selection of CEOs in foreign operations.[10] In Scandinavia, professional qualifications are also the predominant criteria line managers use in selecting personnel for global assignments.[11] Essentially, multinational firms throughout the world tend to focus their selection efforts on finding individuals who exhibit the highest professional or managerial qualifications for global assignments.

While similarities exist between selection processes in the United States and those in Japan, Scandinavia, and Western Europe, there are differences as well. For example, interviews are almost always conducted in the United States (99%) and Western Europe (100%), but are held less frequently in Japan (71%) and Scandinavia (75%). These differences are even more apparent when we consider how frequently spouses are interviewed before decisions about global assignments are made. Spouses are interviewed or briefed sometimes in the United States (52%) and Western Europe (41%), quite rarely in Scandinavia (18%), and never in Japan.[12] These differences, however, do not necessarily result in better or worse assessments of candidates' and spouses' abilities. The differences may stem from unique cultural factors.

In Japan, for example, the family is not an issue in the selection process; if a man is advised to make an international transfer, the effect of the assignment on the family is not considered relevant, because Japanese decision makers believe that a wife will not really be able to influence her husband's decision. Even if a Japanese wife rejected a decision to move overseas, her husband would still be bound to the firm and would have to take the assignment.[13] It is important to note, however, that the cultural homogeneity and paternalistic practices of Japanese business do provide built-in, ongoing mechanisms for identifying potentially difficult situations involving the spouse and the family.

Other cultural reasons may explain why so few Scandinavian firms evaluate spouses. In Scandinavia, strong respect for personal privacy is exhibited, along with an implicit expectation that home life will not be subject to formal, organizational evaluation. As in Japan, however, the smallness of the Scandinavian countries and the relative homogeneity within each one provide opportunities for Scandinavian firms to learn about potentially difficult spouse and family situations without relying on extensive formal evaluations.

There are also differences in the degree to which personality or skill tests are used as selection methods. Line managers and human resource professionals agree that candidates' ability to communicate with and relate to people across cultures is important to successful international assignments, but very few firms actually test these skills formally.[14] Specifically, 24 percent of Scandinavian and 21 percent of Western European firms rely on formal testing mechanisms to evaluate candidates' abilities to relate to people across cultures. In contrast, only 5 percent of U.S. and virtually no Japanese firms administer tests to assess such skills.[15]

U.S. multinationals rely on the suggestions of line managers and human resource staffers, who often have little knowledge of the business and social culture into which the potential expatriate will be placed. Less than 20 percent of companies bother to identify the well-known core personality traits and competencies that make successful expatriates.[16]

Collectively, these findings indicate that the European and especially the Scandinavian firms may be slightly more strategic and systematic in selecting international personnel, since they utilize a wider variety of evaluation methods and pay more attention to cross-cultural skills (in addition to technical qualifications). While it is difficult to draw definite conclusions, Scandinavian and European firms' greater emphasis on assessing cross-cultural skills during the selection process seems to have a positive relationship with expatriate adjustment and performance.

Integrating Strategy into the Selection Process

To acquire or maintain a competitive position in the global marketplace, a firm must seek the highest possible return on its investments in international assignments. The first step is to integrate strategy into the selection process of global employees. As the firm increases its global reach and moves through various stages of globalization, it needs to pay attention to the selection process, which becomes increasingly important. For example, a firm moving from the export stage to the coordinated multinational stage of globalization must plan strategically for the future, since the need for qualified expatriates will be much greater as the firm moves out of the export stage. Without such organizational foresight, the firm will undoubtedly reach a future global expansion point only to discover it has a shortage of qualified personnel for effective staffing. The strategic importance of selecting the right person for a job is further reinforced by examining international joint ventures. The popular press estimates that international joint ventures fail at a rate of 40 to 75 percent and claims that these failure rates are at least partly due to expatriate managers who cannot adjust to local business practices.[17] Furthermore, if firms fail to take a strategic perspective on global assignments, their selection process probably will be doomed to a limited focus on people with technical skills.

In Chapter 1, we discussed three central strategic roles of international assignments: leadership development, coordination and control, and information and technology exchange. In the Emanon case discussed at the beginning of this chapter, Max Eisenhardt's assignment to Stockholm could have served the important strategic function of enhancing information and technology exchange; however, Sue Harris's hasty selection of Max virtually ensured that this objective would not be systematically accomplished. There were unique engineering designs in this case, which Max could have acquired from Swedish engineers and which could have been forwarded to other divisions of Emanon to create market innovations and to increase sales for the entire firm. To learn about and utilize this technology transfer opportunity, however, Emanon would have needed to select and send someone other than Max—someone with more effective cross-cultural communication skills.

Another strategic function—leadership development at Emanon—could have been enhanced if Sue Harris had identified other candidates who had both the ability to solve short-term production-design problems and the potential to develop global leadership skills and outlooks. The selection of a candidate with both abilities could have resulted in the development of a general manager with international experience, who could have assumed important executive positions in Emanon's worldwide operations. Although Max was technically capable, he did not possess the general management potential needed for a position as a future senior executive in the firm. Emanon's mistake (one that many firms make) was to ignore strategic rationales for the global assignment, thereby sacrificing long-term objectives for short-term results. Had the company pursued a more systematic selection process, it could have achieved both its long- and short-term objectives.

When selecting individuals to serve strategic functions during international assignments, firms must remember that these functions are accomplished in unique cross-cultural contexts. Accordingly, specific factors should be considered in the selection of successful international managers.

Selection Factors for Successful Global Assignments

Practicing managers and international researchers have developed relatively long lists of critical factors to consider when selecting candidates for global assignments. In sifting through these lists, we should remember the fundamental purpose of the selection process: to choose individuals who will stay for the duration of their global assignments and accomplish the strategic and tactical purposes of their assignments. Decision makers should consider several categories of expatriate- and spouse-related factors when selecting candidates for global assignments. In contrast to the consistent focus on technical skills, European firms rely more heavily on spouse- and family-related factors when selecting expatriates than do U.S., Scandinavian, or Japanese firms.[18] Differences among geographic regions also seem to exist with respect to language skills and expatriates' adaptability. U.S. firms place the least emphasis on language skills compared to European and Japanese firms.

Selection Factors Predictive of Expatriate Success

While decision makers may consider many potential factors when selecting individuals for global assignments, we have focused on those that are most relevant to success overseas. We chose factors that are related to the strategic functions or the successful completion of an assignment.

Strategic Factors

Before selecting candidates to send overseas, it is very important to assess the critical strategic functions of the international assignment. To be accomplished successfully, each of these functions requires several types of skills, experiences, and contacts. For example, if the primary purposes of the assignment are to improve the control function between headquarters and the subsidiary and to increase the coordination function between subsidiaries, then the candidate should have broad experience in the firm, including a wide array of contacts throughout the company. Another strategic purpose of an international assignment may be to exchange critical information between the foreign operation and headquarters. This exchange may require the movement of information not only from headquarters to a subsidiary but also from the subsidiary back to headquarters.[19] To perform this function, a candidate must have not only the necessary information from headquarters but must also possess excellent cross-cultural communication skills, since the information must be conveyed to the subsidiary, and important information acquired from the subsidiary must be transmitted back to headquarters. If the strategic purpose of an assignment is management or executive development, then the candidate's experience within the firm and advancement potential should be important selection criteria.

Of course, strategic functions are not mutually exclusive, and the selection criteria relevant to performing one function (e.g., coordination) are often relevant to performing another (e.g., information exchange). Decision makers must pay attention first to defining the strategic purposes of the global assignment and then to carefully assessing the skills, knowledge, and experience required to accomplish those objectives.

Professional Skills

Whether the job assignment is for a CEO, a functional department head, or a technical specialist, professional skills (either managerial or technical) are essential. These skills generally include direct knowledge of the job and a grasp of the specific problems to be solved. For example, in the Emanon case, Max Eisenhardt needed engineering and pollution-control knowledge in addition to managerial skills. However, although technical qualifications are necessary, they are often insufficient to guarantee success and maximize the return on a firm's investment in a global assignment.

Conflict Resolution Skills

In domestic as well as international managerial positions, how individuals approach conflict resolution can have a significant impact on an assignment's success. A primary source of stress during global assignments is interpersonal conflict.[20] More importantly, the ways in which expatriates resolve conflict can have a significant impact on their effectiveness. For example, studies of Japanese and Canadian managers found that the inability to deal collaboratively with cross-cultural interpersonal conflicts was related to more effective adjustment.[21] The collaborative approach to conflict resolution is important because it helps individuals focus on understanding other parties (and cultures) instead of forcing others to see situations their way.

Leadership Skills

The leadership styles of expatriate managers can also have a significant impact on their effectiveness during global assignments. Research has demonstrated that high-involvement management, which focuses not only on accomplishing tasks but also on paying attention to people, is generally superior to other managerial styles.[22] Management research has also found that trusting fellow employees and involving them in the decision-making process results in better overall decisions, greater acceptance of decisions, and increased satisfaction in domestic[23] and international management situations.[24]

Communication Skills

The ability to communicate is crucial to expatriates' success in global assignments. Most strategic functions of global assignments require individuals to communicate effectively in other cultures. Research has found several important dimensions of the cross-cultural communication process relevant to expatriate managers. One recent survey found that interpersonal communication skills are one of the most important factors in influencing the success of international assignments.[25] Without some level of proficiency in the host-country language, it is very difficult to communicate genuinely with host-country nationals in a new culture. Language proficiency is a tremendous advantage to operating in a foreign land.[26] As one American expatriate explained: "The 'key' to understanding the host country is the language. I cannot possibly understand why companies do not provide more language training to accomplish this!"

We have also found that willingness to communicate is critical to effective adjustment during a global assignment.[27] While this characteristic may seem obvious, many expatriates are simply unwilling to try to communicate genuinely with host-country nationals; they rely on subordinates and translators to communicate the "necessary information" instead of engaging in significant two-way conversations. Furthermore, this unwillingness to communicate can ultimately frustrate the strategic purposes of the assignment, since it will be difficult to fully coordinate, control, and transfer information without effective communication.

The importance of wanting to communicate is also relevant to spouses overseas, since they often have to work hard to initiate and develop social relationships and must try to communicate with others, even when others may not want to communicate with them. For example, one American spouse told us, "During both my global assignments, I have not once received a warm welcome or strong social support from other bank wives. I knew I would have to build my own life overseas but I expected the first steps to be taken by others in England. My advice to future expatriate spouses? Be prepared and willing to develop contacts and friendships from day one."

Social Skills

A person's social orientation, or ability to develop significant relationships, can also have a positive impact on adjustment to expatriation.[28]

In other words, an abiding interest in developing relationships, regardless of the situation, can help an expatriate reach out during a foreign assignment to develop significant social relationships with host nationals, who can provide critical work- and nonwork-related information and feedback on how the manager is doing.

Researchers have assessed an extensive array of individual characteristics that may be relevant to the selection process of international managers. Perhaps more importantly, however, our own research and that of others has found that certain characteristics are especially critical to cross-cultural adjustment.[29]

Ethnocentricity

How we interpret what is going on around us can have a significant impact on our adjustment to a foreign assignment. We often misinterpret and criticize the behavior of people when we cross cultural boundaries.[30] For example, a Japanese manager negotiating with an older manager from Finland may think that the sound created by the Finn sucking in air through his mouth means that the Finn is responding negatively to the deal, but the Finn may actually be communicating agreement by making the same sound that indicates disagreement in Japan. If an American were involved, he or she might wonder if Japanese and Finnish people have breathing problems. In all likelihood, the Japanese manager is less likely to misinterpret this behavior since virtually all Japanese multinationals insist that their multinational managers have skills in personnel relations. These skills are much less valued in the U.S.[31]

Using our own rules often leads us to misinterpret behavior in other cultures. Accordingly, those expatriates who are less judgmental and less likely to criticize behavior in the new culture have a much easier time adjusting to the new environment.[32] Moreover, those individuals who are less rigid in their evaluations of the "rightness" and "wrongness" of others' behavior are more likely to succeed in global assignments. Individuals who see their way as the only "right" way are referred to as *ethnocentric*. The significance of this characteristic has been reinforced again and again: expatriates and spouses from around the world report that people on global assignments must be flexible and have open minds.

Flexibility

Another important characteristic to look for in potential expatriates is willingness to try new things.[33] These things might include new foods, new sports, new forms of recreation, or new ways of traveling. For example, when Americans visit Japan, are they willing to try sushi or yakisoba instead of a Big Mac and fries? When Swedes come to Miami, are they willing to substitute jai alai for hockey? Opportunities to try something new occur frequently in foreign cultures, and individuals who are adventurous enough to try new things are much more likely to adjust effectively. Families will not find the foods they are used to, but discovering new foods and things to do can be fun. The new culture will not be home, but if families can live with that, they will discover the new country's charm.

Stability

When individuals enter a new culture, a tremendous amount of stress may accompany the tidal wave of new experiences. Being able to cope effectively can be a significant buffer against these stressful experiences. For example, one study found that well-adjusted expatriates developed "stability zones" that functioned like harbors in a storm.[34] These zones included such activities as hobbies, writing in diaries, and contemplation or religious worship. The activities allowed the managers to withdraw temporarily from situations and gain a better perspective on the new culture. The managers were able to break away from the constant struggle of trying to solve complex business problems made even more formidable because they did not fully understand the new culture's language, business customs, political systems, laws, and people.

Gender-Related Factors

We have been discussing the importance of technical, strategic, communication, and individual factors in selecting individuals for global assignments. U.S. firms also pay significant attention to whether the candidate is a man or a woman. Fewer than 15 percent of U.S. human resource directors publicly acknowledge that they intentionally select male candidates more often than female candidates for global assignments, but the reality is that they do, more than 90 percent of the time.[35]

A recent study conducted by the Employee Relocation Council (162 member organizations responding) indicated that females comprise only a small portion of employees on international assignment. Respondents reported that, on average, approximately 10 percent of their total expatriate population is female. Nearly 90 percent of organizations indicated that females comprise 25 percent or less of their international transferees—nearly one-quarter of organizations have *no* female expatriates at all.[36] This bias also exists in Japanese and Finnish selection practices (99 percent and 91 percent, respectively).

In U.S. firms, the reasoning behind the gender-based selection criterion is twofold: foreigners are biased against female managers, and dual-career couples face insurmountable challenges.[37] Neither rationale is completely defensible. Our research in the United States, Japan, and Finland, as well as research by others, presents consistent evidence that women perform just as well as men do, both during and after global assignments.[38] This result is even true for female expatriates in traditionally male-dominated societies such as Japan and Korea. For example, the Japanese view a female executive sent to Japan from IBM corporate headquarters in the United States first as a company representative, second as a foreigner, and third as a woman. The first two factors render the expatriate's gender a non-issue for most Japanese businessmen.

Even if foreigners are not used to having women in the workplace, this cultural bias does not necessarily result in performance problems for female expatriates. Furthermore, our research on U.S. expatriates and spouses has shown that expatriates in dual-career situations are just as likely as single-career couples to complete global assignments and perform effectively after returning home.[39]

U.S. firms should not discount the positive impact that female expatriates can have on profits. As firms attempt to globalize, they should cast an increasingly wider selection net throughout the company to select the very best male and female candidates. The increased level of global competition demands that firms discard their unfounded biases and assess potential female candidates more seriously when making international selection decisions.

Evaluating Selection Factors to Increase Success

After the firm decides which selection criteria are most relevant to a global assignment, it needs to determine how to evaluate candidates effectively on those criteria. Managers have a variety of tools for assessing candidates. Each of these tools has strengths and weaknesses, which are summarized in the answer to the following question: Is the tool reliable and valid?[40]

A selection tool is reliable if it produces similar results in the hands of different people or at different times. For example, if both the human resource department and the line manager have interviewed a candidate for a global assignment and agreed that the candidate has strong communication skills, the method is deemed reliable. If a candidate completes a cross-cultural skills test on two different days and receives very different scores each time, the test is *un*reliable.

The validity of a selection tool depends on the extent to which the tool consistently finds that a particular selection factor is predictive of success during a global assignment. For example, if language skills are deemed relevant to a particular global assignment, then candidates may be assessed with a standardized language test. Even if this test produces reliable or consistent results for a candidate's language ability, it will be considered valid only if variations in test scores predict variations in global assignment success.

Methods of Selection

U.S. firms tend to rely on a very limited range of selection tools, but a variety are actually available. Some of the most effective tools are biographical data, standardized tests, work samples, and assessment centers. Selection interviews and personal references are widely used, but are less effective. We will discuss each of these tools and examine how reliable and valid they are when selecting candidates for international assignments.

Biographical and Background Data

This selection tool consists of background information about candidates' personal and work histories. For example, professional/technical skills are an important selection criterion. These skills can be assessed reliably by reviewing a candidate's history. In the case of Emanon, Sue Harris's selection of Max Eisenhardt was based in part on background data, which indicated that he had significant work experience in pollution-control systems, an area directly related to the problems in the Swedish subsidiary. While lack of technical experience can be a factor in failure, in general, biographical data (e.g., age, gender, race, work experience) and background data (e.g., past jobs and positions) are not strong predictors of international assignment success.

Standardized Tests

Standardized tests can be both reliable and valid methods of screening candidates for international assignments. For example, engineers are often required to take standardized tests for certification in different states or countries throughout their careers. These tests are usually quite reliable and valid predictors of an engineer's knowledge base.

Scientific research has demonstrated that certain individual characteristics are related to international assignment success. These factors, such as conflict-resolution style or willingness to communicate, can be reliably and validly assessed with standardized psychological tests. Unfortunately, U.S. firms, unlike their European counterparts, rarely use standardized tests to assess such selection criteria.[41]

In our own research and work with multinational firms, we have developed a standardized test that assesses several important selection criteria for global assignments. The Global Assignment Preparedness Survey (G-A-P-S™) appraises candidates for six critical criteria: cultural flexibility, willingness to communicate, ability to develop social relationships, perceptual abilities, conflict-resolution style, and leadership style. Our research has found that G-A-P-S results are related to a variety of outcomes, including expatriates' work and nonwork adjustment, job performance, satisfaction, and level of commitment and loyalty.[42]

Many companies using G-A-P-S have found the individual feedback report that is generated to be extremely useful for "self-selection." Rather than using the G-A-P-S results to select and *de*select individuals, the companies send the feedback report to the individuals. The report contains both quantitative and qualitative feedback that gives individuals a good idea of what their strengths and weaknesses are relative to an international assignment and how strong or weak they are overall. For individuals who were choosing to go overseas for the wrong reasons (such as money or no career prospects at home) and who were ill-suited for an international assignment, the G-A-P-S feedback report often helped them to realize that going overseas was a bad idea. For others who had characteristics that made them more likely to succeed, the comprehensive nature of the survey and feedback report helped them better prepare by focusing on areas that needed improvement. Some companies have also had spouses complete a modified version of G-A-P-S to help these spouses self-assess their own cross-cultural strengths and weaknesses. Although none of the firms, nor we the authors, would recommend that G-A-P-S be used as the sole selection mechanism, it can be a reliable and valid component of an overall selection process. Some firms, especially in Asia, are using G-A-P-S to obtain early indications of potential international assignment candidates by having large numbers of young managers complete the survey. Therefore, employees with reasonable prospects have years rather than a few weeks or months to work on bolstering their cross-cultural weaknesses and leveraging their strengths.

Work Samples

This selection tool takes a "slice" of the prospective job and places the candidate in a work situation. For example, one function of the director of Emanon's Stockholm subsidiary is to chair meetings and committees. To determine whether Max was the best candidate for the subsidiary position, it might have been useful to simulate a Swedish business meeting by having Swedish managers or engineers travel to the United States or by having Max travel to Sweden and direct a Swedish meeting. While expensive, this type of method can be both reliable and valid. For example, Max would likely have had difficulty with such a meeting. Max was used to working with New Jersey employees in a very direct fashion. This approach would likely not have worked well with Swedish professionals, who are known in Scandinavia for their ability to hold a meeting, discuss many issues, and make one or more decisions based on subtle and indirect communication. An inexperienced foreigner might not even realize that the decisions have been made. Max's performance in this work situation would have provided Sue with reliable and valid information about his actual ability to manage in Stockholm.

Interviews

Of all the selection tools, interviews are the most utilized by U.S., Japanese, Western European, and Scandinavian multinationals.[43] Unfortunately, an unstructured interview is **not** a highly reliable or valid method for effectively evaluating selection criteria.[44] For an interview to be valid, it needs to be structured in advance and behaviorally focused. In other words, the dimensions to be assessed must be predetermined and defined. In addition, the interview should focus on past behaviors that provide evidence of the presence or absence of the defined characteristics. For example, rather than simply asking the candidate, "Are you flexible?" the interviewer would ask questions about past behaviors. The interviewer might ask, "Describe what you did the last time you had plans in place for a project, things were going fine, and then a key factor outside of your control went in a direction you didn't expect." Firms such as Cendant Intercultural have well-defined behavioral interview techniques, which firms such as

General Motors have used with great success in selecting expatriate managers.

Who Should Evaluate Candidates?

Decision makers must pay attention not only to selection criteria and methods but also to who performs the evaluations. In most U.S. firms, a limited set of decision makers selects candidates for global assignments. Most often, only one individual, the line manager with overall responsibility for the international unit, makes the decision, although others may also be involved in the selection process (for example, representatives from the international unit if the assignment is to a middle- or upper-level managerial position). The human resource department is often underutilized; it usually plays an after-the-fact role, making logistic and compensation arrangements. If firms want to become more strategic in their selection processes, they must learn to incorporate human resource departments' knowledge with that of line managers in home and host countries. In fact, human resource departments could act as decision hubs to ensure that a range of selection criteria are proposed, a variety of selection methods are utilized, and a full complement of candidates is considered.

Who Should Be Evaluated?

Deciding whom to evaluate for a global assignment is not as easy as you might think. Since more than three-quarters of expatriates around the world are married, most selection decisions involve not only the potential expatriate but also the expatriate's spouse and children. On the one hand, inquiring into family matters is a delicate situation. On the other hand, as we will discuss later in great detail, a family's willingness to take an assignment and its ability to complete it successfully can have a significant impact on whether the expatriate performs effectively and completes the assignment. For this reason, firms must obtain some level of accurate information about the family situation. A firm should be straightforward in communicating the pros and cons of a global assignment through an interview or briefing instead of over cocktails. This forum provides an opportunity for the spouse to make a more informed decision. Our research has found that when firms actively and directly seek spouses' opinions about global assignments, the spouses are much more likely to adjust to interacting with host-country nationals and to living in their new culture.[45]

Why Do Candidates Accept or Refuse Assignments?

We have been focusing on the firm's approach to the selection process; however, the candidate's perspective is equally important. What factors influence a candidate's decision to accept or refuse a global assignment?

When considering an offer of a global assignment, candidates ask themselves two fundamental career questions: Will this assignment put me in a strategic business role? Will this assignment lead to my advancement? Since average global managers have more than fourteen years of experience in their parent companies, they want to be certain that an overseas assignment does not leave them out-of-sight and out-of-mind. A good indicator that a global manager will not be forgotten is the firm's clear vision about the strategic importance of an assignment and about how its success will produce tangible results and lead to upper-management visibility for the manager. If the firm takes a "put out the fire" approach to global assignments, however, it will be hard to convince candidates that such assignments present long-term career advantages.

A global assignment can be expected to lead to advancement in the organization if the assignment is clearly defined as strategic before the selection decision is made. In other words, if an assignment is strategically important to the firm's success, then the expatriate has a much higher probability of being promoted after returning home. Our research shows that relatively few global assignments have led to promotion after the return home, even though most expatriates expected them to.[46] Only 11 percent of Americans, 10 percent of Japanese, and 25 percent of Finns received promotions after completing global assignments lasting at least two years. Additionally, 77 percent of Americans, 43 percent of Japanese, and 54 percent of Finns were **demoted** after returning home, meaning they were given positions lower than the ones held overseas.

Other studies corroborate these results, although some executives (such as those featured in a recent *Wall Street Journal* article[47]) attempt to convince the business world that global experience does matter in today's multinational firms. Studies of *Fortune 500* firms have found that executives pay attention to global experience as an important promotion criterion only four to 7 percent of the time.[48] Recent research by the Conference Board showed that 80 percent of surveyed repatriates believed their international experience was not valued by their current companies. The study reported that only

49 percent of participating companies even discussed the promotion with expatriates prior to departure. Furthermore, 87 percent of the responding companies reported that a majority of repatriates do not receive promotions upon return. With these dismal findings, it isn't surprising that 25–50 percent of repatriates leave their companies upon return from their international assignments.[49]

Collectively, these statistics paint a grim picture for potential expatriates and become very important in the selection process, since candidates for the next set of global assignments see returning expatriates not receiving promotions or being demoted. If this is indeed the case, it is quite unlikely that the selection process will result in the best candidates being posted; the best candidates will not want to jeopardize their careers with moves that result in demotion more than half the time. Firms must pay better attention to how they communicate, through words and actions, that global assignments really are strategic and really do count.

Financial incentives have played a significant role in attracting individuals to global assignments; candidates are interested in how a global assignment will affect their overall living situation.[50] In Finland, for example, the high cost of new cars leads many individuals to leave the country on overseas assignments to avoid import taxes and bring home a new automobile. In the past, a global assignment was often seen as an opportunity to live like royalty for several years. This corporate emphasis on the financial rewards of global assignments has created a strong expectation on the part of upcoming expatriates that they have a right to luxury treatment; however, the increasingly competitive global business environment has forced most firms throughout the world to reduce these financial incentives. This compensation-reduction trend reinforces the need for firms to consider the nonfinancial benefits of global assignments, such as completing a strategically important mission for the firm.

Finally, many candidates consider the learning aspect a critical component of the decision to accept a global assignment.[51] In fact, candidates with M.B.A. degrees ranked personal growth and gaining a cross-cultural experience as the first reason they would accept assignments abroad.

The Impact of the Family on Selection and Success

A disappointing scene is being played out in more and more multinational organizations, just as they have begun to recognize the im-

portance of expanding their global operations. An exe━
plum overseas assignment to the best candidate in the ━
to be turned down because the candidate's spouse is unat━
ing to put a career on hold while accompanying an exp ━━ a
global assignment.[52] What can the company do? On the one hand,
management recognizes the need to compete in the international
arena. On the other hand, management is aware of the stress and disruption relocation can cause a family.

As often as this scene is occurring today, we can expect it to
occur even more frequently in the future. Research projections indicate that by the year 2000, 80 percent of all couples will be in dual-
career marriages.[53] Clearly, family conflicts are already a concern
for companies as they try to expand their operations in the ever-
increasing global market. For example, according to a survey of human
resource executives in sixty of the one hundred major multinationals
worldwide, family concerns are among the top three reasons companies are unable to compete on the global scene.[54]

This chapter examines globalization from a family systems
perspective. It addresses several issues that may affect a manager's
decision to accept or reject an offer to relocate internationally. It also
discusses some of the creative relocation assistance programs companies have developed in an effort to make relocation a more attractive
option for the family.

A Systems Approach to Families

Research and experience have shown that the success of a global assignment is highly dependent on the attitudes of a manager's family
at the time an offer is made to relocate and the ability of the family to
adjust during the global assignment. To ensure the greatest chances
of success in the highly competitive global arena, organizations need
to evaluate potential candidates for global assignments on much more
than just their managerial skills and experience. They need to recognize the role of the entire family unit in determining whether the manager will (1) accept the offer, (2) adapt successfully to life and work
in the foreign location, and (3) complete the assignment. Evaluating
the candidate from a systems perspective that includes family as an
integral part achieves this goal.

From a systems perspective, we recognize that an individual's
actions are influenced interactively by the other members of his or her
family as well as by the individual's own past actions.[55] Seen from

this perspective, the potential international manager is viewed as a subsystem of the family, influenced particularly by a spouse's willingness to relocate internationally and the family's ability to adjust while abroad.[56] Spouses develop patterns of interaction that enable each spouse to support the other. These patterns develop through processes of mutual accommodation and influence. An international assignment opportunity is not going to dislodge this process. Consequently, it's unwise to think that work and family life are separate or to disregard the role or influence of the spouse on the decision and the success of the assignment.

Factoring in the Spouse's Opinion

Several studies have shown that a spouse's attitude toward relocating internationally is the most important factor in predicting a manager's willingness to accept an offer of a global assignment. Among the researchers who have studied this issue are Jeanne Brett and Linda Stroh. These researchers surveyed 518 male and female managers and their spouses from twenty multinational U.S.-based corporations to examine this issue. They found that although a manager's own orientation toward moving has a powerful effect on the decision to accept or reject an international relocation offer, a spouse's preferences also significantly influence the decision. In other words, when the manager's spouse is unwilling to relocate, so is the manager.[57]

Spouses often feel that putting their careers on hold will jeopardize their opportunities for future career advancement, and many managers reject offers of global assignments because their spouses express such concerns. One study found that the primary reason managers gave for turning down offers was the negative effect the move would have on their spouses' careers.[58]

At the same time, executives should not eliminate anyone from the pool of potential candidates based on demographic information such as whether a manager's spouse has a career. Short-circuiting the decision to accept an international relocation by presuming that a manager in a dual-career marriage will turn down the assignment or not succeed in the assignment is not advisable for at least two reasons. First, firms need their best and brightest people to gain international experience and cannot afford to remove 80 percent of their married employees from consideration (remember, in the not-too-distant future roughly 80 percent of married individuals will be part of a dual-career couple). Second, even though employees in dual-career couples are more likely to turn down an international assignment, they do not **all** turn them down. Furthermore, dual-career couples who agree to go abroad are equally likely to succeed in international assignments as single-career couples.

Dual-career issues are not as problematic for all multinationals. In Japan, spouse willingness to relocate has less influence on the decision than in Western countries such as the U.S. This situation exists partly because fewer employees are part of dual-career couples in Japan, and partly because decisions and roles relative to work and family are more separated. The breadwinner (usually the man) makes decisions about work, and the spouse (usually the woman) makes decisions about the house, children's education, and other matters, including investments. However, the gender-specific behavior in Japanese families (men = work; women = home and children) is beginning to break down as the number of dual-career couples in the Japanese workforce increases.

Income-Related Concerns

Families dependent on two incomes may also be concerned about the effect of an international transfer on their standard of living. Typically, it is difficult for spouses of expatriate managers to receive permanent working papers in the country to which they are transferred. Thus, not only are spouses often forced to put their careers on hold while they are abroad, but their loss of income may also have serious implications for the family's overall financial future.

Other Family-Related Considerations

Managers often anticipate difficulties in providing for their children's education and safety in international settings and may be reluctant to accept an offer to relocate internationally for these reasons. Managers whose children have special education or health problems may rule out international relocations completely.[59]

One study found that, after spouses' career issues, meeting special family needs (e.g., educational, medical, or social) and concerns about caring for elderly relatives were the main reasons managers turned down offers to relocate or removed their names from consideration.[60] Corroborating these findings, another study found that a candidate's unwillingness to accept an overseas assignment was related to family issues 81 percent of the time.[61]

Ways Companies Can Address Family Concerns

Progressive companies are beginning to recognize that "sweetening the pot" for managers and their families can be an effective way to increase the likelihood that managers will accept offers to relocate internationally, thereby enabling the company to better compete in the international arena.[62] The following section discusses the relocation assistance programs of six companies.

Case 6: Eastman Chemical

Eastman Chemical Company compensates spouses who are unemployed after a move abroad but who were employed before by giving them dislocation payments for as long as they are unemployed, up to a maximum of three years. The first year's payment is 33 percent of the spouse's annual income before the move, up to a maximum of $10,000. If the spouse is still unemployed in the second year, he or she receives 67 percent of the original amount, and in the third year, 33 percent. The first payment is paid at the beginning of the assignment; subsequent payments are made on the anniversary of the move. Policies like Eastman Chemical's, however, are still uncommon. Eighty-eight percent of multinational companies provide no such adjustment, 2 percent do, and 10 percent make other arrangements that are negotiated case by case.

Case 7: Sara Lee

A few companies, however, are following or even improving on Eastman Chemical's example. The Sara Lee Corporation has created what they call "Work and Lifestyle Assistance" and "Work and Lifestyle Supplemental Assistance" policies. At Sara Lee, the human resource department has established links with local employers in the countries in which Sara Lee has international offices. The company contacts these employers for assistance in locating employment for an expatriate's spouse. Staff members also investigate employment opportunities within Sara Lee. As part of this program, the spouse is reimbursed for expenses related to securing employment for the duration of the assignment, for up to $5,000 per assignment period.

Case 8: Quaker Oats

Quaker Oats has similar policies and reimburses spouses up to $5,000 during the assignment for expenses related to seeking employment; however, its policy does not state that the spouse must be unemployed. Eligible expenses covered include, but are not limited to: (1) expenses incurred in obtaining a visa or work permit, (2) assistance in producing a résumé and submitting it to appropriate employment agencies, (3) career guidance and consultation, *and (4) continuing education activities. In addition, both organizations have policies aimed at meeting the needs of single employees, single-parent families, and expatriates with elderly or disabled dependents.*

Case 9: Colgate-Palmolive

Colgate-Palmolive's policy is similar to Sara Lee's and Quaker Oats's in that it reimburses the spouse of an employee on an international assignment up to $7,500 for the duration of the assignment for: (1) assistance in finding a position, (2) career counseling, (3) trips home to meet with business contacts, and (4) seed money to set up a business. This money may also be used to purchase equipment, such as computers, printers, and fax machines. Tuition reimbursement is also provided for noncareer-related and career-related courses.

Case 10: Monsanto

Monsanto's policy is similar in certain respects to both Eastman Chemical's and Sara Lee's; Monsanto provides a dislocation allowance of 33 percent of a spouse's prior six months' earnings after three months on assignment in the foreign country; if the spouse is unable to find employment at the host location, $5,000 is preapproved for the purpose of reimbursing the spouse for career-enhancing expenses. After repatriation, financial assistance is offered in the amount of $1,000 to reimburse the spouse for job search-related expenses. Only spouses who are unable to find employment in the foreign location are eligible. If a spouse finds employment within three months of the assignment, he or she is not eligible for benefits.

Case 11: Motorola

Motorola provides spouses of employees on international assignments with a maximum reimbursement of $7,500 per twelve-month period, rather than per assignment, for expenses related either to maintaining or improving career-related skills or to enhancing employment marketability in the new location. The intent of the policy is not to replace lost income but to recognize the contribution that the spouse makes to the success of the relocation and to provide funds so that adjustment to the new location is even better.

Motorola provides funds for a three-year period or for the duration of the assignment, whichever occurs sooner. Under this policy, the spouse is entitled to reimbursement for: (1) fees to join professional associations; (2) tuition, books, and fees for courses at either the vocational or university level; (3) costs associated with attending career-improvement seminars, including lodging, food, and transportation within the country or to the home country, and seminar costs; (4) costs associated with securing a work permit; and (5) fees required by employment agencies. Expenses incurred prior to the date of expatriation and for six months after repatriation are included.

The Motorola Company has been a vanguard in developing spousal assistance policies. The company's philosophy is that if a company expects its business to be on the cutting edge of the industry, its human resource policies must also be on the cutting edge. Not only was Motorola among the first organizations to offer spousal assistance policies, but it was also the first to evaluate their effectiveness.

Surprisingly, until recently, few Motorola employees were using the program. A study of its spousal assistance programs in China, Hong Kong, Singapore, Japan, the United Kingdom, and the United States revealed that poor communication about the policy and its availability contributed to underuse. Since that study, major changes have been made to ensure that all spouses are aware of the program and its benefits.[62]

Spousal assistance programs like Motorola's are an excellent way for companies to help managers' spouses make the difficult adjustment to life in a foreign location. Since a spouse's adjustment to an international relocation is positively related to the employee's adjustment, instituting such programs should lead to higher productivity and greater likelihood that employees will complete global assignments. Of the Motorola spouses who took advantage of the program, 61 percent said it helped make their adjustment easier. Further, 75 percent claimed the program also contributed to their partners' successful adjustment.[63]

Participation in a spousal assistance program also pays off for spouses upon repatriation. Of the spouses who took advantage of Motorola's spousal assistance program, 79 percent said that they felt better prepared to enter the workforce when they returned home. As one spouse commented, "I have been out of the workforce for four years; I think it will look better to an employer to see I was doing something constructive."[64]

Motorola's experience clearly points to the importance of monitoring spousal assistance programs. Without evaluation, executives at Motorola might have assumed that spouses were not interested in the program. Upon evaluation, however, management realized that many spouses had never received information about the program. Subsequent revisions of the policy guidelines added language that asked human resource staff members to mail all materials related to global managers' spouses directly to them and not via the employee.

Comprehensive Approach to Getting the Right People

This section contains recommendations for how multinational firms can strategically approach the selection process for global assignments. The first stage of this process is summarized in Exhibit 3.1.

Strategic Analysis of Global Assignments

Making global assignments truly strategic requires the foresight to perform a careful analysis of the firm's overall global assignment needs, to define its current global candidate pool, and, most importantly, to assess whether its pool of candidates will be large enough to meet future demands for effective global managers.

Analyzing Current Needs. An analysis of current needs should consider several critical factors. What stage of globalization is the firm in? Companies in the export stage have significantly fewer

Exhibit 3.1
Strategic Analysis of Global Assignments

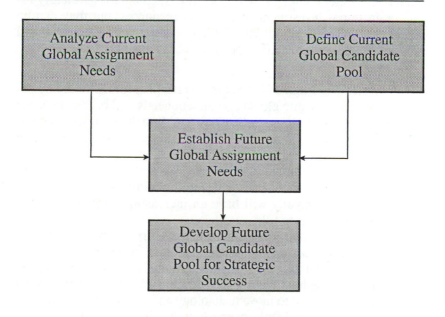

demands for international employees than do firms in the coordinated multinational stage. Another important consideration in assessing global assignment needs is the strategic functions that such assignments should play. Does the firm need to send people from headquarters for purposes of coordination and control? Does the company need to raise the level of communication between headquarters or between subsidiaries? Does the firm need to develop more future executives by giving them global assignments as developmental experiences? Answers to these questions can help a firm decide, from a strategic perspective, what the current needs actually are.

Defining the Candidate Pool. Multinational companies need to know the composition of their current candidate pool of global managers. For many companies, this pool is a "black box," since there is no centralized clearinghouse for collecting and updating information on candidates with relevant skills and linking these individuals with potential needs. Some companies, however, such as Neste Oy, a major Finnish oil and gas firm, have developed comprehensive databases that detail a manager's current assignment, technical qualifications, previous global experience, cross-cultural skills, and management potential within a firm. Such databases clearly require an initial investment of time and resources, but they can be invaluable in searching for the candidates with the best technical and cross-cultural skills to staff a specific global position.

Assessing Future Needs. Firms must plan for the future by deciding what their future global assignment needs will be. Again, these needs will be a function of a firm's future globalization stage and of the necessary strategic functions for sustaining a global competitive advantage. If a firm is currently at the multidomestic stage, with uncoordinated operations in two or three countries, but intends to become a coordinated multinational with operations in several more countries, that company will have an increasing number of global assignment positions to fill.

In addition to its globalization stage, a firm must consider what its key strategic functions will be in the future to assess future needs accurately. For example, if a firm intends to make several key strategic acquisitions throughout the world to develop additional technological synergies, it will need to move technology and information from operation to operation and from overseas to headquarters. The effective flow of information may well require more global assignments.

Developing the Candidate Pool for Strategic Success. The final strategic step in preparing for the future is the development of a firm's candidate pool. To develop a sufficient pool of qualified candidates for global assignments, a company must implement regular assessments of employees' managerial and cross-cultural skills. In addition to examining managerial advancement potential through traditional succession-planning mechanisms, the firm should regularly assess a variety of skills and individual characteristics associated with successful global assignments, including communication skills, conflict-resolution skills, leadership style, foreign-language skills, stress-reduction capacity, and cultural flexibility. An analysis of these important cross-cultural skills could be incorporated into traditional assessment center programs or management-training courses. The skills could also be assessed with surveys such as G-A-P-S.[66]

In addition to regularly assessing managerial and cross-cultural skills, firms should create strategies and plans for systematically developing skills in which many employees may be weak. For example, the Lord Corporation, a medium-sized, privately held U.S. manufacturing firm, was preparing to set up production operations in France, so the company offered free French language classes on company time to interested employees. Lord also held "French Day" at corporate headquarters once a week. On French Day, the corporate cafeteria served French foods so that people could try previously unknown gastronomic delights. This relatively simple but strategically thought-out tradition helped many employees develop greater cultural flexibility and improve their spoken French. These activities may seem minor, but combined with other programs, they help communicate the genuine importance of global competence to employees and provide them with opportunities to develop the skills necessary to complete international assignments.

Selection Process for Specific Assignments

After conducting a strategic analysis of global assignments within a firm, managers must face the reality of selecting appropriate individuals for specific global assignments. To assist managers in the decision-making process, Exhibit 3.2 demonstrates a flow chart of key activities that should lead to more successful and strategic outcomes.

Creating a Selection Team. The first step in the selection process is to create a selection team. This team should include at least three members: a home-country manager, a host-country manager, and a human resource department representative. The home- and host-country managers help ensure that headquarters and subsidiaries are both served in the selection process. Furthermore, the home-country manager might be designated as the expatriate's "sponsor" for the global assignment. The human resource representative can offer several important functions to the selection team, such as ensuring that a range of selection criteria are utilized and helping to locate a broad slate of candidates for the position.

Exhibit 3.2
Global Assignment Selection Process

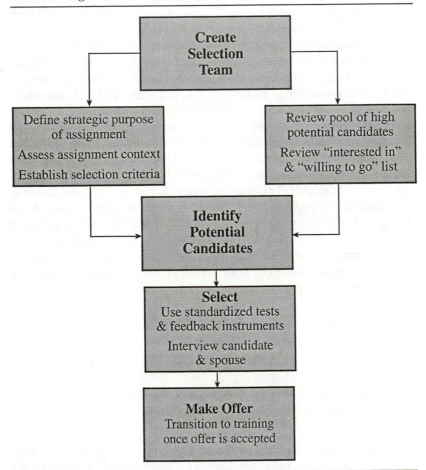

Defining Strategic Purposes for Global Assignments. The next step is for the team to determine the strategic purpose of the global assignment. Currently most assignments are short-term problem-solving experiences, so firms must be more reflective in deciding the strategic functions of an assignment before the assignment is made.

Assessing the Context. What will the cultural context of the assignment be? If an assignment requires extensive interaction with host-country nationals, cross-cultural communication and language skills will be important. If the general culture of the host country will be unique and, therefore, more challenging to candidates, this factor may have a significant impact on the selection criteria and decision.

Establishing Selection Criteria. The selection team should define the criteria that match the technical needs of the job, the strategic functions of the assignment, and the cross-cultural context of the position. For example, specific engineering knowledge may be needed; if the assignment is also developmental, then potential for advancement as a manager is a crucial criterion. If extensive interaction with host-country nationals is also required, the selection team should pay attention to cross-cultural communication skills. Finally, the more difficult the general culture of the foreign country, the more attention the selection team should pay to issues such as flexibility and ethnocentricity.

Review Pool. To ensure that those managers considered for international assignments are not simply the employees that a given individual happens to know, many leading-edge companies have created pools of high-potential candidates. The companies also survey employees every couple of years to identify who is interested in and willing to go on an international assignment. In global companies such as Colgate-Palmolive, the list of high potentials and those interested in going on an international assignment are nearly identical. However, because of particular circumstances at a given time, not everyone in the high potential and interested group is willing to go now. This information allows Colgate to avoid reviewing candidates or making offers to candidates who can't accept now. This approach also helps avoid the negative affects of the candidate appearing to turn down an international assignment.

Defining the Candidate Pool. Once appropriate selection criteria have been developed, the firm can utilize references, internal job postings, and a global candidate pool database (if available) to match the highest number of potential candidates with a particular assignment.

Utilizing Standardized Tests and Feedback Instruments After a candidate pool has been defined, the human resource member of the selection team can facilitate the use of a variety of selection methods. An overseas assignment will be both costly and risky, so the expense of utilizing a standardized feedback instrument, like G-A-P-S, to ensure a sound selection process is an investment in the future rather than just an immediate expense. Since most decision makers tend to use selection methods that are unreliable or invalid (such as one-on-one interviews), the selection team should decide which methods are most effective for evaluating which selection criteria for a particular assignment.

Interviewing the Candidate and Spouse. At this stage, the selection team will have narrowed the field to one or two potential candidates who, it is hoped, have both the technical and the cross-cultural qualifications for the global assignment. An in-depth interview that outlines the strategic purpose of the assignment and its relationship to the candidate's career path within the firm and that includes an honest assessment of living in the foreign country can provide a realistic preview for the candidate. In addition, interviews or briefing sessions with the spouse, to provide him or her with realistic expectations about life in the foreign country and to determine unique dual-career and family needs, can significantly enhance the chances for success in a global assignment. The importance of providing a realistic preview of the job and of living overseas cannot be overemphasized. Interviews must be conducted in a context where both the organization representative and the candidate can honestly share perspectives on overall aspects of the job and the foreign country.

Making the Offer. If the selection team approves the candidate after utilizing several selection methods and conducting interviews with the candidate and the spouse, and if the candidate and the spouse are favorable to the assignment after having been given a realistic preview, an offer can be made. This decision will be based on more relevant, factual, and comprehensive information than most companies currently use to select individuals for global assignments.

Making the Transition to Training and Preparation. The final stage of the selection process entails the transition from acceptance of the assignment to preparation for it. Generally, if the selection process has been strategic and not tactical, the assignment will be made well enough in advance for appropriate training and preparation to be initiated.

Selection Decisions: The Key to Future Success

Two fundamental points should be made about the selection process for global assignments. First, the selection process must be ahead of the firm's globalization process. In other words, as the firm increases its level of globalization (for example, from a primarily export to a global firm), it must already have a sufficient pool of international human resources, or potentially successful international managers, to sustain its global expansion. Second, acting strategically is the key to keeping ahead of the globalization process. Conducting strategic assessments of needs and developing a strong candidate pool can enhance the global competitiveness of the firm and the success of the individual. Otherwise, decision makers easily lapse into ineffective selection practices, such as using technical qualifications as the only selection criterion or relying on interviews as the only selection method. By maintaining a strategic orientation at each stage of the selection process, the firm is much more likely to receive a positive return on its high-cost investment as it selects expatriates with the necessary technical and cross-cultural skills who can solve short-term problems and accomplish long-term strategic objectives.

Notes

1. Miller, "The International Selection Decision: A Study of Managerial Behavior in the Selection Decision Process"; Nicholson and Ayako, "The Adjustment of Japanese Expatriate to Living and Working in Japan"; Katz and Seifer, "It's a Different World Out There"; Deller, "Expatriate Selection: Possibilities and Limitations of Using Personality Scales"; Ones and Viswesvaran, "Personality Determinants in the Prediction of Aspects of Expatriate Job Success."
2. Windham International & the National Foreign Trade Council, Global Relocation Trends 1995 Survey Report.
3. Black and Stephens, "Expatriate Adjustment and Intent to Stay in Pacific Rim Overseas Assignments"; Gregersen and Black, "A Multifaceted Approach to Expatriate Retention in International Assignments"; Ioannou, "Unnatural Selection."
4. Miller, "The International Selection Decision."
5. Black and Stephens, "Expatriate Adjustment"; Gregersen and Black, "A Multifaceted Approach to Expatriate Retention"; Deller, "Expatriate Selection: Possibilities and Limitations of Using Personality Scales"; Mount and Barrick, "The Big Five Personality Dimensions: Implications for Research and Practice in Personnel and Human Resource Management."
6. Miller, "The International Selection Decision"; Ioannou, "Unnatural Selection."

7. Windham International and the National Foreign Trade Council, Global Relocation Trends, 1995 Survey Report.
8. Ibid.
9. Miller, "The International Selection Decision."
10. Tung, "The New Expatriates"; Nicholson and Ayako, "The Adjustment of Japanese Expatriates to Living and Working in Japan."
11. Bjorkman and Gertsen, "Selecting and Training Scandinavian Expatriates: Determinants of Corporate Practice"; Gertsen, "Expatriate Training and Selection"; Kainulainen, "Selection and Training of Personnel for Foreign Assignments."
12. Bjorkman and Gertsen, "Selecting and Training Scandinavian Expatriates: Determinants of Corporate Practice"; Nicholson and Ayako, "The Adjustment of Japanese Expatriates to Living and Working in Japan"; Katz and Seifer, "It's a Different World Out There: Planning for Expatriate Success Through Selection, Pre-Departure Training and On-Site Socialization."
13. White, *Japanese Overseas*.
14. Deller, "Expatriate Selection: Possibilities and Limitations of Using Personality Scales"; Ones and Viswesvaran, "Personality Determinants in the Prediction of Aspects of Expatriate Job Success"; Zeira and Banai, "Selection of Managers for Foreign Posts."
15. Bjorkman and Gertsen, "Selecting and Training Scandinavian Expatriates: Determinants of Corporate Practice."
16. Ioannou, "Unnatural Selection."
17. Schell and Solomon, *Capitalizing on the Global Workforce: A Strategic Guide to Expatriate Management*.
18. Nicholson and Ayako, "The Adjustment of Japanese Expatriates to Living and Working in Japan"; Tung, "The New Expatriates."
19. Gupta and Govindarajan, "Knowledge Flows and the Structure of Control Within Multinational Corporations."
20. Clarke and Hamer, "Predictors of Japanese and American Job Success, Personal Adjustment, and Intercultural Interaction Effectiveness"; Hammer, Gudykunst, and Wiseman, "Dimensions of Intercultural Effectiveness: An Exploratory Study"; Hammer, "Behavioral Dimensions of Intercultural Effectiveness"; Mendenhall and Oddou, "The Dimensions of Expatriate Acculturation."
21. Abe and Wiseman, "A Cross-Cultural Confirmation of Intercultural Effectiveness"; Black, "Personal Dimensions and Work Role Transitions: A Study of Japanese Expatriate Managers in America"; Hawes and Kealey, "An Empirical Study of Canadian Technical Assistance."
22. Blake and Mouton, *The Managerial Grid*; Clarke and Hamer, "Predictors of Japanese and American Job Success, Personal Adjustment, and Intercultural Interaction Effectiveness."
23. Cotton, Vollrath, Froggatt, Kengnick-Hall, and Jennings, "Employee Participation: Diverse Forms and Different Outcomes."
24. Negandi, Eshghi, and Yuen, "The Managerial Practices of Japanese Subsidiaries Overseas."
25. Clarke and Hamer, "Predictors of Japanese and American Job Success, Personal Adjustment, and Intercultural Interaction Effectiveness."
26. Bjorkman and Gertsen, "Selecting and Training Scandinavian Expatriates: Determinants of Corporate Practice"; Brewster, *The Management of Expatriates*; Kainulainen, "Selection and Training of Personnel for Foreign Assignments."

27. Black, "Personal Dimensions and Work Role Transitions"; Church, "Sojourner Adjustment"; Clarke and Hamer, "Predictors of Japanese and American Job Success, Personal Adjustment, and Intercultural Interaction Effectiveness"; Mendenhall and Oddou, "Dimensions of Expatriate Acculturation."

28. Black, "Personal Dimensions and Work Role Transitions"; Church, "Soujourner Adjustment"; Clarke and Hamer, "Predictors of Japanese and American Job Success, Personal Adjustment, and Intercultural Interaction Effectiveness"; Hammer, Gudykunst, and Wiseman, "Dimensions of Intercultural Effectiveness"; Hawes and Kealey, "An Empirical Study of Canadian Technical Assistance"; Mendenhall and Oddou, "Dimensions of Expatriate Acculturation."

29. Mendenhall and Oddou, "Dimensions of Expatriate Acculturation."

30. Gibson, "Do You Hear What I Hear? A Framework for Reconciling Intercultural Communication Difficulties Arising from Cognitive Styles and Cultural Values"; Lin, "Ambiguity with a Purpose: The Shadow of Power in Communication." Oddou and Mendenhall, "Person Perception in Cross-Cultural Settings: A Review of Cross-Cultural and Related Literature"; Triandis, Vassilou, and Nassiakou, "Three Cross-Cultural Studies of Subjective Culture."

31. Ioannou, "Unnatural Selection."

32. Black, "Personal Dimensions and Work Role Transitions"; Ruben and Kealey, "Behavioral Assessment of Communication Competency and the Prediction of Cross-Cultural Adaptation."

33. Black, "Relationship of Personal Characteristics with Adjustment"; Mendenhall and Oddou, "Dimensions of Expatriate Acculturation."

34. Mendenhall and Oddou, "Dimensions of Expatriate Acculturation"; Hawes and Kealey, "An Empirical Study of Canadian Technical Assistance."

35. Adler, "International Dimensions of Organizational Behavior"; Adler, "Women in International Management: Where Are They?"; Adler, "Expecting International Success: Female Managers Overseas"; Black, "Work Role Transitions: A Study of American Expatriate Managers in Japan"; Black and Gregersen, "When Yankee Comes Home"; Gregersen and Black, "A Multifaceted Approach to Expatriate Retention."

36. ERC, "International Relocation Issues."

37. Adler, "Do MBAs Want International Careers?"; Adler, "Women Do Not Want International Careers: And Other Myths About International Management"; Brett and Stroh, "Managers Willingness to Relocation Internationally."

38. Adler, "Pacific Basin Managers: A Gaijin, Not a Woman"; Adler and Izraeli, *Women in Management Worldwide*; Black and Gregersen, "When Yankee Comes Home"; Jelenik and Adler, "Women: World-Class Managers for Global Competition"; Adler, "International Dimensions of Organizational Behavior."

39. Brett and Stroh, "Managers Willingness to Relocate Internationally"; Stephens and Black, "The Impact of the Spouse's Career Orientation on Managers During International Transfers."

40. Hall and Goodale, *Human Resource Management.*

41. Bjorkman and Gertsen, "Selecting and Training Scandinavian Expatriates"; Tung, *The New Expatriates*; Katz and Seifer, "It's a Different World Out There."

42. Global Leadership Institute, "1997 Technical Report."

43. Bjorkman and Gertsen, "Selecting and Training Scandinavian Expatriates"; Katz and Seifer, "It's a Different World Out There"; Tung, *The New Expatriates*; Dowling Schuler, and Welch, "International Dimensions of Human Resource Management."

44. Hall and Goodale, *Human Resource Management*; Katz and Seifer, "It's a Different World Out There."

45. Adler, *International Dimensions of Organizational Behavior*; Black and Gregersen, "The Other Half of the Picture: Antecedents of Spouse Cross-Cultural Adjustment"; Black and Gregersen, Antecedents to Cross-Cultural Adjustment for Expatriates in Pacific Rim Assignments"; Black and Stephens, "Expatriate Adjustment"; Stephens and Black, "The Impact of the Spouse's Career Orientation"; Stroh, Dennis, & Cramer, "Predictors of Expatriate Adjustment."

46. Black and Gregersen, "When Yankee Comes Home"; Stroh, "Predicting Turnover Among Repatriates"; Stroh, Dennis, and Cramer, "Predictors of Expatriate Adjustment."

47. Bennett, "Going Global."

48. Global Leadership Institute, 1997 Technical Report.

49. Gates, "Managing Expatriates' Return: A Research Report"; Stroh, "Predicting Turnover Among Repatriates"; Stroh and Lautzenhiser, "Benchmarking Global Human Resource Practices and Procedures."

50. Black and Gregersen, "The Other Half of the Picture"; Black and Gregersen, "When Yankee Comes Home."

51. Adler, "Do MBAs Want International Careers?"

52. Harvey, "The Impact of the Dual-Career Expatriate on International Human Resource Management"; Swaak, "Today's Expatriate Family: Dual Career and Other Obstacles."

53. U.S. Bureau of the Census, "Household and Family Characteristics"; Harvey, "Impact of the Dual-Career Expatriate."

54. Stroh and Caligiari, "Increasing Global Competitiveness Through Effective People Management."

55. Kanter, *Work and Family in the United States*; S. Minuchin, *Families and Family Therapy*; Brett and Stroh, "Willingness to Relocate Internationally."

56. Brett and Stroh, "Willingness to Relocate Internationally."

57. Ibid.

58. Swaak, "Today's Expatriate Family."

59. Brett and Stroh, "Willing to Relocate Internationally."

60. Swaak, "Today's Expatriate Family."

61. Windham International and National Foreign Trade Council, "International Relocation Trends Survey."

62. Pellico and Stroh, "Spousal Assistance Programs."

63. Pellico and Stroh, "Spousal Assistance Programs: An Intregal Component of the International Assignment."

64. Pellico and Stroh, "Spousal Assistance Programs."

65. Ibid.

66. Global Leadership Institute, 1997 Technical Report.

4

Training: Helping People Learn to Do the Right Things

Case 12: Recor Engineering

Ordinarily, Mel could bring into focus even the most complicated problem by ruminating over it during his commute home from the office. "I must be out of my league on this one," Mel thought. He had faced many challenges as vice president of human resources since arriving at Recor Engineering, but none had nagged at him so persistently.

Recor Engineering, a leader in the U.S. domestic construction industry, had just sealed a joint-venture pact with one of Japan's largest construction firms, Dentsu Hogen K.K. Recor, a San Francisco-based company, and had agreed to send a large team of American experts to work in Osaka with a special group of Dentsu Hogen's best engineers. The Americans were to team up with their Japanese counterparts to bid on a project to expand the runway at Osaka Airport, as well as related ventures. This arrangement would solve two problems. For Dentsu Hogen, it would buffer pressure from the Japanese government to allow American construction firms into the bidding process for the expansion. For Recor, it would mean some of its employees would gain experience working in the Japanese construction industry, thereby helping management at the firm decide whether to attempt to enter that market in the future.

The project manager, who had been selected by Recor, was Larry Runolfsson. Larry had vast experience in all aspects of the construction industry and had overseen four projects in the United States, from the idea and bidding stages to completion.

All of Recor's engineers—a total of eighteen—had agreed to relocate to Japan after being assured that their families' financial positions and standards of living would not suffer as a result of the three-year assignment. None of the engineers, most of whom were married, had indicated any reluctance on their spouses' part concerning the relocation. Nevertheless, Mel's secretary—his hidden ears in the company—had told him three weeks earlier that she knew of at least eight spouses who were "less than thrilled" about disrupting their children's education and relocating. Five of the spouses had also indicated that they were not pleased about having to quit their jobs to move overseas, even though the international assignment compensation package was good. Mel had seen to that by ensuring that the compensation package was comparable to what most firms provided for expatriates in Japan.

Mel quickly discovered that guaranteeing his people good pay was much easier than his next task—deciding how much and what kind of predeparture training to give them. His phone calls to colleagues had yielded mixed responses. Some felt that no training was necessary, some felt a little "area briefing" was sufficient, and a few had heard of consulting firms that offered comprehensive training packages, although none knew whether the programs were truly helpful or cost-effective.

"I don't have time to figure out all the particulars—they leave in three months," Mel had told his training manager, Maria. "Find out what kind of training these people need—or if they need any at all." He asked the manager to give him a report in a week.

Included in the manager's report were price quotes given to her for training by consultants on the West Coast. But providing the training, Maria noted, would push the upper limits of the quarterly training budget. She had also talked with people at a variety of firms that had managers in Japan. None had provided any in-depth predeparture training. Maria concluded that Recor should follow the lead of other companies: offer a good financial package and leave it at that.

Mel ejected his Mozart disc and found a news station on his car radio. He tried to relax as he listened to the news, but the nagging feeling that Recor needed to do more for the team would not go away. "We're sending these guys into a strange, totally unfamiliar culture," he thought. "Or at least it seems strange to me. Shouldn't we do something to prepare them? Other firms don't do much, if anything ... but if this joint venture melts down, I'll be in a tight spot. On the other hand, the people being sent have all been successful here, especially Larry Runolfsson ... They should do fine. Besides, if they're worth what we're going to pay them, they should be able to work through whatever problems come up." Mel put his thoughts on hold and turned his attention to the weather report.

Was Mel justified in being concerned that Recor's managers needed predeparture training? How much training do managers sent on global assignments usually receive? Management research has uncovered the following facts across industries:

1. About 62 percent of U.S. firms offer some type of cross-cultural preparation. This figure is significant, but it means that 38 percent of U.S. firms send their "troops" overseas with no "combat training."[1]

2. On average, those who receive training get less than a day of it.

3. Of the firms that offer cross-cultural training, 32 percent offer programs for the entire family, 27 percent for the expatriate and spouse only, and 3 percent for the expatriate only.[2] Watching films, reading books, and talking with people who have lived in the country to which the manager is being sent are the most common activities included in the training. Few firms offer in-depth, rigorous, skill-centered cross-cultural training.[3]

4. Fifty-seven percent of the companies that offer cross-cultural training indicated that most future expatriates who are eligible for the training participate. [4]

5. Empirical evaluation studies have shown that cross-cultural training programs enhance global managers' job performance, adjustment to their new cultures, and cross-cultural managerial skills.[5]

With so many individuals and families receiving no training or less training than necessary, it is no wonder so many global managers struggle in their overseas assignments. The question is not whether firms should allocate time and resources to training their global managers, but rather *how* firms should construct such training to ensure that it meets their global managers' needs. We do not advocate the use of "canned" programs; instead, a firm's thoughtful responses to a variety of training issues should drive the nature of the training offered.

Understanding How People Learn and Adapt to New Cultures

An understanding of how individuals learn and adjust to new business and social cultures is critical to developing effective cross-cultural training. Much research, which is covered in detail in Chapters 2 and 5, has been done on this subject. The process of adapting to a new culture involves several learning principles that need to be accounted for when designing cross-cultural training.[6]

Three-Step Learning Process

These principles are presented as a series of learning steps. Associated with each step is an example from the experiences of an expatriate manager, Earl Markum, who was in charge of a large ranching operation in New Zealand.

Step 1: Attention. Before managers can alter their behavior so that it conforms to the norms of the host culture, they must first see, attend to, and become aware of how the locals behave. Typically, people need to view behavior and think about it before they can decide whether they want to try it out.

For example, the Polynesian employees of a ranching operation regularly held parties on the weekends. An integral part of the get-togethers was the *hangi,* which basically consists of cooking food on white-hot rocks in a hole in the ground. Flax leaves are placed over the heated rocks, then meat is laid on the flax, then more flax leaves are placed on top of the meat. The process is then repeated with a variety of vegetables. Finally, dirt is put over the food until the hole is filled in. Later, when the food is cooked, the "oven" is dug up and the food is distributed to everyone. The Polynesian managers, supervisors, and workers viewed these get-togethers as culturally very important. A lot of singing, dancing, storytelling, and renewing of family and community ties took place. Being together and the warm feelings associated with being part of a social unit were important; people who did not come to the parties or who were unwilling to loosen their inhibitions and sing, dance, and so on were viewed as cold, aloof, and untrustworthy. The American manager, Earl Markum, sensed all this and realized that attending the get-togethers as well as sponsoring them would be important if he was to be effective.

Step 2: Retention. During the second step, managers typically think about what they have learned, seen, or heard regarding culturally appropriate behavior in their new country. The more they think about what they have seen, the more they develop a "cognitive map" regarding when to produce certain behavior, under what circumstances it is acceptable and unacceptable, whether it is all right for foreigners to produce the behavior, the penalties for not producing the behavior, and so on. Examples of the behavior in question get locked into memory and become a reference point for understanding and reproducing the behavior.

During the early part of the retention process, important new behaviors and the norms surrounding them must be quite conscious. Eventually, as the new behaviors and their norms are understood more completely, that knowledge settles into memory and spurs reactions in social and business situations naturally and unconsciously. This process is not unlike driving in a city that's new to you. Without a map, you get lost easily. To avoid this, you look at the map often and keep it close while driving. Slowly, over time, you learn where streets are, the shortest routes to work, and so on until you no longer need the physical map because you've made a mental map. Likewise, in a foreign culture, with effort, the culture becomes less new after a while and behaviors become more predictable because we develop "cognitive cultural maps" that inform us what to say and do.

In the New Zealand example, Earl Markum continued to attend the parties hosted by his workers and their relatives and carefully observed the process of the *hangi,* participating selectively when the Polynesians called on him to do so. Mainly, he blended into the group and carefully observed everything that was going on, developing an understanding of the rules, their purpose, and the behavior expected of participants. He observed that important conversations took place at each stage of the *hangi* and that food was an important stimulant to the social norms that caused cohesiveness in the work group and among members of their extended families and friendship networks. The dances, singing, and conversation all revolved around the construction of the oven, the preparation of the food, the length of time the food was cooked, and the eating of the food afterward. Even cleanup of the oven provided "quiet time" for the male volunteers to spend together.

Step 3: Trying Out the New Behavior. Basically, once international behavior has been observed and managers have gained a mental understanding of the rules associated with the behavior, they must decide to try out, or not to try out, the behavior. As managers experiment with new behavior, they check their performance against their "cognitive maps" until they become expert at the behavior. If trying it out causes embarrassment or negative reactions from host nationals, the managers may never try the behavior again and thus risk never adjusting to their new culture. The closer managers' cognitive maps accurately reflect the culture, the more likely they will reproduce new behaviors successfully.

Having finally decided that he was ready to host a *hangi,* Earl Markum invited all the Polynesians in the community to his house. When they arrived, they saw smoke rising out of the ground. The festivities began, and all were having a good time. When the *hangi* was ready to be unearthed, the Polynesians began to ask each other who had helped their American boss host the party. After a while, it became obvious that no one had. All eyes focused on Earl, who simply smiled and yelled, *"Haere Mai Kita Kai!"* ("Welcome, come and get the food!"). His ability to influence and gain compliance from his workers increased dramatically—literally overnight—for no other American had ever attempted to prepare a *hangi* before.

Training and the Three-Step Learning Process

The case just presented highlights three areas on which training for global managers must focus—namely, helping managers (1) become aware that behaviors vary across cultures and the importance of observing these cultural differences carefully; (2) build cognitive cultural maps so they can understand why the local people value certain behaviors and how those behaviors may be appropriately reproduced; and (3) practice the behaviors they will need to reproduce to be effective in their overseas assignments. Without training, some global managers will succeed at negotiating the three-step learning process by themselves, but many won't. Good training can be a tremendous help in learning about new cultures.[7]

Designing Cross-Cultural Training

Research shows that an important factor in the success of a cross-cultural training program is its *rigor*—the degree of mental involvement and effort that the trainer and the trainee must expend for the trainee to learn the required concepts. The ability of a firm to determine the degree of rigor that is appropriate is the key to the design of valid cross-cultural training.[8]

Low-rigor training includes activities such as watching films, listening to lectures and area briefings, and reading books. By contrast, more rigorous training requires the trainee to learn skills passively but also to practice them. More rigorous training would include role modeling, videotaped sessions to demonstrate success at mastering skills, and language training. High-rigor approaches extend the degree of participation on the part of the trainee through the use of assessment centers, interactive language training, and sophisticated cross-cultural simulations. Exhibit 4.1 illustrates the close relationship between training rigor and participant involvement.

Rigor is also associated with the length of time spent on training. A training program that required trainees to participate for twenty-five hours over five days would be less rigorous than a program that spanned 100 total hours over three weeks. Even though the time and expense involved usually increases with the rigor of the training, so does the level of what is learned and retained. For example, people generally only remember about 17 percent of what they hear in a lecture. In contrast, retention from more rigorous training methods such as simulations is often in excess of 85 percent. Consequently, it is important not to cheat global managers by offering them "quick-and-dirty" programs. It's also important **not** to assume that just because a program is offered it is effective. Viewing training as an expense rather than an investment often results in inadequate and inappropriate training. Training for international assignees and families is an investment that pays off best when the rigor of the training is appropriately matched to the nature and requirements of the assignment.

Exhibit 4.1
Training Rigor

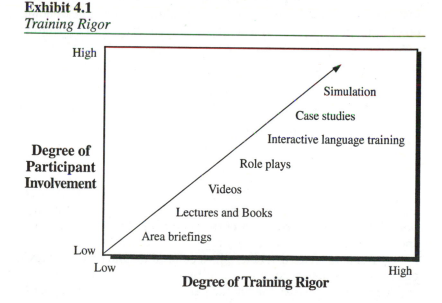

Once key decision makers understand the need to offer global managers rigorous training, the critical question is how rigorous the training should be. To help firms answer this question, we offer a framework based on the findings of the best research studies.[9] Basically, three dimensions must be taken into account when deciding what methods should be included in the training design. These dimensions are the degrees of *cultural toughness, communication toughness,* and *job toughness* required of the manager in the overseas assignment. A careful analysis of these three dimensions is necessary before valid training can be designed. Otherwise, the wrong training will be given to people.

Cultural Toughness

Some cultures are more difficult or tough to adjust to than others. The underlying values that determine the way business is done are more different from American norms in some countries than in others. A manager going to Japan will have a tougher time and the learning curve will be longer than a manager going to Australia. Both expatriates will encounter cross-cultural problems, but the challenges facing the manager in Japan will be more severe. The tougher the new culture is to adjust to, the more assistance, through rigorous training, the global manager will need to adjust and be effective.

How does one determine which cultures are toughest? Research suggests that the following regions of the world, in descending order of toughness, are the most difficult for Americans to adjust to[10]:

1. Africa
2. Middle East
3. Far East
4. South America
5. Eastern Europe/Russia
6. Western Europe/Scandinavia
7. Australia and New Zealand

Individual countries within regions vary in cultural toughness, and there are within-country differences as well, but this simplification of the research provides a fairly good idea of the need, amount, and rigor of training necessary by region of assignment.

The next factor that determines cultural toughness is the previous overseas experience of the specific candidate for the global assignment. The more experience the person has had with the specific culture to which he or she will be assigned, even if that experience was in the distant past, the more the person should be expected to be able to cope with the challenges in the new culture. Someone who has already lived and worked in Nairobi for three years and is reassigned there after being home for five years will need less rigorous training than someone who has never lived or worked in Nairobi before.

Both the duration and the depth or quality of a manager's past overseas experiences influence training needs. An expatriate will find the Indonesian culture less tough if he or she has lived there before than will the candidate who has not. Likewise, an expatriate who had frequent, in-depth interactions with Indonesians during a three-year stay will find the cultural toughness less of an obstacle during a later visit than will the expatriate who had infrequent, superficial contact with Indonesians during a similar three-year assignment. Because it is dangerous to assume that superficial experience will lead to positive results, both the quantity *and* the quality of a candidate's experience should be examined before deciding on the training required. While this point may seem obvious, we have seen far too many cases like the following one.

Recently the general manager for a joint venture in Japan between a large U.S. telecommunications company and a Japanese company was selected in part on his three-year experience in Japan as a U.S. naval officer. Unfortunately, the fact that the individual had little direct interaction with Japanese during that time and lived on base was not carefully considered. The manager's previous limited experience did little to help prepare him for all the cross-cultural management intricacies of running the joint venture. He was sent without any training. Because key company officials did not think about the quality of this individual's previous experience, they were surprised when he encountered significant cross-cultural adjustment and management difficulties.

Communication Toughness

Another issue that should determine the training rigor is how much the global manager will be expected to interact with the local populace.[11] The more interaction required, the higher the level of communication toughness. For example, an oil rig expert sent to Saudi Arabia may only rarely have to speak to a Saudi, either on or off the job, whereas a marketing manager in Peru may be in constant contact with local clients, advertising agencies, and people in the media. Obviously, the manager in the former situation does not require nearly the rigorous cross-cultural training that the manager in the latter situation does.

The extent of communication toughness in the global assignment can be determined by examining the extent to which the overseas job requires communicating with the local nationals. Responses to the following questions will help you understand the degree to which such interaction will be necessary[12]:

Communication Toughness Questions

1. Are the rules and norms for communicating very different from those in the home country, or are they quite similar?

2. Will the manager have to communicate frequently or infrequently with local workers?

3. Does the candidate speak the local language? Do local nationals speak the candidates native language? If not, how difficult is the foreign language to learn?

4. Will the manager have to communicate mainly in one direction (e.g., giving orders, delegating, giving presentations, and so on), or will the nature of the job require intensive two-way communication (e.g., consultations, parties, business negotiations) with local nationals?

5. What will be the main form of communicating with local nationals—face-to-face communication (intimate daily discussions with subordinates) or technical communication (memos, mail, and so on)?

6. How long will the manager be on the assignment? Six months? One year? Three years?

7. What will be the main type of interaction—formal (aloofness from subordinates, figurehead authority style, authoritative order giving) or informal (personal influence with clients, relationships with government officials, and so on)?

As the intensity of interactions increases, the need for rigor in the training program increases proportionately. For example, if the communication will be frequent, two-way, face-to-face, and informal, the training should be more rigorous than in the opposite situation.

In assessing communication toughness, it is important to recognize that, even if the expatriate does not have a high level of interaction on the job, he or she may still have to undertake high levels of communication with locals outside the workplace. For example, a manager in Korea (a culture known for its high degree of communication toughness) may not have a great deal of daily interaction with local nationals but may have high levels of interaction as he or she manages the personal necessities of life. To ensure that managers and their families adjust to life in Korea, predeparture training should address communication both inside and outside the business arena.

Job Toughness

Many global managers are promoted when they are sent overseas. The promotion often means a job challenge because the manager is working in a new area and has more responsibilities, more autonomy, and new challenges. The tougher the tasks of the new job, the more assistance the manager will need through rigorous predeparture training. The elements of job toughness can be discerned in the answers to the following questions[13]:

Job Toughness Questions

1. Are the performance standards the same?
2. Is the degree of personal involvement in the work unit the same?
3. Is the task the same or quite different?
4. Are the bureaucratic procedures similar?
5. Are the resource limitations the same?
6. Are the legal restrictions similar?
7. Are the technological limitations familiar?
8. Is the freedom to decide how the work gets done the same?
9. Are the choices about what work gets delegated similar?
10. Is the freedom to decide who does which tasks the same?

An examination of the answers to these questions should enable a rough estimate to be made regarding the job toughness of the overseas assignment. If the job toughness is moderate to high, the manager will need job-specific training, as well as cultural training in how jobs get done and how people are used to being managed in the country of assignment. If the demands of the job are quite different from the job the manager has had at home, if the constraints are greater, and if there is less freedom, then the job toughness will be greater, as will the required level of training rigor.

Applying the Principles

Let us return to Mel, the manager at Recor. His predicament is very common across industries and in firms of all sizes. Remember that Mel was trying to put together a training program for eighteen engineers who were being sent to Japan. Let's look at his situation and apply the principles discussed in this chapter to the design of an effective cross-cultural training program.

Analysis and Application

To do this, we will take a look at each of the three major determinants of training rigor—cultural toughness, communication toughness, and job toughness.

Cultural Toughness. Looking at the list of seven regions, Mel quickly determined that the Far East was the third-most difficult, in both business practices and culture, for Westerners to adjust to. After speaking with local university professors and local businesspeople who had had dealings with the Japanese, and after consulting a few recommended books, Mel learned that the Japanese accept power differences in organizations and are more influenced by matters of hierarchy and status than Americans are. He also learned that the Japanese are less risk-oriented than Americans, are more comfortable working in groups, accept traditional sex-role differences, and have a stronger work ethic than Americans. The language is difficult to learn, and few Japanese speak fluent English.

Many of Mel's people had vacationed once or twice overseas (mainly in Europe and the Caribbean), but none had lived or worked abroad or in Japan. Thus, their previous experience would not reduce the cultural toughness or the need for rigorous cross-cultural training. Mel expected his people to experience serious culture shock on their arrival in Japan and that it would take some time for them to adjust to living and working there.

Communication Toughness. At first, Mel thought that except for Larry Runolfsson, the project manager, his people would have a fairly low degree of interaction with host nationals. Upon reflection, however, Mel realized that the group-oriented nature of the Japanese organization and the practice of group decision making increased the likelihood that all of Recor's people would be interacting frequently with the Japanese at work. Thus, Mel decided that Larry would have a higher level of required interaction, but that it was likely to be quite high for the others as well. Mel surmised that his team of engineers would be working in a business culture with different communication rules, where they would need to interact frequently with the Japanese, communicate with people speaking a difficult foreign language, and be expected to carry out tasks that would require two-way, face-to-face, informal communication. Communication toughness would be high.

Job Toughness. By contrast, it appeared, on the surface, that the job toughness in Japan would *not* be high. Larry Runolfsson had managed four projects before, and all the engineers had considerable professional experience; they did not need to learn any new technical skills. Nevertheless, there was a good chance that performance standards, tasks involving training or working with the Japanese, the ways in which decisions are made, and the bureaucratic procedures that have to be followed would all be somewhat different. Closer examination of the various aspects of the job suggested that job toughness would probably be moderate rather than low.

So far, Mel's analysis focused on the engineers. What about their families? Several people had stressed to Mel that family issues should not be overlooked; overseas assignments frequently get aborted because the spouse and the family are unable to adjust to the new culture. In general, family members react to cultural toughness as much as managers do, so the family needs predeparture training, too. Children under thirteen seem to have less difficulty adjusting to new cultures than teenagers do, but ideally the cross-cultural training teenagers and spouses receive should be as rigorous as the training given managers. Nonworking spouses find the adjustment to cultures that are high in communication toughness especially difficult: the inability to communicate, both verbally and nonverbally, can lead to depression, alienation, and loneliness. Telling people to "snap out of it" is simply not enough. Mel has to weigh all these issues before deciding on the training design. His budget may be limited, but, if at all possible, he needs to ensure that the engineers' spouses and other relevant family members are included in the training program.

Mel's Conclusions. What conclusions can Mel reach from his analysis of the culture in which his team will be working? His findings can be summarized as follows:

1. Cultural toughness = high
2. Communication toughness = high
3. Job toughness = moderate

Framework for Developing Cross-Cultural Training

Exhibit 4.2 illustrates a framework for selecting a training program.[14] The reasoning behind it is straightforward: the greater the cultural toughness, communication toughness, and job toughness, the greater the need for rigorous cross-cultural training. Adjustment along each of these dimensions is not equally tough, however. Research shows that adjustment to a new culture and to interacting with local nationals is more difficult than adjusting to the new job.

Mel realized that this group would need at least training at the high end of "moderate." He had no in-house expertise and could get the team members together for only three to five days of training. After examining several programs offered by various consulting firms, Mel found only one highly rigorous program. Mel encouraged the spouses to attend the training, and all did but two.

Exhibit 4.2
Determining Cross-Cultural Training Vigor

Low Training Rigor *(Duration = 4–20 Hours)*	Moderate Training Rigor *(Duration = 20–60 Hours)*	High Training Rigor *(Duration = 60–180 Hours)*
Lectures Films Books Area Briefings	Methods in previous box, plus: Role Plays Cases Assimilators Survival-level Language	Methods in previous box, plus: Assessment Centers Simulations Field Trips In-depth Language

Mel and the members of the consulting firm agreed that the focus of the training would be the development of cross-cultural interaction skills. Among the specific methods used were role plays, short simulations, culture assimilators, and case studies. Mel arranged for the engineers and their families to take lessons in the Japanese language after arriving in Japan. In addition, Mel gave them a list of books on Japanese culture, compiled after his assistant consulted with Japanese experts at the local university.

Mel felt that follow-up training once the engineers were settled in Japan might be useful. Later, he would have to decide whether to hire an American or a Japanese consulting firm to provide this training. He also thought that, to reduce costs, he could send over one or two professors whom he had met at the university to keep his people updated and to help them with any adjustment problems they might be having.

Mel's last idea brings up an important consideration that is overlooked by virtually all consulting firms that do cross-cultural training. Learning about the new culture is useful before leaving on a global assignment, but truly effective training requires rigorous, in-depth, cross-cultural training after global managers are "in country" (see Exhibit 4.3).

To understand why this is the case, think about Mel's group of engineers before and after they arrive in Japan. Before they leave their home country, it is more difficult for them to imagine what the trainers are trying to explain. For example, it is one thing to imagine what it is like to have a subordinate in Japan say, "Yes, I understand what you want me to do" and then do nothing because in fact he did not understand. It is another thing to have such an interaction and then learn about the cultural reasons behind it. In-country training has several advantages: (1) trainees are more highly motivated; (2) they have a higher level of baseline experience with the local culture as a foundation for learning deeper cultural values, norms, and ideas; (3) the trainees can immediately apply what they learn; and (4) the environment itself makes the training content real.

Predeparture training should focus mostly on basic, day-to-day, survival-level concerns. These are the things that the assignee and family will encounter as soon as they step off the plane. Predeparture training should also include some of the deeper aspects of the culture, but should not attempt to cover every segment at the deepest levels. In addition to the reasons we have already mentioned, without some actual experience in the culture many managers will simply find it hard to believe that "things could really be that different."

The bulk of in-depth culture training should take place after the assignee has been in the country for at least a month but not more than six months. The reason to wait at least a month is simple. During the first month after arrival, the assignee and family are so involved in all the logistics of getting settled, that there is precious little energy or mental capacity to absorb in-depth cultural training. The rationale for not waiting more than about six months is equally straightforward. After several months in the country the assignee and family will begin to form judgments and conclusions about the culture—what the norms are, what motivates people, and so on. Even if they are wrong, changing their minds at that point is difficult at best, impossible at worst.

After arrival in the host country, global managers and their families will need to focus less on day-to-day survival issues. With proper predeparture training, the basics will be mastered quite quickly. Mastery of culturally tough concepts is not automatic, however, so postarrival training is needed. The ideal place to master cultural skills is in the host culture.

Exhibit 4.3
Cross-Cultural Training: Content and Timing

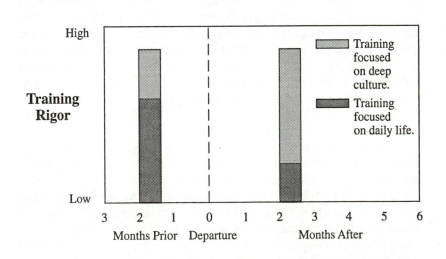

Linking Corporate Orientation to Training

Chapter 1 discussed the importance to firms that are "going global" of maintaining a fit between their globalization stage, their competitive strategy, and their people management. Each of the five functions of people management (in this case, the training function) must support the others and not detract from them.

Internal Fit

Spending a lot of time and money carefully searching for key people to send to specific countries can turn out to be a waste of an investment if the company uses an invalid, generic, ineffective training program. Likewise, offering no training at all is certain to inhibit the effectiveness of the selection process. Thus, the training function is an important link between good selection and good management development in the process of establishing internal fit.

A companywide, "canned" cross-cultural training program may not support the function of management development either. Imposing a one-dimensional approach on all international assignees, with no regard to their current strengths and weaknesses, to the unique situations they will find themselves in overseas, or to the kinds of skills they need to learn, will simply create frustration, unmet expectations, and poor management on the part of the global managers themselves when they are overseas.

External Fit

Cross-cultural training, like all the other functions of people management, must be designed with the firm's globalization stage in mind. Consider two global managers, both assigned to Nigeria. One works for a firm at the export stage of globalization, while the other works for a multinational corporation. Even if both jobs appear similar in cultural toughness, communication toughness, and job toughness, the globalization stages of the respective firms should also influence how training is designed. These relationships are illustrated in Exhibit 4.4.

The matrix in Exhibit 4.4 overarches what we have discussed to this point. The assumption in designing this matrix was that cultural toughness, communication toughness, and job toughness were always identical. This was done to illustrate how the globalization stage should influence the design of cross-cultural training. In general, the more a firm is moving out of the export stage of globalization, the more rigorous the training should be. Breadth of content also

Export Stage	MDC Stage
Degree of Rigor: Low to Moderate	*Degree of Rigor:* Moderate to High
Content: Emphasis should be on interpersonal skills, local culture, customer values, and business behavior. *Host-Country Nationals:* Low to Moderate training of host nationals to understand parent country products and policies.	*Content:* Emphasis should be on interpersonal skills, local culture, technology transfer, stress management, and business practices and laws. *Host-Country Nationals:* Low to Moderate training of host nationals; primarily focusing on production/service procedures.
MNC Stage	**Global Stage**
Degree of Rigor: High-Moderate to High *Content:* Emphasis should be on interpersonal skills, two-way technology transfer, corporate value transfer, international strategy, stress management, local culture, and business practices. *Host-Country Nationals:* Moderate to High training of host nationals in technical areas, product/service systems, and corporate culture.	*Degree of Rigor:* High *Content:* Emphasis should be on global corporate operations/systems, corporate culture transfer, customers, global competitors, and international strategy. *Host-Country Nationals:* High training of host nationals in global organization production/efficiency systems, corporate culture, business systems, and global conduct policies.

Exhibit 4.4
Stage of Globalization and Training Design Issues

___

increases as the firm moves from the export stage to the global stage; in other words, more rigorous training is needed. As firms move from the export and multidomestic stages, global managers also need to be able to socialize host-country managers into the firm's corporate culture and other firm-specific practices; this managerial responsibility requires rigorous training.

___

Case 13: Nestlé

As an example, let's examine some of the training issues that arise at a company like Nestlé as a result of its globalization orientation. Nestlé is a firm that responds well to local markets and that has relatively low levels of co-ordination of activities across borders. The company sees itself as an international firm and is profitable and innovative. Thus, in many ways Nestlé could be classified as a multidomestic organization. In-depth knowledge of each culture and market where the firm operates is critical, since production and product innovations take place in a variety of countries. Although local nationals would be more expert than expatriates in local cultural and market subtleties, Nestlé global managers retain control of these operations. Consequently, the number of managers Nestlé sends overseas is higher than if Nestlé were simply exporting.

In this context, the rigor of the training offered to the global managers whom Nestlé deploys ranges from moderate to high (see Exhibit 4.1). The primary reason for this level of training is that, to be effective, a global manager must have specific knowledge of the target foreign market and culture. Thus, the training needs to emphasize skills related to local business practices and cross-cultural communication, stress management, and so on. Training that included tactics for socializing local nationals to the Nestlé philosophy, implementation of worldwide corporate systems, and other firm-homogenizing practices would not be particularly useful, since such practices do not fit the globalization orientation of the firm as a whole.

Whether a firm has a pattern of globalization that requires many or few managers to be in positions around the world, those managers need to receive training appropriate to the contexts of their assignments. To maintain external fit, the training function must be flexible enough to deal with all potential contexts that derive from globalization patterns. A rigid, mechanical training philosophy will not benefit global managers to the greatest extent possible. Following the framework presented in this chapter, wise training decisions can be made despite constraints in the organization and the environment.

Notes

1. Windham International and National Foreign Trade Council, *Global Relocation Trends 1995 Survey Report* 1996.
2. Ibid.
3. Oddou and Mendenhall, "Succession Planning in the 21st Century."
4. Windham International and National Foreign Trade Council, *Global Relocation Trends 1995 Survey Report* 1996.
5. Black and Mendenhall, "Cross-Cultural Training Effectiveness: A Review and Theoretical Framework for Future Research."
6. Bandura, *Social Learning Theory*; Black and Mendenhall, "Cross-Cultural Training Effectiveness"; Manz and Sims, "Vicarious Learning: The Influence of Modeling on Organizational Behavior."

  7. Black and Mendenhall, "Cross-Cultural Training Effectiveness."

  8. Black and Mendenhall, "Selecting Cross-Cultural Training Methods: A Practical Yet Theory-Based Model"; Mendenhall and Oddou, "Acculturation Profiles of Expatriate Managers: Implications for Cross-Cultural Training Programs"; Mendenhall, Dunbar, and Oddou, "Expatriate Selection, Training, and Career-Pathing."

  9. Mendenhall and Oddou, "The Dimensions of Expatriate Acculturation."

10. Torbiörn, "Living Abroad"; Hofstede, "Culture's Consequences: International Differences in Work-Related Values."

11. Mendenhall and Oddou, "Acculturation Profiles of Expatriate Managers."

12. Black and Mendenhall, "Selecting Cross-Cultural Training Methods."

13. Ibid.

14. Ibid.

5

Adjusting: Developing New Mental Road Maps and Behaviors

In Chapter 2, we addressed the issue of culture and how people adjust when they are sent on foreign assignments. Chapters 3 and 4 discussed whom to select and how to train people for international posts. In this chapter, we examine some additional factors that help or hinder successful cross-cultural adjustment among expatriates.

You may recall that in Chapter 2, we pointed out that one of the key aspects of culture is a common set of rules, values, and assumptions. These rules, values, and assumptions are passed from one generation to another and influence behavior; they are also evident in other ways. We have also pointed out that this view of culture raises two important implications. First, the most powerful components of culture are invisible rather than visible; consequently, the most important aspects of foreign cultures are hard to recognize, understand, and adjust to. Second, being immersed in a new culture disrupts familiar and established routines and threatens self-image. The result is usually ego-defensive countermeasures and feelings of anger, frustration, and anxiety. For many people, returning home early is the easiest way to escape these feelings and the situations that cause them. Most people, however—perhaps because of fear, determination, or both—continue to live and work in the foreign country, struggling to adjust.

The process of cross-cultural adjustment consists of two interrelated components. The first component involves creating a new set of mental road maps and book of traffic rules, or *predictive control*.[1] These maps and rules enable people to predict what behaviors are expected in specific situations, how people will probably respond, what behaviors are not appropriate, and so on. By enabling expatriates to predict what to do in a variety of situations, these maps and rules allow people in foreign cultures to feel a measure of control in their new environments.

The second component of cross-cultural adjustment involves mastering new behavior, or *behavioral control*.[2] For example, it is one thing to know that the Chinese communicate more indirectly than Americans but quite another to be able to change one's own style of communication from direct to more indirect. The challenge is equally difficult for Chinese who must change their indirect style to a more direct one when transferred to the United States. Cross-cultural adjustment involves figuring out what the new cause-and-effect contingencies are in the foreign culture and mastering the behavior necessary to produce desired rewards and to avoid unwanted punishments.

It's important to keep in mind, however, that adjustment does not necessarily mean total and permanent transformation. People can effectively adjust to a foreign culture without having to embrace and accept all its assumptions, values, and behaviors. The key to cross-cultural adjustment is the ability to express appreciation and respect for the local culture without rejecting their own native culture. The most respected expatriates in an international business community are bicultural. They speak the local language, are well integrated into both the local culture and the community of expatriates, and understand the host culture as well as their own.

What Factors Influence Cross-Cultural Adjustment?

Most research on cross-cultural adjustment has focused on Americans working overseas.[3] Recently, however, work has also been done on Japanese managers on international assignments and on European managers in foreign posts. Consequently, although the major influences on cross-cultural adjustment we will talk about are based on the experiences of American managers overseas, we will also discuss the extent to which these factors are true for other nationalities as well.

Dimensions of Cross-Cultural Adjustment

When scholars first started researching adjustment among expatriates, they focused on their adjustment to the more visible aspects of their new cultures, such as food, transportation systems, daily customs, and so on. More recently, our team of researchers has discovered three related but separate aspects or dimensions of cross-cultural adjustment: adjustment to the job, adjustment to interacting with host-country nationals, and adjustment to the general nonwork environment. Interestingly, our research has found strong evidence that the same three dimensions of cross-cultural adjustment apply to other nationalities of managers sent on foreign assignments.[4] These three dimensions are represented in the far right-hand box of Exhibit 5.1.

Adjustment to Work. Generally, this is the easiest of the three dimensions of adjustment for expatriate managers, primarily because job adjustment is aided by similarities in procedures, policies, and requirements of the task in the foreign operation and in the home-country operation. But although adjustment to the job is the easiest adjustment to make, it is not necessarily easy.

Aspects of the foreign operation's corporate culture, as well as its national culture, are often dramatically different from those back home and exert an influence on managers' tasks and responsibilities. Consequently, although a manager from New York may be expected to perform basically the same task in Hong Kong, elements of the foreign operation and the host-country culture may make it necessary to perform the task in a slightly, or even dramatically, different manner to achieve similar results and success.[5] In the United Kingdom, for example, a systems engineer may be able to interview workers to find out their needs and expected uses of a proposed computer program. By contrast, in India, workers may simply expect to be told how they are to use the new program and may be confused when someone asks for their input. A British expatriate may find that asking Indian workers how they would use the program will generate information that is incomplete and inaccurate. Adjustment to work may also be affected by gender relations, compensation levels, and promotability of the work in the host country.[6]

Adjustment to Interacting with Host-Country Nationals. Regardless of the expatriate manager's nationality, interacting is generally the most difficult of the three adjustment dimensions, primarily because differences in mental maps and rules show up in interactions with host-country nationals. Time spent with other expatriates prior to the assignment and the novelty of the new culture significantly affect adjustment along this dimension.[7]

Adjustment to the General Nonwork Environment. This dimension, which has typically been the focus of many researchers studying cross-cultural adjustment, includes adjustment to food, transportation,

Exhibit 5.1
Dimensions of Cross-Cultural Adjustment

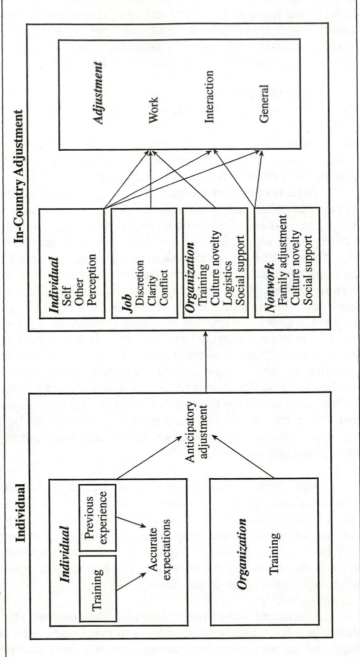

entertainment, health care, and other issues. In general, international assignees have an easier time adjusting to the general environment than to interactions with host nationals and have more difficulty adjusting to the general environment than to the job.[8] Several factors affect adjustment to the general environment, including international experience, time spent with other expatriates, and the novelty of the new culture.[9]

Case 14: Fred Bailey: An Innocent Abroad

One of the easiest ways to understand the three dimensions of adjustment is to examine a real (but disguised) case of an expatriate manager. Fred Bailey and his family had been recently assigned to the Tokyo office of a Boston-based U.S. consulting firm.[10]

Fred Bailey gazed out the window of his twenty-fourth-floor office at the tranquil beauty of the Imperial Palace amidst the hustle and bustle of downtown Tokyo. It had only been six months since Fred arrived with his wife and two children for his three-year assignment as director of Kline & Associates' Tokyo office. (Kline & Associates was a large multinational consulting firm in Boston, with offices in nineteen countries.)

Fred was trying to decide whether he should simply pack up and tell the home office that he was leaving or try somehow to convince his wife (and himself) that they should stay and finish the assignment. Fred had thought they all were excited to begin with, so it was a mystery to him how things had reached this point. As he reflected back on a variety of incidents, one stood out in his mind as particularly frustrating.

Not long after his arrival in Japan, Fred had a meeting with representatives of a top Japanese multinational firm concerning a potentially large contract. Those present included Fred; the lead American consultant for the potential contract, Ralph Webster; and one of the senior Japanese associate consultants, Kenichi Kurokawa, who spoke perfect English. The Japanese team had four members: the vice president for administration, the director of international personnel, and two staff specialists. After some awkward handshakes and bows, Fred said that he knew the Japanese gentlemen were busy and he did not want to waste their time, so he would get right to the point. Fred then had Ralph Webster lay out the firm's proposal for the project and what the project would cost. After the presentation, Fred asked the Japanese team for its reaction to the proposal. The Japanese team did not respond immediately, so Fred launched into his summary version of the proposal, thinking that the translation might have been insufficient. Again, although he asked several direct questions, the Japanese team offered only vague responses.

*After five months, a contract between the firms had yet to be signed.
"I can never seem to get a direct response from the Japanese," Fred complained.*

*Fred decided that the reason little progress had been made was that
he and his group did not know enough about the client to package the proposal in a way that was appealing. He called in Ralph Webster and asked
him to develop a report on the client so the proposal could be reevaluated
and changed as necessary. Jointly, Fred and Ralph decided that one of the
more promising young Japanese research associates, Tashiro Watanabe,
would be the best person to take the lead on this report. To impress upon
Tashiro the importance of this task and the great potential they saw in him,
they decided to have the young Japanese associate meet with them. In the
meeting, Fred had Ralph describe the nature and importance of the task.
Fred then leaned forward in his chair and said, "You can see that this
assignment is important and that we are placing a lot of confidence in you
by giving it to you. We need the report by this time next week so we can
revise and present our proposal again. Can you do it?"*

*After a pregnant pause, Tashiro responded hesitantly, "I'm not sure
what to say."*

*At that point Fred smiled, got up from his chair, walked over to the
young Japanese associate, extended his hand, and said, "Hey, there's nothing to say. We're just giving you the opportunity you deserve."*

*The day before the report was due, Fred asked Ralph how it was
coming. Ralph said that since he had heard nothing from Tashiro, he
assumed everything was under control but that he would double check.
Ralph later ran into one of the American research associates, John Maynard.
Ralph knew that John had been hired because he was fluent in Japanese and
that, unlike the other Americans, John often went out after work with some
of the Japanese research associates, including Tashiro. Ralph asked John if
he knew how Tashiro was coming along on the report.*

*John recounted that the night before at the office, Tashiro had asked
him if Americans fire employees for being late with reports. John, sensing
that the question was not hypothetical, asked Tashiro why he wanted to
know. Tashiro did not respond immediately. Since it was 8:30 p.m., John suggested they go out for a drink. At first Tashiro resisted, but John assured him
that they would grab a drink at a nearby bar and come right back. At the bar,
John got Tashiro to open up.*

*Tashiro explained the nature of the report he had been requested to
produce. He continued to explain that, although he had worked late every
night, it was impossible to complete the report in a week, and that he had
doubted from the beginning that he could complete it that soon. Furthermore,
Kenichi Kurokawa, who was four years senior to Tashiro, had originally been*

involved in the project but apparently nothing had been said to him about Tashiro's assignment.

At this point, Ralph asked John, "Why the hell didn't he say something in the first place?" Ralph did not wait to hear whether John had an answer to his question. He headed straight to Tashiro's desk.

The incident got worse. Ralph chewed Tashiro out and then went to Fred, explaining that the report would not be ready and that Tashiro had not thought it could be from the start.

"Then why didn't he say something?" Fred asked. No one had any answers, and the whole thing left everyone more suspicious and uncomfortable.

The problem centered around different communication styles and assumptions. Fred's operating assumption was that if you wanted someone to understand your idea, opinion, etc., it was your responsibility as the speaker, not the listener, to clearly and explicitly communicate what you had to say. In Japan, the cultural assumption regarding communication is quite different. Tashiro assumed that the listener (Fred in this case) had significant responsibility for hearing what was not said. Tashiro assumed that Fred would hear Tashiro's worries even if they were implicit rather than explicit. When asked why he hadn't voiced his concerns about the feasibility of completing the project on time, Tashiro responded, "I did," meaning he expressed his concerns without explicitly stating them. A good Japanese manager would have picked up on these implicit, unvoiced concerns. In fact, it would have been the Japanese manager's responsibility to do so.

Fred found himself frustrated in interactions with Japanese customers and co-workers because the two cultures hold very different assumptions about communication. In general, Americans expect explicit communication and place most of the responsibility on the speaker. In contrast, Japanese value implicit communication and place responsibility for effective communication on both the speaker and the listener.

An encounter the Baileys had at a Japanese resort illustrates the potential challenges of adjusting to the general environment. After a few months into the assignment, the Baileys were looking forward to a long weekend vacation, and everyone in the office had advised Fred to stay at a famous hot springs north of Tokyo. Fred, Jenny, and their children arrived and were proceeding to the front desk to check in when an elderly Japanese man started making gestures with his hands and speaking rapidly in Japanese. Fred and Jenny stopped in time, but the two girls had stepped up to the main floor with their shoes on before the man could bring them slippers. Once they all had their multicolored slippers on and their shoes securely stored in lockers, the Baileys proceeded to check in.

This accomplished, two elderly Japanese women escorted the Baileys to their room. After walking down a long hall, the women stopped in front of a wooden door, slid it back, and waited for the Baileys to enter. The hall door opened into a small entry room, about three feet wide and five feet long. The Japanese women indicated that they should all remove their slippers, but once again, the girls had opened a door and stepped up into the main room. After removing their slippers, Fred and Jenny gazed in amazement at the big, empty room; there were no beds and no furniture. The Japanese women showed the Baileys the closet in which the futons, *or sleeping mattresses, and blankets were stored, and they rattled off several comments in Japanese. As the Japanese women prepared to leave, Fred tried to tip them. Both women covered their mouths and waved their right hands back and forth in front of their faces.*

Later, Fred decided to take a soak in one of the hot springs. He went downstairs to the locker room and took off his clothes. Two doors led out of the locker room, and the signs above them were in Japanese. Fred decided to take the door on the right and entered a large room. On the right side was a line of short wooden stools and small buckets lined up in front of a row of water faucets. At one of the faucets, a Japanese man was seated, vigorously washing his hair. In the center of the room was a large tub about the size of a swimming pool. At about the same time Fred noticed this, he also noticed giggles coming from three young women sitting in the water on the left side of the tub. Fred had stumbled into the "co-ed" section of the hot spring. He quickly retreated, got dressed, and returned to his room.

Later that evening, Fred and his family decided to have a fresh fish dinner. After a few strange appetizers, a big fish was brought in on a large platter. As the fish was placed on the table in front of the Baileys, Fred noticed a movement. As he looked closer, Fred could see the gills of the fish slowly opening and closing in a futile attempt to breathe. The body of the fish had been masterfully sliced into little fillets that lay all along its torso. Christine shrieked, "Daddy, it's still alive! They've sliced it open, and it's still alive!" Suddenly no one was hungry.

What the Baileys failed to appreciate was that by quickly "gutting" and skillfully slicing the fish into sashimi *(raw fish fillets), and serving it before the reflexes of the fish stopped it from opening and closing its gills demonstrated absolute freshness. This was a skill and level of service that very few resorts could offer.*

Categorization of Influential Factors

One of the important reasons for distinguishing among the three dimensions of cross-cultural adjustment is that not all important factors are related equally, or even at all, to all three dimensions of adjustment. For example, a certain factor may influence work adjustment more than interaction adjustment and have no influence at all on general nonwork adjustment. In discussing these factors, we have organized them into two categories—those that influence adjustment before departure and those that influence adjustment after arrival. These factors are represented in Exhibit 5.1 by two separate boxes.

We have further divided the factors that influence adjustment after arrival into four separate categories: factors related to the individual, to the job, to the organization, and to nonwork issues. The following section discusses, for each of these categories, specific factors that researchers have found are important, and details the adjustment dimensions on which the factors tend to have the strongest influence. Exhibit 5.1 illustrates the various relationships.[11]

Factors That Affect Adjustment Before Departure

One of the most important advances in the understanding of cross-cultural adjustment is the realization that people make adjustments in advance of actually transferring overseas. Expatriates should really want to work abroad, even to the point of being idealistic or having a sense of mission. Only candidates who show high levels of enthusiasm and involvement are likely to make the necessary sacrifices and to be committed to achieving real understanding and acceptance of the conditions in the host country. The expatriate who has absolutely no desire to go on a foreign assignment is the least likely to make necessary adjustments in advance of the assignment (*anticipatory adjustment*) and ultimately is the least likely to adjust overseas.[12]

The process of anticipatory adjustment is primarily psychological; that is, people begin to adjust their mental maps and rules (*anticipatory expectations*). For example, if individuals know in advance that the Japanese drive on the left side of the road, they can make mental adjustments before actually traveling to Japan. Likewise, if people know that the Swiss take gifts of flowers or chocolate when invited to someone's house for dinner, they can mentally adjust in advance of receiving an invitation. Generally, three aspects of anticipatory adjustment help actual in-country adjustment: (1) making a large number of mental adjustments in advance, (2) focusing the process of anticipatory adjustment on important aspects of the new culture, and (3) refining the advance adjustments so that they are accurate. In a domestic context, significant research has been conducted on realistic previews of future jobs and assignments and the impact on adjustment.[13]

Individual Factors. Research has found that two specific factors facilitate the formation of accurate expectations and mental adjustments. The first factor is one we have already discussed in some detail—cross-cultural training. (In particular, issues concerning the content and rigor of training were examined in Chapter 4.) Because individuals can provide predeparture training for themselves or can receive it through their firms, training can be categorized as either an individual or an organizational factor.

The second individual factor that can help someone develop accurate expectations is previous overseas experience. Many writers have speculated that having lived in a foreign country has a positive impact on the formation of accurate expectations about another foreign experience. The assumption is that learning how to live and work in France is applicable to learning how to live and work in Malaysia. Research suggests, however, that although previous international experience can be positively related to all three forms of adjustment,[14] assuming that because someone has lived in one country he or she will adjust to another country is too simplistic.[15] Previous overseas experience can have a positive impact on anticipatory adjustment, but because various aspects of living and working in one foreign country are not always applicable to another, the positive impact is moderate at best.

The impact of previous international experience is strongest when the last international experience was relatively recent and when the degree of interaction with host-country nationals and involvement in the foreign culture was relatively high. For example, consider the case of the French manager who had lived in Africa for two years before his current assignment there. His previous assignment in Africa was fifteen years ago, and he lived in a neighborhood dominated by families of French diplomats. He really did not have to interact with the local people and culture at all. In his current assignment, he will be managing a joint venture between a government ministry and his firm, and he will be living in a native neighborhood. Under these conditions, his previous experience will *not* have a significant impact on the formation of accurate predeparture expectations and, therefore, will not really facilitate his successful adjustment or job performance. Because someone worked overseas many years ago is not an accurate predictor of success in an impending assignment.

Organizational Factors. Training is one of the more critical organizational factors that can help individuals form accurate expectations in advance of being sent overseas.[16] As discussed in Chapter

4, however, basic logistical issues occupy the minds of most managers before their overseas departure. Since most of them will not have had recent previous experience in the countries to which they are being sent, their level of motivation and general capacity to relate to deep cultural information are often not ideal just before transfer. Therefore, although research evidence suggests that predeparture cross-cultural training can have a positive impact on the development of cross-cultural skills, adjustment, and job performance, some (if not most) of the deep cross-cultural training should be provided after the individual has been in the country for a month or so. Research also suggests that besides training, whether expatriates receive company assistance and support is a positive predictor of their adjustment.[17] When companies show genuine concern for the well-being of the expatriate and the family, the chances are much better that they will adjust well to their new culture.[18]

Factors That Affect Adjustment After Arrival

This section discusses factors that affect adjustment after arrival at the foreign assignment (*postarrival* or *in-country factors*). Many of these factors can be influenced by organizations, but require planning and design before individuals are sent overseas. (Steps that organizations can take to facilitate successful cross-cultural adjustment are discussed in more detail at the end of this chapter.)

Individual Factors. Individual factors that influence cross-cultural adjustment were discussed in Chapter 3, but they can be summarized in terms of three broad categories.[19]

The first category consists of *self-oriented factors.* These individual characteristics relate to people's proclivity to believe in themselves and to be confident in their ability to deal effectively with foreigners and new surroundings. As discussed earlier, disrupted routines are a strong blow to ego and self-image. Although arrogance or an inflated self-image do not help in the process of cross-cultural adjustment, people who believe strongly in themselves tend to persevere even in the face of mistakes, ask questions about mistakes they make, learn from their mistakes, and do not make the same mistakes repeatedly.[20] Thus, individuals with strong, healthy self-images tend to persist in adjusting their behaviors, even when these adjustments are less than perfect and produce negative consequences. The more they try to master new behavior, the more they have the opportunity to receive both positive and negative feedback about how they are doing and to refine their behavior until it is effective.

The second category of individual factors are *other-oriented* or *relational factors*. These characteristics are associated with the ability to meet new people, interact with them, and empathize with them. This orientation toward developing relationships is powerful because host-country nationals are the best source for teaching foreigners how to navigate in their country successfully.

The third group of individual factors are *perceptual-oriented factors,* or an individual's ability to grasp and understand a culture's invisible maps and rules. People are not equal in this ability. For example, some people cannot comprehend what is not visible. Others are much better able to appreciate and understand the invisible and subtle determinants of people's behavior.

Although much research remains to be done on the relative strength of specific individual factors, our studies suggest that G-A-P-S is an effective way to measure characteristics that have a positive influence on all three dimensions of cross-cultural adjustment.[21]

Job Factors. Job factors tend to have their strongest influence on work adjustment, and tend to have little spillover effect on interaction or general nonwork adjustment.

The job factor that has the strongest impact on work adjustment is the amount of freedom individuals have in their jobs, or *job discretion.* A person who has a great deal of job discretion has flexibility in determining what work to do, when and how to do it, and whom to involve. People with greater job discretion are able to configure their work so they can use past successful behaviors and approaches more easily, which in turn facilitates job adjustment and performance.[22]

Another aspect of the job that helps improve work adjustment is the extent to which what is expected of the individual is clear and unambiguous, or *job clarity.* It is hard to adjust to something that is unclear or ambiguous. Consequently, job ambiguity generally hurts job adjustment and performance, while job clarity has a positive impact on both outcomes.[23]

Yet another aspect of the job that influences work adjustment is the extent to which conflicting demands or expectations are placed on the worker. This is called *role conflict,* not to be confused with job ambiguity. In the case of job ambiguity, what is expected is unclear; in the case of role conflict, what is expected is clear but different people have conflicting expectations of the manager. Role conflict generally hinders work adjustment.[24]

Organizational Factors. Four specific organizational factors have a significant impact on adjustment to an international assignment. These factors tend to be related most strongly to work adjustment, rather than to interaction or general nonwork adjustment.

The first of these organizational factors is postarrival cross-cultural training. If the content of the training focuses on the job, interacting effectively with host nationals, and on the general environment, then the training tends to have an impact on all three aspects of adjustment.[25] Training can help individuals gain the necessary mental maps and understand the rules of a culture; it can also help them practice and develop the behaviors and skills necessary to operate effectively in the foreign culture. Too often, firms simply use training as a means of conveying information. Understanding a culture's rules is a necessary but insufficient step in the process of cross-cultural adjustment and competence. People also need to be able to behave appropriately. (As discussed in Chapter 4, developing these skills and behaviors requires more rigorous training.)

The second organizational factor that can affect work adjustment is the extent to which the organizational culture in the foreign operation is different from the organizational culture at home. The greater the difference, the more difficult the adjustment, and the longer it ultimately takes.[26]

As anyone who has had to move from one country to another will attest, the logistics involved are tremendous, especially for a family. Thus, the third organizational factor that affects adjustment is the extent to which the organization provides logistical support. By providing this support, a company can significantly reduce the uncertainty associated with finding housing, schooling, and so on. Since much of this support concerns nonwork issues, it tends to have more of an effect on general nonwork adjustment than on work adjustment.[27]

The fourth organizational factor involves the extent to which members of the foreign operation provide social support to the newcomer. Supportive co-workers can provide both information about how to get along in the organization and emotional support while the newcomer learns the ropes. Expatriates with higher levels of social support from their co-workers have lower levels of role ambiguity and role conflict and higher levels of work adjustment than those expatriates who lack such support.[28]

Nonwork Factors. The research on managers sent on international assignments has also identified three other important factors that contribute to adjustment. With the marked exception of the family's adjustment (primarily the spouse), these factors tend to be strongly related to the general nonwork environment.

The first nonwork factor is the spouse. Studies show a consistent and strong relationship between the adjustment of the manager and his or her spouse.[29] At this point, it is impossible to determine the exact cause-and-effect relationship between the adjustment of the employee and that of the spouse. The relationship is most likely reciprocal, and the adjustment of the employee and the spouse mutually influence each other.

Like differences in organizational culture, general nonwork differences between the native and the host culture increase expatriates' uncertainty about how to behave appropriately, leading to adjustment difficulties. These differences hinder interaction and nonwork adjustment more than they hinder job adjustment.[30] These differences have been referred to by various authors as *culture novelty, culture toughness,* and *culture distance.*

Culture novelty has a negative impact on interaction and general nonwork adjustment for two reasons. The first reason is that the greater the number and degree of differences between two cultures, the more mistakes people can make as they try to live and work in the new culture. The more depressed people get about making these mistakes, the more defensive and angry they become toward host-country nationals, who are often seen as the cause of their troubles. The second reason culture novelty has a negative impact on adjustment is that the ways in which differences are discovered or learned, the way mistakes are recognized, or how apologies for mistakes are made **may also be different!**

For example, Japanese and American cultural differences have received a lot of scholarly and popular attention. Business-related differences, such as the use of merit versus seniority pay systems or individual versus group decision making, have been discussed in several popular books. Much of the academic and popular press suggests that the differences between American and Japanese people are so numerous and significant that conflict is inevitable when they get together. But conflicts occur among Japanese in Japan and among Americans in the United States. So what is the big deal if conflicts arise between Japanese and Americans working together? The problem is not only that Japanese and Americans do things differently and as a result create conflicts, but that they also resolve conflicts differently, which in turn creates conflicts that neither side can agree on how to solve.

The final nonwork factor that has an important relationship to cross-cultural adjustment is the extent to which expatriates receive social support from host-country nationals outside the workplace. Such support can provide both information about how to get along in the culture and emotional support while the newcomers are learning the ropes. Expatriates with higher levels of support had significantly higher levels of interaction and general nonwork adjustment.[31]

What Factors Influence Spouses' Cross-Cultural Adjustment?

By comparison with what is known about employees, very little is known about the specific factors that affect the cross-cultural adjustment of their spouses. Nevertheless, it is clear that, unlike the employee, who has the built-in structure of an organization and a job, the spouse generally is left alone to figure out how to survive and succeed in the new environment and culture. As a result, the spouse often feels isolated. In general, however, it appears that having a spouse for social support is an advantage for expatriates versus expatriates who are single. Still, poor spouse adjustment is the single greatest cause for expatriates terminating their foreign assignments early.[32]

We conducted a study of spouses in which we tried to systematically examine a number of factors and their impact on cross-cultural adjustment.[33] We found that although managers are often excited about the career potential of an international assignment, their spouses may not be. For spouses, a move to a foreign country may simply represent a disruption of their own careers or long-term social relationships. Not surprisingly then, our study found that the more the spouse was in favor of making the move overseas, the more he or she tried to learn about the country and its culture. This self-initiated pre-departure training in turn was positively related to the spouse's interaction adjustment. Further, those spouses who were interviewed by a human resource professional from the firm before the assignment had the highest levels of adjustment. This correlation may be due to the fact that spouses received a more thorough description of the assignment and country in an interview than they received from their spouse (i.e., the employee who is the candidate for the assignment).

Given the bashing (or at least bruising) effect a cross-cultural move can have on ego, we expected that whether spouses had social support would be an important factor in their cross-cultural adjustment. Our study found that both family support and support from host-country nationals helped the interaction adjustment of spouses.

Support from host-country nationals was particularly helpful, because host-country nationals could provide information about the culture, and feedback to the spouse on how well he or she was doing and what changes could lead to more effective functioning in the culture.

Our research identified two other factors that were significantly related to the spouses' general nonwork adjustment. The first of these factors was culture novelty. As with employees, the greater the cultural difference between the home and host cultures, the more difficulty spouses had adjusting to the general environment.

The second factor was a function of the spouses' particular circumstances. Even though many spouses who worked full time before moving overseas find work when they are abroad, most spouses do not work during an international assignment.[34] Consequently, most spouses have to deal with the family's general living conditions all day, day in and day out. It is perhaps not surprising then, that living conditions equal to or better than those at home, have a positive effect on spouses' general adjustment.

Maximizing the Chances of Successful Adjustment

For executives involved in or responsible for the international movement of human resources, a key question is, What steps can we take to maximize the success and minimize the failure of international transfers? This question is especially important, since some factors that affect cross-cultural adjustment are not under the executives' control (e.g., the level of organizational or cultural novelty, which is not really under anyone's control). So what effective steps can be taken? Exhibit 5.2 summarizes these actions.

Selection

Chapter 3 discussed at length how firms can more effectively select employees for global assignments. Three points are worth emphasizing. First, provide feedback to both candidates and spouses on their cross-cultural strengths and weaknesses through standardized instruments. Knowing where they are strong and weak can help employees and spouses maximize the effectiveness of any preparation offered by the firm and any they do on their own. In addition, the feedback may be an important catalyst and motivation for these education and preparation efforts. Second, certainly not all but a majority of candidates for global assignments are married. It is clear that the spouse's opinion can significantly affect both self-initiated predeparture training and

Action Category	Action
Selection	• Provide feedback to both the employee and spouse about their cross-cultural strengths and weaknesses through a standardized instrument. • Interview the spouse to investigate the level of motivation he or she has for the assignment. • Take greater care in assessing the employee and the spouse when the assignment is to a highly different culture or to a remote and more harsh locale.
Training	• Provide more rigorous training as the level of communication, job, and cultural toughness increase. • Provide, whenever feasible, both predeparture and postarrival training, and focus the postarrival training on the more complicated aspects of the culture. • Extend whatever training is provided to both the employee and the spouse.
Job Design	• To the extent possible, give the employee considerable discretion and freedom in the job. • To the extent possible, try to clarify the job expectations, responsibilities, and objectives. • Provide overlap with the job incumbent whenever possible. • Know and attempt to align any conflicting expectations concerning the job, objectives, or performance standards.
Logistical Support	• Provide first-class logistical support so that both the employee and the spouse can focus on the challenging and important aspects of effectively living and working abroad. • Monitor logistical programs and solicit expatriate feedback concerning outside vendors.
Social Support	• To the extent possible, encourage local national employees to provide support to new international assignees and families. • Provide comprehensive information about various social, community, or religious organizations that may create opportunities to meet people and develop social support networks.

Exhibit 5.2
Effective Steps for Successful Adjustment

in-country adjustment, yet only about 30 percent of U.S. firms take the opportunity to elicit spouses' thoughts and questions about the move.[35] An employee and a spouse may not be equally motivated to accept an international assignment, so it is probably not wise to rely on an employee's report of the spouse's opinion. Third, although executives cannot control the extent of organizational or cultural novelty expatriates will experience in their host countries, executives can factor it into the process of selecting candidates for expatriation. The greater the cultural novelty, the more careful the selection decision should be.

Training

Although we discussed this topic at length in Chapter 4 and in this chapter, as the level of communication, job, and cultural toughness increase, provide more rigorous training. Whenever feasible, provide both predeparture and postarrival training. If both are provided, predeparture training should focus on the daily living aspects of the new country, and postarrival training should focus on the more complicated aspects of the culture. If only predeparture training is provided, then both daily living and the culture need to be addressed. Finally, whatever training is provided should be extended to both the employee and the spouse. Many training providers now have excellent programs for children, and these should be taken advantage of whenever possible.

Job Design

Research shows that greater job discretion and clarity and less role conflict facilitate work adjustment. Providing job discretion, making role expectations clear, and eliminating conflicting demands seem like three simple steps executives can take when designing an overseas position. Their execution, however, is actually quite complex.

Let us consider the issue of role clarity. One easy but rarely utilized technique for increasing role clarity is to build in job overlap— that is, to allow the new expatriate and the incumbent in the expatriate's new job several days or perhaps weeks to work together. During this time, the incumbent teaches the new entrant. The more complex the job and the less experienced the new entrant, the longer the overlap should be. Theoretically, the incumbent should be able to clarify all aspects of the job. In interviews, several expatriates specifically mentioned that this approach was a relatively low-cost means of facilitating adjustment and effectiveness. American expatriates in countries such as Japan, Korea, Singapore, and Saudi Arabia have also mentioned that time with their predecessors was necessary for making the proper introductions to customers, suppliers, business partners, and government officials.

Key executives can also enhance the ROI of an international assignment by reducing role conflict. The primary source of role conflict for expatriates is conflicting expectations between the parent firm and the local operation. Interestingly, efforts to clarify the job may actually uncover previously hidden role conflict. Thus, firms must consider the need to increase job clarity and decrease role conflict simultaneously. This action requires that both the parent firm and the foreign operation have a clear understanding of what is expected of the expatriate manager and that they work to align those expectations.

Even a firm's best efforts may not eliminate role ambiguity and conflict. This is probably why job discretion tends to be the single strongest factor affecting work adjustment. Even if role ambiguity and role conflict exist, having a fair amount of freedom to decide what tasks to do, how to do them, when to do them, and who should do them facilitates an expatriate manager's ability to cope effectively with ambiguity and conflict. Thus, one way to solve all of these problems is simply to give expatriate managers a lot of job discretion and freedom. Unfortunately, this may not be as easy as it sounds. Too much discretion without clear objectives may cause the manager to choose objectives that are not in the best interest of the parent firm, the foreign operation, or both. Therefore, the firm needs to consider all three elements of an expatriate's job simultaneously.

Even though research indicates that job clarity, role conflict, and job discretion are important to work adjustment, we believe that it is best to think of these aspects of the expatriate manager's job not as targets of manipulation but as outcomes of broader policy and strategic processes. If a firm wants to make significant, long-term effective changes in the expatriate manager's job, this goal is best achieved through a careful assessment of the following issues:

1. Why is this specific expatriate being sent to this particular post? (Because there are no host-country nationals capable of fulfilling the job? To provide the expatriate with needed developmental experience?)

2. What are the criteria by which success in the job will be measured? What is really desired of the person in this particular position?

3. Are the objectives and goals of the parent firm and the foreign operation consistent? Are they consistent in the foreign

operation and in the particular department where the individual will work?

4. How much coordination and control are needed between the parent firm and the foreign operation? How much freedom and autonomy ought to be incorporated into the foreign unit? Is job discretion consistent with coordination needs?

Without an assessment of these strategic issues, the firm may adjust its expectations in ways that are dysfunctional for the overall strategy and for the relationship between the parent firm and the foreign operation. For example, a firm may provide overlap time that only reinforces deep and severe expectation conflicts between the parent and the local organizations, or the firm may give too much freedom to expatriate managers when much more control and coordination are required. Adjustments made independently, without regard for the broader competitive strategy, are likely to have short-term positive results at best and severe negative results at worst. By contrast, an analysis that begins with the broader competitive business strategy and context naturally leads to understanding of and appropriate adjustments to the expatriate manager's job and to a higher probability of successful adjustment at work.

Logistical Support

While most firms would rate themselves as quite good at providing logistical support, employees and families are not so generous. The critical thing to remember is that excellent logistical support is generally money well spent because it frees the employee and the spouse to focus on other targets of adjustment, such as to the job and interacting with host nationals, that yield both greater negative consequences if not accomplished well and significant payoffs if achieved.

Social Support

Evidence consistently indicates that social support can facilitate cross-cultural adjustment for both employees and their spouses. The evidence is particularly strong concerning social support from host-country nationals with respect to interaction adjustment. Although the firm cannot directly control the amount of social support particular families or employees receive, it can take steps to enhance the probability of their receiving it. Some firms have adopted the practice of asking a host-country national employee and family in the foreign operation to help the expatriate and family have a "soft landing." Generally, this assistance has focused on logistical issues such as housing, schools, and shopping. Although friendships cannot be mandated, some companies have made it clear that helping families (especially spouses) become involved in social or cultural activities is appreciated. Other firms have taken a more indirect approach. They simply provide stacks of information on local social and cultural activities and groups in which expatriate managers and families can become involved.

Summary

This chapter and Chapter 2 have outlined a definition of culture, a process of adjustment, and a set of specific factors that provide a beginning framework for understanding the complexities of successfully moving human resources around the world. We have emphasized the difficulty and importance of understanding and adjusting to the invisible aspects of culture and the factors that either enhance or detract from that process. We have argued that factors such as organizational and cultural novelty, although not under the direct control of firms, should at least be factored into the decisions (e.g., selection and training) that are under firms' control. Chapters 6, 7, and 8 focus on expatriates' commitment, performance, and compensation and rewards during assignments. All these aspects of the international assignment are discussed separately, but these issues are very much interrelated. Firms that enjoy the greatest success in sending people on international assignments deal effectively with all of these issues.

Notes

1. Belle and Staw, "People as Sculptors Versus People as Sculpture: The Roles of Personality and Personal Control in Organizations"; Greenberger and Strasser, "Development and Application of a Model of Personal Control in Organizations."
2. Bell and Staw, "People as Sculptors."
3. Aycan, "Expatriate Management: Theory & Research"; Black, Mendenhall, and Oddou, "Toward a Comprehensive Model of International Adjustment: An Integration of Multiple Theoretical Perspectives"; Osland, "The Adventure of Working Abroad."
4. Black, "Work Role Transitions: A Study of American Expatriate Managers in Japan"; Black, "Factors Related to the Adjustment of Japanese Expatriate Managers in America"; Black and Gregersen, "Antecedents to Cross-Cultural Adjustment for Expatriates in Pacific Rim Assignments."
5. Black and Porter, "Managerial Behaviors and Job Performance: A Successful Manager in Los Angeles May Not Succeed in Hong Kong"; House, Wright, and Aditya, "Cross-Cultural Research on Organizational Leadership: A Critical Analysis and a Proposed Theory."
6. Aycan, *Expatriate Management: Theory and Research*; Parker and McEvoy, "Initial Examination of a Model of Intercultural Adjustment."

7. Parker and McEvoy, "Initial Examination of a Model of Intercultural Adjustment"; Stroh, Dennis, and Cramer, "Predictors of Expatriate Adjustment."
8. Black, "Factors Related to the Adjustment of Japanese Expatriate Managers"; Black and Gregersen, "Antecedents to Cross-Cultural Adjustment."
9. Aycan, "Acculturation of Expatriate Managers: A Process Model of Adjustment and Performance"; Parker and McEvoy, "Initial Examination of a Model of Intercultural Adjustment."
10. Black, "Fred Bailey: An Innocent Abroad."
11. Black, Mendenhall, and Oddou, "Toward a Comprehensive Model of International Adjustment."
12. Brett and Stroh, "Willingness to Relocate Internationally"; Osland, "Working Abroad: A Hero's Adventure."
13. Wanous, *Organizational Entry*.
14. Osland, "Working Abroad: A Hero's Adventure."
15. Black, "Work Role Transitions"; Black and Gregersen, "Antecedents to Cross-Cultural Adjustment"; Brett and Stroh, "Willingness to Relocate Internationally."
16. Aycan, "Acculturation of Expatriate Managers: A Process Model of Adjustment and Performance"; Black and Mendenhall, "Cross-Cultural Training Effectiveness: A Review and Theoretical Framework for Future Research"; Chao and Sun, "Training Needs For Expatriate Adjustment in the People's Republic of China."
17. Osland, "Working Abroad: A Hero's Adventure."
18. Stroh, Dennis, and Cramer, "Predictors of Expatriate Adjustment"; Stroh, "The Family's Role in International Assignments."
19. Mendenhall and Oddou, "The Dimensions of Expatriate Acculturation: A Review."
20. Aycan, "Acculturation of Expatriate Managers: A Process Model of Adjustment and Performance"; Bandura, *Social Learning Theory*; Graen, Hui, Wakabayashi, and Wang, "Cross-Cultural Research Alliances in Organizational Research: Cross-Cultural Partnership-Making in Action."
21. Aycan, *Expatriate Management: Theory & Practice*; Black, "Personal Dimensions and Work Role Transitions: A Study of Japanese Expatriate Managers in America"; O'Hara-Devereaux and Johansen, *Global Work: Bridging Distance, Culture & Time*; Earley and Erez, *New Perspectives on International Industrial/Organizational Psychology*.
22. Black, "Work Role Transitions"; Black and Gregersen, "Antecedents to Cross-Cultural Adjustment"; Black, "Factors Related to the Adjustment of Japanese Expatriate Managers."
23 Ibid.
24. Black, "Work Role Transitions"; Black and Gregersen, "Antecedents to Cross-Cultural Adjustment"; Stroh, Dennis, and Cramer, "Predictors of Expatriate Adjustment."
25. Black and Mendenhall, "Cross-Cultural Training Effectiveness."
26. Black, Mendenhall, and Oddou, "Toward a Comprehensive Model of International Adjustment"; Chao and Sun, "Training Needs for Expatriate Adjustment in the People's Republic of China"; Stroh, Dennis, and Cramer, "Predictors of Expatriate Adjustment."
27. Black, Mendenhall, and Oddou, "Toward a Comprehensive Model of International Adjustment."
28. Black, "Locus of Control, Social Support, Stress, and Adjustment to International Transfers."

29. Black and Gregersen, "The Other Half of the Picture: Antecedents of Spouse Cross-Cultural Adjustment"; Black and Stephens, "Expatriate Adjustment and Intent to Stay in Pacific Rim Overseas Assignments"; Pellico and Stroh, "Spousal Assistance Programs"; Brett and Stroh, "Willingness to Relocate Internationally"; Arthur & Bennett, "The International Assignee: The relative importance of factors perceived to contribute to success."

30. Black, "Work Role Transitions"; Black and Gregersen, "Antecedents to Cross-Cultural Adjustment"; Black and Stephens, "Expatriate Adjustment."

31. Black, "Locus of Control."

32. Aycan, "Acculturation of Expatriate Managers"; Feldman and Tompson, "Expatriation, Repatriation, and Domestic Geographical Relocation: An Empirical Investigation of Adjustment to New Job Assignments"; Pellico and Stroh, "Spousal Assistance Programs."

33. Black and Gregersen, "The Other Half of the Picture."

34. Stephens and Black, "The Impact of the Spouse's Career Orientation on Managers During International Transfers."

35. Black and Gregersen, "The Other Half of the Picture"; Pellico and Stroh, "Spousal Assistance Programs"; Brett and Stroh, "Willingness to Relocate Internationally."

6

Integrating: Balancing Dual Allegiances

Each year, hundreds of thousands of managers all over the world find themselves torn between their allegiance to their parent firms and their allegiance to foreign operations. To understand this tension, consider the following situation.

A Dutch expatriate manager in a multinational consumer products firm is faced with a parent firm that wants a set of products introduced to the host country (a large developing nation) as part of its global brand-image strategy, on the one hand, but on the other hand, the host-country government wants high technology transferred into the country, not just consumer products placed on store shelves. Market research suggests that the local consumers are interested in a certain subset of the core products but not in others and are also interested in products not currently part of the parent firm's core set. The parent firm has a philosophy and a set of policies encouraging participative decision making, but host-country employees expect managers to make all the decisions and not burden subordinates with those responsibilities.

Faced with serving two masters, many expatriate managers end up directing their allegiance too far in one direction or the other and create serious costs and consequences, both for themselves and for their organizations. If individuals are unbalanced in their commitment to a foreign operation, it is difficult for the home office to coordinate with them. A senior executive from Honda commented to us that they had incurred "nontrivial" costs trying to coordinate their global strategy for the new Honda Accord because some expatriate managers were too focused on the local situation of their country of assignment. On the other hand, expatriates who are unbalanced in their commitment to the parent firm often implement policies or procedures from the home office inappropriately and meet considerable resistance and delays at the local level. Today's multinationals need managers who are highly committed to both the parent firm and the foreign operation and who try *and* are able to integrate the demands and objectives of both organizations.

Unfortunately, very little research has been done on the problems of dual allegiance during international assignments. One of the few studies that has addressed this issue was recently conducted by two of the present authors and involved over 300 managers in eight different countries.[1] The good news is that we now have a good idea about the influential factors, underlying dynamics, and actions that firms can take to manage the dual allegiance of international managers more effectively. The bad news is that expatriate managers with high dual allegiance seem to be rare.

In this chapter, we describe the patterns, causes, and consequences of expatriates' dual allegiance. Let's start with a look at the four general patterns of commitment or allegiance. Expatriate managers can be grouped into one of four patterns of allegiance. They can be too committed to the parent firm or to the local operation; they can be highly committed to both organizations or to neither. These four basic patterns are presented in Exhibit 6.1.

Much more important than the patterns of dual allegiance, however, are the factors that cause them and the related organizational and individual consequences. We describe the causes and

Exhibit 6.1
Patterns of Allegiance

| | | ALLEGIANCE TO THE PARENT FIRM | |
		Low	*High*
ALLEGIANCE TO THE LOCAL FIRM	*Low*	Expatriates who see themselves as **Free Agents**	Expatriates who leave their **Hearts at Home**
	High	Expatriates who **"Go Native"**	Expatriates who see themselves as **Dual Citizens**

consequences associated with each cell in the Exhibit 6.1 matrix and illustrate them with actual cases generated through numerous interviews and surveys (most of the managers asked that their names and the names of their firms be disguised). We also examine what firms are doing now and what they can do in the future to manage the dual allegiance of their expatriates more effectively.

Expatriates Who See Themselves as Free Agents

Paul Jackson was a vice president and general manager of the Japanese subsidiary of a large West Coast bank. This was his fourth position and firm in the ten years since he had earned his master's degree. Paul had been an Asian studies undergraduate major. He spoke and wrote Chinese reasonably well at the time of his graduation from college. As an undergraduate, he had also spent two years studying in Japan. In that time, his speaking and listening ability had reached a nearly professional level in Japanese. After graduate school, he was hired by a major East Coast bank. Two years later, he was sent on a three-year assignment to Hong Kong.

The compensation package that Paul and his family received made life in Hong Kong very enjoyable, but Paul felt very little loyalty to the parent firm or to the local operation in Hong Kong. Paul was committed to his career first and foremost. Because he was such a hard charger, the bank had invested a substantial amount of time and money in his linguistic and technical training. He worked hard but always kept an eye out for better jobs and better pay. Two years into his Hong Kong assignment, he found a better position in another firm and took it. Four years into that assignment, he took a job with a different U.S. bank and its operation in Taiwan. After another four years, he took the job in Japan.

In the interview in which Paul related his work history, he said, "I can't really relate to your question about which organization I feel allegiance to. I do my job, and I do it well. I play for whatever team needs me and wants me. I'm like a free agent in baseball or a hired gun in the old West. If the pay and job are good enough, I'm off. You might say, 'Have international expertise, will travel.'"

Hired-Gun Free Agents

Paul was part of a network we discovered of hired-gun free agents in the Pacific Rim. The network consisted of a group of about ten managers, hired as expatriates (not as locals), who were either bilingual or trilingual and who had spent over half of their professional careers in the Far East (Japan, China, Hong Kong, Taiwan, Singapore, Korea, Malaysia, and Indonesia). These free agents helped one another by passing along information about various firms that were looking for experienced expatriate managers for their Far East operations.

This type of expatriate has a low level of commitment to the parent firm *and* to the local operation. These free agents are primarily committed to their own careers. Asked what long-term career implications this approach might have for them, these expatriates commonly indicated that it would be very difficult for them to "go back home" and move up the hierarchy in any firm. This situation was not considered a drawback, though, because most of the expatriates reported that they did not want to go back home for several reasons. First, they felt that the experience their children were receiving, both in private schools and in life in general, was far superior to what they would have had back home. Second, they would have been worse off financially if they had gone home and had to give up the extra benefits of their expatriate packages. Third, most were confident that they would not be given jobs back home with the status, freedom, and importance of those they held overseas. Most of these hired guns seemed content with their lives and free-agent careers overseas.

Firms tend to view such expatriates with some ambivalence. On the one hand, even though these hired guns are given special benefit packages, they are often slightly less expensive to a firm than expatriates sent from home. Furthermore, these expatriates have already demonstrated that they can succeed in global settings, and they have specialized skills (such as in language) that may be lacking in the firm's internal managerial or executive ranks. This may be especially important to U.S. firms. For example, when Kentucky Fried Chicken launched its first restaurant in China, it had only three Mandarin Chinese-speaking employees, and only one of them had business experience that even came close to what was required to head up the new venture.

On the other hand, free-agent expatriates often leave with little warning. Replacing them is usually costly and difficult and can have negative consequences, both for the parent firm and for the local operation. Sometimes in their commitment to their own careers, hired guns take actions that serve their own short-term career objectives but do not necessarily serve the long-term best interests of the local operation or the parent firm. Since few are willing to repatriate, integrating their general international experience or specific regional knowledge into the firm's global strategy formulation process is next to impossible.

Plateaued-Career Free Agents

We also uncovered another type of expatriate with low commitment to the parent firm and the foreign operation. This type usually comes from the ranks of home-country employees, rather than from the ranks of hired international experts. This individual is generally not committed to the parent firm before leaving for the overseas assignment and does not develop commitment to the local operation during the assignment. Lack of commitment to the parent firm often stems from the fact that the individual's career has "plateaued" prior to the international assignment. These managers take global assignments because they do not see themselves going anywhere at home and they hope that a global stint will change things, or they may simply be attracted by the financial package offered. Unfortunately, many of the same factors that led to low commitment to the parent firm before the assignment result in low commitment to the local operation during the assignment. We have termed these managers "plateaued-career free agents."

Several contributing factors may create this type of expatriate. If a firm simply allows candidates for overseas assignments to self-select, it opens the door for plateaued managers to nominate themselves. As one expatriate said, "I figured I was stalled in my job in North Carolina, so why not take a shot at an overseas assignment, especially given what I'd heard about the high standard of living even midlevel managers enjoyed in Jakarta?" As this quote indicates, not all individuals who want to go on an international assignment have either the right motivations or the right personal characteristics. The chances of the wrong person nominating or self-selecting themselves increases to the extent that the company does not provide self-assessment feedback through standardized instruments. If an unrigorous selection process is combined with a relatively low value placed on global operations within the company, the chances increase that plateaued managers will apply for international assignments. At the same time, the chances decrease that high-potential managers will apply.[2] The high-potential managers know, since the global operations are devalued, that overseas is not the place for them to get ahead. Lack of predeparture cross-cultural training can also reinforce low commitment to the parent firm and to the local operation. U.S. firms may be particularly vulnerable to this factor, *since 40 to 50 percent of American expatriates receive no predeparture cross-cultural training;* the resulting attitude is, "The company doesn't care about me, so why should I care about it?" Lack of training can also inhibit the expatriate's understanding of the foreign culture and people, which has a negative impact on commitment to the local operation.

Unlike the hired-gun free agents, many of the plateaued-career free agents are not happy in their overseas assignments. Given their low commitment, they often make little effort to adjust to local operations and cultures. In the most dramatic cases, this lack of effort and adjustment can lead to failed assignments and their associated costs. Generally, a failed overseas assignment does not facilitate career advancement and can strike a severe blow to individual identity and self-confidence. There are also significant costs to the firm. Beyond the $100,000 needed to bring the employee and the family home and send out a replacement, the firm incurs damage to relationships with clients or suppliers because of the expatriate's poor adjustment and performance while overseas. The leadership gap that often occurs during the replacement process can also damage internal and external relations, and the firm may find that failed overseas assignments generate rumors that an international post is the kiss of death for a career.

Even if this dual lack of commitment does not result in a failed assignment, it can still be costly to the person and the organization. An interview with a manager of a major international aircraft manufacturer, who is stationed in Taiwan, revealed some of the more subtle but important personal and organizational costs. Bob Brown, a typical plateaued manager, transferred overseas three years ago. Bob was *not* excited about living in Taiwan, and neither was his family; his wife and daughter repeatedly asked to go home. Bob pointed out that there was really no job for him to go back to. His daughter became so distraught with life in Taiwan that she began doing extremely poorly in school. This and other pressures put a severe strain on Bob's relationship with his wife. Bob summed up the situation by stating that his home life was in shambles and that work was merely a paycheck. Perhaps the parent firm and the local operation were getting their money's worth from Bob, and perhaps firms in general do get their dollar's worth, yen's worth, or pound's worth from these types of expatriate managers, but we doubt it.

Expatriates Who "Go Native"

Another pattern of allegiance is found in expatriate managers who have high allegiance to the local operation but low allegiance to the parent firm. Because the local operation is embedded in the foreign country, its culture, its language, its business practices, and its values, these expatriates usually form a strong identification with and attachment to the larger cultural context. Consequently, these expatriates are often referred to as having "gone native."

Gary Ogden had been with a large computer company for fifteen years, and Paris was his third global assignment. He was the country manager for the firm's instrument division in France and had been there for about eighteen months. Of his fifteen years with the parent firm, a little under half had been spent overseas. Since this was the family's third international post, it had not taken long for Gary, his wife, and their three young daughters to settle in. Although Gary's French was not perfect, it was decent. His girls' language proficiency however, was amazing. They had enrolled in regular French schools when they moved to Paris, and now they were fluent for their ages. The Ogdens frequently took trips to museums, nearby cities and villages, and other points of interest. In fact, the Ogdens loved France so much that Gary had already requested an extension, even though his contract required him to stay only another six months. When asked to describe his commitment to the parent firm and to the local operation, he responded, "My first commitment is to the unit here. In fact, half the time I feel like headquarters is a competitor I must fight, rather than a benevolent parent I can look to for support."

Our research found that individuals like Gary Ogden, who have spent a number of years overseas and are skilled at adjusting to foreign cultures, are the most likely to "go native" and have high allegiance to local operations and relatively low allegiance to their parent firms. Part of the explanation of this tendency is that as managers spend more time away from home offices and the home-country operations, they begin to experience less and less of their identity as tied to their parent firms.[3] This literal and psychological distance, in combination with their ability to relate to and understand foreign cultures and people, tends to lead these expatriates to identify strongly with local operations at the expense of parent firms. The lack of formal communication with home offices through mechanisms such as sponsors (individuals assigned to keep in touch with specific expatriates during overseas assignments) also reinforces this pattern of commitment. Firms with international divisions and cadres of career internationalists who move from one international post to another may be particularly vulnerable to this pattern of lopsided commitment.

What are the consequences of "going native" in terms of the expatriate's allegiance? The easiest way to answer this question is to return to our earlier case. Gary Ogden often felt that the parent firm was a competitor he had to fight. Because he knew that any global assignment was temporary, and that his career was to some extent a function of evaluations made of him back at corporate headquarters, he had to fight the parent firm in subtle ways. "Sometimes I would simply ignore their directives if I didn't think they were appropriate or relevant to our operations," he said. "If it's really important, eventually someone from regional or corporate will hassle me, and I have to respond. If it isn't important, or if they think I implemented what they wanted, they just leave me alone. As long as the general results are good, it doesn't seem like there are big costs to this approach." Gary also indicated that on occasion he has had to fight more overtly. While this may have cost him back home, fighting and especially winning these fights helped him gain the trust and loyalty of the French employees. Their greater loyalty made it easier for him to be effective. His effectiveness often scored points and created lenience at corporate headquarters.

Gary said that he had nearly left the firm both times he was repatriated after his previous global assignments. He complained about the lack of responsibility back home, compared to what he had enjoyed overseas, and about the general lack of appreciation and utilization of his global knowledge and experience after repatriation. Low commitment to the parent firm heightened the salience of these factors as justification for quitting. Gary said that what kept him from actually leaving the firm both times was a granted request for another overseas assignment.

The Negative Aspects of Going Native

From the parent firm's point of view, one common problem associated with expatriates who go native is the difficulty of getting corporate policies or programs implemented in foreign operations. Intense commitment to the foreign operations often leads these expatriates to implement what they think is relevant in ways they deem appropriate and then ignore or fight the rest. This approach can be very costly, especially when the parent firm is trying to coordinate activities closely across a variety of countries for the good of global objectives, such as global brand management or global quality control and consistency.

To the extent that low commitment to the parent firm contributes to repatriation turnover, the parent firm also loses the opportunity to try to incorporate the knowledge and experience of these expatriates into global strategy or to incorporate some of these individuals into succession plans. Interestingly, our research has found that the vast majority of expatriates, regardless of commitment pattern, do not feel that the global knowledge and experience they gained overseas is valued by their firms. This finding suggests that firms in general are not utilizing valuable resources in which they have already invested substantial sums.

The Positive Aspects of Going Native

Despite various negative aspects of expatriates who go native, many corporate executives recognize that these expatriates have advantages as well. Their high allegiance to foreign operations generally leads these expatriates to identify with and understand host-country employees, customers, and suppliers and their feelings and values. This can mean that new products or services, or adapted products or services, are well targeted to the local market and that managerial approaches are suited to the host-country employees. The importance of a managerial style suited to host-country employees must not be overlooked. Many firms assume that good managers in Paris will do fine in Tokyo or Hong Kong and select expatriates primarily on the basis of their domestic performance. However, as we have already pointed out, managerial characteristics related to good performance at home are not necessarily related to good performance in foreign countries.[4]

Expatriates with relatively high allegiance to foreign operations may be particularly beneficial in other ways, too. In the case of multidomestic firms, for example, each overseas unit usually tries to compete in its specific national or regional market independent of other units in other countries. In this case the primary information flow is within the local operation, rather than between it and the parent firm or between it and other foreign subsidiaries. At this stage of globalization, a premium is placed on understanding local markets and the host-country people and culture. Expatriates who go native often have valuable insights into local operations, culture, and markets and can implement or adopt procedures, products, or managerial approaches to fit local situations. However, these expatriates rarely return home to contribute their "local" knowledge to broader regional or global strategic plans.

Expatriates Who Leave Their Hearts at Home

Another type of expatriate manager has high allegiance to the parent firm but little allegiance to the foreign operation. We refer to such expatriates as those who leave their hearts at home. This group identifies much more strongly with the parent firm than with the foreign operation or the foreign country and its culture, language, and business practices.

Earl Markus was the managing director in the European head-quarters of the "do-it-yourself" retail division of a large building-supplies firm. This was Earl's first global assignment in his twenty-two years with the firm. He was married and had two children, both of whom were in college and had *not* moved with their parents to Belgium. Earl had worked his way up from store manager to Southwest regional manager and eventually to vice president of finance.

The European operations were fairly new, and Earl saw his mission as expanding the number of retail outlets from the current nine in Belgium to fifty during the next three years all over western Europe. The parent firm had assigned a sponsor, Frank Johnson, to work closely with Earl during his three-year assignment.

One year into the assignment, Earl was on schedule and had opened fifteen new outlets in three countries but was still very frustrated. He mentioned that he had seriously considered packing up and going home more than once during the past year. He claimed that Europeans were lazy and slow to respond to directives. Asked about his feelings of allegiance and commitment, he said there was no contest: he was committed first and foremost to corporate headquarters, and when the assignment was finished, he would be headed back home. As an example of how things had gone, Earl described the implementation of the inventory system.

About eight months into his assignment, Frank Johnson had suggested that Earl implement the new computerized inventory system that had just been phased into all the U.S. outlets. Frank was very excited about the cost-saving and theft-reducing aspects of the new system and had high expectations of its use in Europe. For proper operation, the system required the daily recording of sales and a weekly random physical inventory of specific items. These reports needed to be transferred within forty-eight hours to the central office, where total and store-by-store reports and evaluations could be generated. The forms and procedural manuals were printed, and a two-day seminar was conducted for all the European store managers, the director of operations, and members of his staff. Two months later, when Earl asked his managers how the system was operating, he discovered that it was not. All he got from his managers, he said, were "lame excuses" about why the system would not work, especially in Belgium.

This case briefly illustrates some of the main causes and consequences of expatriates' allegiance being tilted strongly toward parent firms. Our research has found that a long tenure with the parent firm in the home country is significantly related to leaving one's heart at home.

All the investment of time, sweat, and heartache has been in the parent firm. High commitment to the parent firm is partly a function of expecting to receive a return on that investment. Such an investment, over time, also intertwines the identity of the manager with the parent firm. The natural consequence is high allegiance to the parent firm.[5]

Our research has also found that two other factors contribute to this pattern of allegiance. First, poor adjustment to the host country and culture, in part fostered by selection processes that primarily consider domestic performance, is an important factor. Because these expatriates cannot relate to the broader culture and people of the host country, it is difficult for them to feel strong allegiance to the local operation. Second, having a sponsor in the home office creates a formal tie which, in combination with the tie that many years of experience in the parent firm have created, directs attention and allegiance toward the parent firm and away from the local operation.[6]

What are the personal and organizational consequences of this pattern? Earl Markus thought about leaving several times during the first year, and it was basically his fear of negative career consequences that kept him from actually doing so. Expatriates who leave their hearts at home generally fail to identify with foreign operations, host countries, host-country employees, customers, suppliers, and their values. As a result, they often try to implement and enforce inappropriate programs, or they implement them in a way that offends employees, customers, or suppliers. Earl Markus's attempt to implement the inventory system is an example. His implementation effort antagonized the employees and created an adversarial relationship that hampered the other changes and programs he later tried to initiate.

Not all the consequences of leaving one's heart at home are bad, however. Our research has found that American expatriates with high commitment to their parent firms during global assignments were more likely to want to stay with their firm after repatriation. Thus, to the extent that expatriates who leave their hearts at home are able to gain valuable experience, knowledge, and skills during their global assignments, their stronger intent to stay with their parent firms after repatriation provides the firm an important opportunity to gain future returns on substantial human capital investments. Unfortunately, however, low commitment to the foreign operations generally reduces the net return on these investments because this low allegiance inhibits learning about the foreign markets, suppliers, business partners, competitors, government officials, regulatory processes, and so on.

Nevertheless, expatriates who leave their hearts at home often make it easier for home offices to coordinate activities with subsidiaries. Because of Earl's "homeward-looking" orientation, it was very easy for the corporate purchasing agent to utilize the buying power of headquarters' centralized purchasing activities for the European operations; this coordination resulted in substantial savings over prices that the European operation could have obtained on its own.

The ability to coordinate easily with the home office may be particularly beneficial for a firm at the export stage of globalization. The primary objective of most firms at this stage is to sell in foreign markets products developed and manufactured in the home country, and the primary direction of information flow is from the parent firm to the foreign operation. Thus, being able to work easily with headquarters may be especially useful for a firm at the export stage because of the primacy of the home-country operations and the key coordinating role that the home office plays. An expatriate with relatively high commitment to the parent firm is less likely to resist working with and following the coordination efforts of the home office than an expatriate with low commitment to the parent firm might be.

In summary, for the individual and the parent firm there are both pros and cons to a high parent/low local level of allegiance. Expatriates who leave their hearts at home are relatively easy for the home office to work with and can be very valuable in coordinating purchasing, marketing, or other strategic activities. They are also more likely to stay with the firm upon repatriation and can be a valuable resource in global strategic planning activities or succession plans. There are negative consequences as well, however. Their low level of commitment to the local operation may lead them to not make the efforts usually necessary to adjust to the host culture. If these expatriates can figure out how to avoid the negative career consequences of returning prematurely, they may decide to leave the foreign assignment early. This action can then result in a host of substantial direct and indirect costs to the parent company. Finally, these expatriates may implement home office policies in a manner that offends the local employees, clients, or suppliers, or which may be inappropriate for the local operations. The damaged relationships that result can, in turn, have substantial short-term and long-term negative consequences for both the local foreign operation and the parent firm.

Expatriates Who See Themselves as Dual Citizens

The final category of expatriate managers consists of those who have high allegiance to both the parent firm and the foreign operation. We describe these expatriates as dual citizens. We chose the word *citizens* because it seems to reflect the active behavior, attitudes, and emotions that this group exhibits. These managers tend to see themselves as citizens of both the foreign country and the home country, as well as of both the foreign operation and the parent corporation. As dual citizens, they feel a responsibility to try to serve the interests of both organizations.

John Beckenridge was director of the Japanese office of a prominent U.S. consulting firm. This was John's second global assignment in his thirteen years with the firm; his first assignment had been a one-year special-project stint in Singapore, seven years before. John was one of three candidates considered for the job in Japan and had been selected not only on the basis of his past performance but also on the basis of interviews and assessments by outside consultants who assessed his personal characteristics and the demands of the job in Japan. Because the job required work in a very novel culture and a high degree of interaction with host-country nationals, John was given five months' notice before departing for Japan. During this time, he received about sixty hours of cross-cultural training. In addition, John's wife received about ten hours of survival briefing before the assignment. Approximately four months after arriving in Japan, John also received another forty hours of cross-cultural training specifically related to Japan—its culture, business practices, and so on. He also took advantage of language training, paid for by the parent firm, after he arrived in Japan.

John had a clear set of objectives for his assignment in Japan. The foreign office of the consulting firm had been established to serve the Japanese subsidiaries of U.S. clients, but the growth of the Japanese office was limited by the slowed expansion of the U.S. client firms. John was given the job of developing Japanese clients to serve two objectives: (1) increase the growth potential of the Japanese office and make it easier to secure Japanese firms' U.S. subsidiaries as clients, and (2) facilitate the growth of the large U.S. domestic operations.

John found relatively little conflict between the expectations placed on him by the parent firm and by the foreign operation. Perhaps the most significant consistency involved the time and expense that everyone realized would be needed to cultivate effective contacts and relationships in Japan. For John, there was no tension between corporate "bean counters" going crazy over entertainment expenses in Japan and local staff members constantly floating "contact opportunities."

In addition, it was clear how this assignment in Japan fit into John's overall career path and how his repatriation would be handled.

Although he was not guaranteed a specific job or position upon repatriation, John knew what the process of repatriation would involve and what general opportunities would be his if he met his objectives while in Japan.

Perhaps most importantly, John was given a great degree of discretion and autonomy in achieving the objectives that were set. According to John, this job discretion often gave him the flexibility to deal with inevitable conflicts between the parent firm and the local operation or with the various ambiguities that cropped up in his job.

Asked about his commitment or allegiance to the parent firm and the Japanese operation, John commented, "I feel a strong sense of allegiance to both. Although they sometimes have different objectives, I try to satisfy both whenever I can." When objectives or expectations were in conflict between the two organizations, John generally worked to bring them together, rather than simply choosing to follow one or the other.

The personal and organizational consequences of John's dual orientation were primarily positive. At the personal level, John indicated that it was sometimes frustrating to feel torn in two directions, but that the clarity of his objectives, the latitude he had to pursue them, and the relative infrequency and small magnitude of the conflicts made it quite rewarding and personally satisfying to work for the benefit of both organizations. John did well in his five-year assignment in Japan and upon repatriation received a rather substantial promotion to a position where some of what he learned was utilized in the firm's domestic and international expansion plans. At the organizational level, John's dual orientation facilitated solid relationships with Japanese clients and governmental officials and aided the home office in establishing new contracts with the U.S. subsidiaries of Japanese client firms. John felt that he had achieved other results with his dual focus, including a greater ability to recruit high-quality Japanese employees (something the firm's competitors struggled with).

Our research has found that roughly one-fourth of our sample of American expatriate managers had high commitment to both the foreign operation and the parent firm. It would be inaccurate to say that none of these expatriates ever returned home early, left the firm after repatriation, or had adjustment or performance problems during global assignments. Still, high dual allegiance led to a higher probability that the managers would stay in their foreign assignments for the expected length of time, would stay with the firm upon repatriation, and would adjust well during the overseas stay. These expatriate managers were interested in fully understanding needs, objectives, constraints, and opportunities with respect to both the foreign operation and the parent firm. They talked of trying to use their understanding to find solutions that would satisfy and benefit both organizations. This approach created two possibilities: (1) effectively implementing home-office policies in the foreign operation, and (2) passing information and guidance from the foreign operation to corporate headquarters—information that could shape more effective strategy and policy development in all the firm's foreign operations.

As we have seen, role conflict is an important factor in determining whether expatriate managers have low or high commitment to both the parent firm and the foreign operation: the higher the role conflict, the lower the managers' commitment to both organizations,[7] and the lower the role conflict, the higher the managers' commitment to both organizations. Interviews with dual-citizen expatriate managers indicated that the single most common source of role conflict was conflicting expectations, demands, or objectives between the parent firm and the foreign operation. In other words, it was clear what was expected of the expatriate, but the expectations of the two organizations were different. The greater these conflicts, the less managers felt responsible for outcomes, and the less they felt committed to either organization. As one expatriate put it, "It's hard to feel responsible for what happens when you're being torn in opposite directions." The greater the consistency in demands, expectations, and objectives between the two organizations, the more responsible expatriate managers felt for what happened, and the more they felt committed to both organizations.

A similar dynamic was true for role ambiguity.[8] Role conflict involves clear expectations that are in conflict; role ambiguity involves expectations from both organizations that simply are not clear. Interviews with expatriate managers indicated that poor coordination between the parent firm and the foreign operation was a common source of role ambiguity. When we asked one expatriate manager how much responsibility he felt for what happened on his job, he replied, "How can I feel responsible when I don't really even know what I'm supposed to do or what's expected of me?" The greater the role clarity, the more the expatriate managers felt responsible for what happened at work and the more they felt committed to both the parent firm and the foreign operation.

Another factor related to high allegiance to both the parent firm and the foreign operation was clarity of repatriation programs.

Unfortunately, over 60 percent of U.S. firms have no systematic or formal repatriation programs.[9] When such programs do exist, however, their clear communication facilitates high commitment to both the parent firm and the foreign operation.[10] Clear repatriation programs seem to free expatriates from worrying about going home and allow them to focus on their jobs. This approach, in combination with clear, nonconflicting job expectations, facilitates allegiance to the foreign operation. At the same time, clear repatriation programs seem to communicate to expatriates that the parent firm cares about them and has thought about issues of reintegration. This message, in turn, creates a greater sense of commitment and obligation in the expatriates toward the parent firm.

We found that the most powerful job factor in creating dual allegiance was role discretion,[11] which is simply the freedom that the manager has to decide what needs to be done, how it should be done, when it should be done, and who should do it. The more discretion expatriate managers have, the more they feel responsible for what happens at work, and the more they feel committed to the local operation. Because they generally view the parent firm as ultimately responsible for the amount of freedom they enjoy, however, this also translates into a greater sense of obligation and commitment to the parent firm. Part of the reason why discretion was consistently the most powerful factor lies in the fact that most expatriate managers experience some level of role conflict and role ambiguity. Greater role discretion allows the manager the flexibility and freedom to try to define more clearly what is expected and to resolve conflicting expectations.

Although dual-citizen expatriate managers are desirable for any firm at any stage of globalization, they are most critical for firms at the coordinated multinational stage. Firms at this stage need information to flow back and forth between the home office and the foreign subsidiaries and from one foreign subsidiary to another. They need managers who identify both with the people back at the parent firm and with those in the foreign operation. They need managers who try to integrate and meet the needs of both organizations. They need expatriate managers who will not leave after repatriation, so that their international experience, knowledge, and skills can serve as assets in the global strategy and policy-making activities of the corporate office. Expatriate managers who are highly committed to both the parent firm and the foreign operation are critical in filling these needs. Exhibit 6.2 summarizes the positive and negative aspects of each of the four patterns of allegiance.

Exhibit 6.2
Allegiance Pattern Pros and Cons

Allegiance Pattern	Pros	Cons
Free Agent	• Typically have superior and demonstrated international capabilities (e.g., language, negotiation, management). • Often somewhat less costly than traditional expatriates.	• Often leave with little warning. • Replacement costs may be significant. • May serve self-interests more than company interests.
Go Native	• Typically adjusts well and quickly to the local culture and environment. • Usually is effective in the local environment, including interactions with employees, customers, suppliers, and government officials.	• May fight global initiatives. • May be slow to implement directives from headquarters. • More likely to leave the firm after repatriation.
Heart at Home	• Facilitates the coordination of global initiatives. • Quick to implement directives from headquarters. • More likely to stay with the firm after repatriation.	• Typically adjusts poorly and slowly to the local culture and environment. • Often is not effective in the local environment managing employees, customers, suppliers, or government officials. • Likely to inappropriately implement directives from the parent organization.

Exhibit 6.2 (continued)

Allegiance Pattern	Pros	Cons
Dual Citizen	• Typically adjusts well and quickly to the local culture and environment. • Usually is effective in the local environment, including interactions with employees, customers, suppliers, and government officials. • Facilitates the coordination of global initiatives. • Responsive to directives from headquarters. • More likely to stay with the firm after repatriation.	• They require serious thought and commitment from the company to create. • They are a rare breed and may be quite attractive to other firms who may try to steal them away.

Guidelines for the Effective Management of Dual Allegiance

Although most multinational firms and their executives are aware of the issues concerning expatriates' dual allegiance, our research revealed very few expatriates who said that the firm had a clear understanding of the causes and consequences of the different patterns or had systematic means of developing dual-citizen expatriates. Instead, many firms seem to have found ways to try to counterbalance expatriates' tendencies to be too committed to one organization or the other. Before addressing what firms can do to counterbalance "lopsided" allegiance, and proposing steps that firms can take to develop dual-citizen expatriates, we want to examine a "strategic alignment" that can capitalize on the positive aspects of each of the four patterns of allegiance while reducing the negatives.

Strategy 1: Matching Subsidiaries and Expatriates

The thrust of this strategic alignment is that by matching a particular pattern of expatriate allegiance to a particular strategic orientation of a foreign subsidiary, it may be possible to capture most of the positives associated with each of the four patterns while avoiding most of the negatives.

You may recall that in Chapter 1 we introduced the idea that a given foreign subsidiary may have a particular strategic function relative to the flow of information. To remind you, the diagram that we presented in Chapter 1 is reproduced below.

Island subsidiaries are those whose strategic function is to focus on the domestic market. Information, knowledge, technology, and so on neither flow in nor out in heavy volume. Implementor subsidiaries are those whose strategic function is to focus on the domestic market by implementing information, knowledge, technology, products and so on sent by the parent organization. Innovator subsidiaries are those whose strategic function is to serve the domestic market but to focus on the world market by generating information, knowledge, technology, and products and sending those innovations out to the parent organization and other foreign subsidiaries. Integra-

Exhibit 6.3
Foreign Subsidiary Strategic Function

	Information Flow	
	Low Flow In	*High Flow In*
Low Flow Out	**Island**	**Implementor**
High Flow Out	**Innovator**	**Integrator**

tor subsidiaries are those whose strategic function is to focus both on the domestic and world market by implementing information, knowledge, technology, products, and so on sent by the parent organization and by generating information, knowledge, technology, and products to send out to the parent organization and other foreign subsidiaries.

Exhibit 6.4 illustrates how each of the four patterns of strategic subsidiary roles matches with each of the four patterns of expatriate allegiance.

Because island subsidiaries by their strategic function do not require high information and knowledge flows in or out, free-agent expatriates' few connections with or little loyalty to the overall organization is of less consequence. An island subsidiary's need to focus on the domestic market matches well with the free agent's proven language, cross-cultural management, and other skills. While it is understandable that some firms may choose not to use free agents, the best strategic fit for them is in an island subsidiary.

Implementor subsidiaries need someone who has the connections into and orientation toward the source of the information, knowledge, technology, products and so on that are to be implemented. A heart-at-home expatriate may be the ideal fit for this requirement. Conversely, a free-agent or go-native expatriate would be a very poor fit for this strategic situation.

Exhibit 6.4
Strategy and Allegiance Alignment

	Information Flow		
	Low Flow In	*High Flow In*	
Low Flow Out	**Island** *Free Agent*	**Implementor** *Go Native*	**Low**
High Flow Out	**Innovator** *Heart at Home*	**Integrator** *Dual Citizen*	**Allegiance to the Parent Firm** **High**
	Allegiance to the Local Firm		

Innovator subsidiaries draw from the local context to produce the information, knowledge, technology, products, and innovations to send out to the parent organization and other foreign subsidiaries. This arrangement may be the result of a local environment with a superior pool of scientists, or a general environment that contributes to innovation (e.g., some people claim this about Silicon Valley). A go-native expatriate may be a great fit for this strategic situation. Their natural affinity for and knowledge of the local environment can be just what the doctor ordered in terms of networking and tapping into the local talent pool.

The dual directional flow of information, knowledge, technology, and products within integrator subsidiaries requires dual-citizen expatriates. An integrator subsidiary cannot afford for key expatriates to favor one and neglect the other of these high flows in and out, as a go-native or heart-at-home expatriate would. While dual-citizen expatriates might function effectively in any of the four strategic subsidiary patterns, no other type of expatriate other than a dual citizen would work as effectively in an integrator subsidiary.

This strategic alignment perspective points to several important implications. For example, not all firms need the same ratio of dual citizen versus other patterns of allegiance. Firms with a multidomestic strategic orientation would need fewer dual citizens than a firm well into an integrated global strategy. In fact, a firm in the midst of an integrated global strategy probably has fewer dual citizens than it needs and will likely need to do all it can to develop them. In addition, even if most of the firm's foreign subsidiaries are of a particular strategic orientation, not every one is identical. Therefore, the critical issue is ensuring that managers of a particular commitment profile are matched with the appropriate assignment and subsidiary.

Strategy 2: Counterbalancing the Tendency to Go Native

Even if the firm does the best it can matching expatriates with the appropriate assignment and subsidiary, it still may find that it has too many managers who have a go-native tendency. Consequently, the firm may need to try to "rebalance" these managers by counterbalancing their go-native tendencies.

The managers who are most likely to go native and who have high allegiance to the foreign operation and low allegiance to the parent firm are those who have had several years of previous international experience and who have been successful in adjusting to the general nonwork environment of foreign cultures. Ironically, these managers are also good candidates for overseas posts in terms of lowering the risk and associated costs of failed assignments and premature returns.[12]

One action that Honda takes to counterbalance this tendency is to have expatriates return home to Japan for a few years before they are sent overseas again. This practice reinforces the link between the individual expatriate and the parent firm and counteracts the tendency toward overcommitment to the foreign operation. Honda's view is that it is not logical to expect career internationalists who move from one foreign assignment to the next to be highly committed to the parent firm.

Firms could also counterbalance this tendency by sending expatriate managers who have longer tenure in the parent firm. The longer managers have been with the parent firm, the more they have invested in it, the more they identify themselves with it, and the more they are committed to it. This recommendation becomes problematic, however, for firms such as General Electric (GE), General Motors (GM), and Ford, which increasingly utilize global assignments as developmental experiences for younger, high-potential managers.

Consequently, GE takes a broader approach to counterbalancing the tendency to go native through its system of sponsors. In some GE divisions, this approach even involves a prior commitment to hire the expatriate manager back to a specific position. More often, the system of assigned sponsorship involves assessing the expatriate's career objectives, choosing a senior manager (often in the function to which the expatriate is likely to return) who is willing to serve as sponsor, maintaining contact between the sponsor and the expatriate throughout the assignment (including face-to-face meetings), evaluating the performance of the expatriate during the assignment, clarifying career objectives and abilities before repatriation, and providing career advice and helping to find a subsequent position before the manager's repatriation.

We talked with executives at several firms that have sponsorship programs, and they offered additional advice. Overall, they recommended that sponsor assignment should be systematic. First, the sponsor should be senior enough to the expatriate to provide a broad view of the organization. Second, the sponsor should be given specific guidelines about keeping in touch with the expatriate (e.g., form, content, and frequency of contact). Too often, the sponsor is simply assigned, and that is all. If the sponsor takes the initiative and fulfills the responsibility, things go well; otherwise, the assigned sponsor exists in name only. Third, the responsibility of planning for the expatriate manager's return and of finding a suitable position should not be solely that of the sponsor but must be incorporated into the career systems of the firm.

Although most U.S. firms do not provide rigorous, well-planned cross-cultural training for expatriates before or after their arrival in global assignments, our research indicates that such training is an effective mechanism for counterbalancing the tendency to go native. Intuitively, you might think that predeparture or postarrival training would only encourage the expatriate manager to identify with the host culture. Although good training does help expatriate managers adjust and perform better,[13] this training provides a more powerful sense of obligation and commitment to the parent company that paid for the training. The training demonstrates the firm's care and concern for the expatriate.

In summary, a firm can counterbalance the tendency to go native by having managers come home for several years before sending them overseas again, by selecting managers with longer tenure in the parent firm, by instituting a systematic sponsorship program, and by providing predeparture and/or postarrival cross-cultural training for managers. Once these counterbalancing moves have been taken, policies that facilitate high commitment to both the foreign operation and the parent firm can be employed.

Strategy 3: Counterbalancing the Tendency to Leave One's Heart at Home

Many executives seem relatively unconcerned about counterbalancing the tendency to leave one's heart at home. However, the negative consequences are serious. The managers most likely to leave their hearts at home are those who have many years of tenure with the parent firm and little international experience. Thus, such firms as GE, GM, Colgate-Palmolive, and Ford, which are increasingly sending younger managers overseas as part of career development, are perhaps unintentionally counterbalancing expatriates' tendency to leave their hearts at home.

Helping expatriate managers adjust to the general nonwork environment is another powerful counterbalancing force. Ironically, many of the perks (e.g., company car and driver, company housing, and so on) given to senior expatriate executives may isolate them and inhibit their adjustment. Another major factor related to the expatriate's adjustment to the general environment is the family's adjustment.[14] Family members (especially spouses) are often exposed more directly to the general environment because they do not enjoy the insulation that the corporate structure provides. Therefore, a firm's efforts to facilitate the family's (especially the spouse's) adjustment to the general environment can have a positive effect on the expatriate manager's adjustment and counterbalance the expatriate's tendency to leave his or her heart at home.

How can the firm facilitate the family's adjustment to the general environment? One factor that helps families also helps expatriates—interacting with host-country nationals. Because host nationals are the best source of information about their own culture, the more families interact with them in general, and the more the expatriate managers interact with them outside of work, the greater the expatriate's adjustment to the general environment of the foreign country.[15]

Ford is one of the few U.S. firms that consistently tries to provide training and preparation for families (especially spouses) of expatriates. Executives at Ford did not decide to do this to provide a counterbalance to the heart-at-home tendency, but our research suggests that this practice does so nonetheless.

A preparation program can facilitate interaction between host-country nationals and newly arrived expatriate managers and their families, but it does not guarantee it. An additional step that a firm can take is to ask host-country employees and their families to help specific expatriates and their families during the first few months after arrival. Obviously, care should be taken to match the sponsoring host-country family's characteristics with those of the expatriate family. Several Japanese auto firms, for example, have hired Americans who speak Japanese to help Japanese expatriate managers and families adjust to life in the United States.

Strategy 4: Creating Dual Citizens

The most important steps for firms to take are those that have a strong impact on creating high dual allegiance—steps that develop dual-citizen expatriates. The work environment represents the most powerful factor for fostering dual citizens. The specific steps to be taken may seem trivial or obvious at first, but they are probably much more involved for most firms. Greater role clarity, greater job discretion, and lower conflict are the most powerful factors related to high dual allegiance.

As we discussed in Chapter 5, enhancing job clarity, reducing role conflict, and determining the appropriate level of discretion or freedom is not as simple as it seems. Still, to foster dual citizens, nothing is more powerful. However, keep in mind, as we discussed in Chapter 5, you cannot effectively try to turn these three "dials" independently; rather, you need to think about all three factors simultaneously.

The assessment and design of an expatriate's job must account not only for the technical aspects but also for the strategic dimensions. Without an assessment of the strategic dimensions, the firm may unintentionally design dysfunctional job requirements. By contrast, an analysis that begins with the broader strategy and context naturally leads to understanding and appropriate design of the expatriate manager's job and to a higher probability of dual allegiance.

Some readers may be saying to themselves, "We are a global firm, and we need managers who are not just capable of dual citizenship but of world citizenship. We need global managers." Clearly, many firms are moving in this direction. However, despite the perceived glamour of world citizenship, most expatriate managers actually struggle to reach the level of high dual allegiance. Consequently, the first practical step toward global firms and global managers is to develop managers who are at least capable of being dual citizens. This plan may be especially critical in firms that have reached or are working to reach the coordinated multinational stage of globalization. In this case, dual-citizen expatriates are best developed through careful selection processes, predeparture and postarrival cross-cultural training programs, well-planned strategies that translate into career systems with clear and consistent job expectations and appropriate levels of freedom and discretion, and repatriation programs that reintegrate expatriates and effectively utilize their knowledge, skills, and experience. These steps will help firms manage dual allegiance more effectively and help expatriates serve two masters more successfully.

Notes

1. Gregersen and Black, "Antecedents to Commitment to a Parent Company and a Foreign Operation."
2. Black, "Repatriation: A Comparison of Japanese and American Practices and Results"; Clague and Krupp, "International Personnel: The Repatriation Problem"; Harvey, "Repatriation of Corporate Executives: An Empirical Study"; Kendall, "Repatriation: An Ending and a Beginning."
3. Mowday, Porter, and Steers, *Employee-Organization Linkages: Psychology of Commitment, Absenteeism, and Turnover.*
4. Black and Porter, "Managerial Behaviors and Job Performance: A Successful Manager in Los Angeles May Not Succeed in Hong Kong"; Miller, "The International Selection Decision: A Study of Managerial Behavior in the Selection Decision Process."

5. Glisson and Durrick, "Predictors of Job Satisfaction and Organizational Commitment in Human Service Organizations"; Mowday, Porter, and Steers, *Employee-Organization Linkages;* O'Reilly and Chatman, "Organizational Commitment and Psychological Attachment: The Effects of Compliance, Identification, and Internalization of Prosocial Behavior."

6. Mowday, Porter, and Steers, *Employee-Organization Linkages.*

7. Glisson and Durrick, "Predictors of Job Satisfaction and Organizational Commitment."

8. Jackson and Schuler, "A Meta-analysis and Conceptual Critique of Research on Role Ambiguity and Role Conflict in Work Settings."

9. Harvey, "Repatriation of Corporate Executives."

10. Gomez-Mejia and Balkin, "Determinants of Managerial Satisfaction with the Expatriation and Repatriation Process."

11. Glisson and Durrick, "Predictors of Job Satisfaction and Organizational Commitment."

12. Black, "Work Role Transitions: A Study of American Expatriate Managers in Japan."

13. Black and Mendenhall, "Cross-Cultural Training Effectiveness: A Review and Theoretical Framework for Future Research."

14. Black, "Work Role Transitions"; Black and Stephens, "Expatriate Adjustment and Intent to Stay in Pacific Rim Overseas Assignments."

15. Black, "Work Role Transitions."

7

Appraising: Determining if People Are Doing the Right Things

Compared to other aspects of international assignments, most companies report they could do a much better job at performance appraisal. Specifically, 53 percent of companies reported that they are average or below average at effectively assessing the performance of expatriate managers.[1] On the domestic front, however, most companies indicated they do a much better job. In this chapter, we address the general challenges of conducting effective performance appraisals and examine these issues from a global perspective to determine what unique challenges arise in the development of valid performance appraisal systems for international managers. We then offer prescriptions for companies, to assist them in constructing sound international performance appraisal programs.

Wayne Casio, a longtime researcher in human resource management, best summed up the problematic nature of performance appraisal systems: "Performance appraisal has many facets. It is an exercise in observation and judgment, it is a feedback process, it is an organizational intervention. It is a measurement process as well as an intensely emotional process. Above all, it is an inexact, human process."[2]

The Purpose of Performance Appraisals

Organizations conduct performance appraisals for two main reasons—evaluation and development. Unfortunately, these two purposes are often mutually exclusive and cause friction within the organization. Evaluation goals for performance appraisal systems are as follows:[3]

1. To provide feedback to managers so they will know where they stand.
2. To develop valid data for pay and promotion decisions, and to provide a means of communicating these decisions.
3. To help management in making discharge and retention decisions, and to provide a means of warning subordinates about unsatisfactory performance.

Consider the development goals of a performance appraisal system:[4]

1. To help managers improve their performance and develop future potential.
2. To develop commitment to the company through discussion of career opportunities and career planning with the manager.
3. To motivate managers via recognition of their efforts.
4. To diagnose individual and organizational problems.

As Exhibit 7.1 illustrates, these two sets of goals often come into conflict. When performance appraisal is being conducted for evaluation purposes, the system is a tool by which managers make

Exhibit 7.1
Conflicts in Performance Appraisal

	Firms	**Individuals**
Evaluation Purpose	Want valid information on performance of individuals on which to base rewards and punishments.	Want valid feedback on their performance to know what rewards and punishments to expect.
Development Purpose	Want to develop people and encourage their growth and development.	Want opportunities and encouragement to grow and develop.

difficult judgments that affect their subordinates' futures. This function can create an adversarial relationship and low trust, which then works against the coaching and development purposes of performance appraisal."[5]

Exhibit 7.1 also illustrates the conflict within those who are being evaluated. They desire feedback about their performance to reduce uncertainty about their standing in the organization; yet, conversely, they want only to hear good news about their performance. This psychological tug-of-war can exacerbate poor performance due to worry, stress, and a constant focus on appearance versus substance, and quantity versus quality of performance. These stresses and strains of competing purposes within the organization and of competing needs within individual employees partly cause and reinforce the knotty dilemmas and problems encountered when designing and implementing performance appraisal systems.

Challenges to the Design of Valid Appraisal Systems

We would need an entire book to cover all the issues of performance appraisals, so this section solely focuses on "problem dimensions." Each dimension has within it a large number of specific issues that cause performance appraisal systems to fail. The dimensions are really "umbrella" concepts that encompass a variety of dysfunctional organizational behaviors. Seasoned managers know that these dimensions are virtually impossible to eradicate totally in organizations. The best an organization can do is minimize the extent these dimensions hurt organizational and individual growth and performance.

Invalid Performance Criteria

It is not unusual for companies to measure people on behavior that actually does not assist the organization in attaining its goals. For example, it is probably not logical to give significant weight to punctuality in arriving at work as a performance criterion to measure the job performance of a software designer or a commercial artist, yet this dimension is included on standardized appraisal forms used in some companies. Isolating the key factors of success for any managerial position in a company is not as easy as it seems. The more complex the job, the more difficult it is to isolate what the important behaviors are that enable someone to achieve the task in an outstanding manner.

Rater Competence

The rater must have the technical background and the experience necessary to evaluate employees' behavior correctly. When raters have limited contact with those whom they evaluate, invalid ratings usually occur. The same holds true if raters do not have a clear idea of the actual complexities of the work environment. For example, it would be foolhardy to expect a manager who only understood sales results to effectively evaluate salesmen who must develop junior salesmen, jointly design systems with clients, and work with marketing research. A complex system of "little things" often must be done well for a complex task to be accomplished. Misunderstanding of the complexity of the job tends to cause inaccurate appraisal.

Rater Bias

Rater bias occurs when the rater's values, perceptions, and prejudices replace organizational standards as the basis for evaluation. This bias can take many forms. For example, a manager may "protect" a valued subordinate by giving him or her lower ratings than deserved so that the subordinate will not be promoted or transferred from the rater's organizational unit; or a rater may give an employee who is actually doing a good job a low rating because of how the employee dresses, speaks, and generally acts around the office. Thus, personal preference overcomes performance standards. Moreover, since raters are to some degree evaluated on the performance of their subordinates, it is in their best interests to have subordinates who are "above average." In this case, an entire staff may receive undeserved positive ratings. Another rater bias is reflected when recent events (positive or negative) get more emphasis in evaluations than past events do. The longer the interval between evaluations, the greater the effect of this "recency bias." In short, rater bias can take many forms, depending on the personal needs of the rater.

Challenges to Valid Appraisal Systems in the International Context

The problem dimensions just outlined exist in the international arena as well as in the domestic context. The pertinent issue, however, is whether the manifestations of these problems are different or more severe for international assignments. To answer that question, we need to explore the international aspects of each problem dimension.

Two of the authors of this book conducted one of the few studies that has evaluated performance appraisals and international assignments with the assistance of nearly seventy multinational firms. The statistics reported in the next several sections are based on that study.

Invalid Performance Criteria

For a performance appraisal system to work, a clear link must be established between what it takes to be successful on the job and what is measured by the appraiser. Too often, the criteria of success at home may not make sense in a foreign setting.

Common performance criteria that managers are measured on at home involve profit and loss, rate of return on investment (ROI), cash flows, efficiency (input-output ratios), market share, conformity to authority, and physical volumes. It would seem, on the surface, that expatriate managers should be evaluated by the same criteria, which are easily measured and straightforward enough to lead to clear performance standards. After all, companies want their managers to achieve the same goals no matter where they are in the world. In our study, 37 percent of the companies emphasized these types of "hard" performance criteria. Nevertheless, simply superimposing the same criteria at home and abroad can cause problems.

It is unfair to compare global managers against domestic performance standards on these criteria, because external factors often influence the financial and organizational performance of the international assignee's area of responsibility. The following environmental factors can distort the appearance of financial and other performance standards in ways that the home office often cannot foresee:

- Rapid exchange-rate fluctuation
- Price controls
- Control over the revaluation of assets
- Depreciation allowances
- Costs assessed by the parent company and other associated firms against the foreign subsidiary (e.g., price of materials, general overhead charges)
- Availability of local debt financing
- Local currency evaluation of foreign-source assets invested

The problems of assessing current profit and loss from liquidation of assets and investments can sometimes cause home-office evaluators to make invalid performance evaluations of global managers.[6] Severe inflation for months or years, with no devaluation of the local currency, can help a subsidiary earn high profits, but the profits are more attributable to the inflation rate than to good management. Conversely, when currency is devalued against the home currency, the subsidiary, although well managed and profitable in terms of local currency, may show a loss in a given accounting period when its income statement is translated into the home currency. The experience of a global manager who was stationed in Chile illustrates this problem:[7]

> In Chile he had almost single-handedly stopped a strike that would have shut down their factory completely for months. . . . In a land where strikes are commonplace, such an accomplishment was quite a coup, especially for an American. . . . However, because of exchange-rate fluctuations with its primary trading partners in South America, the demand for their ore temporarily decreased by 30 percent during the expatriate manager's tenure. Rather than applauding the efforts this expatriate executive made to avert a strike and recognizing the superb negotiation skills he demonstrated, the home office saw the expatriate as being only somewhat better than a mediocre performer.

This global manager's home office placed important emphasis on sales figures, without understanding the context that influenced sales in Chile. As a result, all the other accomplishments of this manager were downgraded. Unfortunately, only 10 percent of the firms surveyed actively incorporate these types of contextual factors in their appraisals.

The foreign subsidiary may be measured on traditional criteria, but corporate headquarters may make it difficult to achieve the performance standards for several reasons, such as delays in decisions from headquarters, cumbersome reporting procedures that headquarters has superimposed on the subsidiary, or complete disregard of suggestions made by the foreign subsidiary for changes that would enhance the probability of its success. Transfer pricing can force some subsidiaries to show profits that are allocated to them but that have not really been earned by them. Global managers of the subsidiaries from which the profits were actually taken may be evaluated less highly than they deserve, especially if regional headquarters staff members are doing the evaluating and are not informed by corporate headquarters about transfers that haven taken place.

The evaluation goals of performance appraisal are to isolate the truly great performers in a company and to reward them for their efforts. When this does not happen, word gets around, and global managers begin to play games with statistics to make themselves look good to the home office instead of focusing on what really needs to be done. Sometimes the real keys to success in foreign settings are unique, such as:

- Relationships with individuals in the local government
- Relationships with union leaders
- Public image of the firm in the local environment
- Local market share
- Employees' morale and job satisfaction
- Interpersonal negotiation skills
- Cross-cultural skills
- Community involvement

Many of these important aspects of a global manager's job are not easily quantified or measured. If they are not measured and evaluated, however, managers soon learn that it does not pay to concentrate on them.

Rater Competence

In a domestic setting, managers are evaluated by people who work fairly closely with them and with whom they have had a fair amount of interpersonal interaction. For global managers, the situation is somewhat different. The global manager may be evaluated by a regional, area, or corporate executive with whom the global manager has had little face-to-face contact. Also, the evaluator may have little international experience and therefore may not understand the totality of the work situation of the global manager. In our survey, 25 percent of the top executives had international experience and only 11 percent of the human resource managers had such experience. In 21 percent of the firms, none of the top executives had international experience and in 59 percent of the firms, none of the top human resource executives had international experience. Yet these same executives may feel perfectly capable of evaluating international assignees.[8]

The previously cited example of the global manager in Chile illustrates this problem. He was evaluated by someone in the home office who did not understand the business environment of Chile. A high-potential global manager sent to Japan by a large semiconductor firm had the following experience:[9]

> He barely kept his head above water because of the difficulties of cracking a nearly impossible market. On returning to the United States, he was physically and mentally exhausted from the battle. He sought a much less challenging position and got it because top man-

agement . . . believed [it] had overestimated his potential. In fact, top management never did understand what the expatriate was up against in the foreign market.

Global managers frequently indicate that their home offices deal with them from an "out-of-sight, out-of-mind" philosophy and do not understand what they encounter overseas. In a 1981 Korn-Ferry report,[10] 69 percent of the global managers surveyed reported they felt isolated from their domestic operations and home-office superiors. More recent surveys have found similar results.[11]

A competent rater who understands the reality of the business situation can compensate for a poorly designed performance appraisal system that measures the wrong things, but the combination of a poorly designed system and a rater who does not understand the business situation of the ratee almost inevitably leads to invalid performance evaluations. When top management does not understand the realities of the overseas business environment, invalid performance evaluations, either formal or informal, are liable to occur.

Rater Bias

People from different cultures often misinterpret one another's behavior. For example, a research study that investigated how global managers from Britain, Japan, and the United States, and their host-country employees in Singapore perceived one another, found the following:[12]

1. American and Japanese global managers perceived themselves to be more technically competent than the British and Singaporeans perceived them to be.
2. The British global managers perceived themselves to be more technically competent than any of the other groups perceived them to be.
3. The American global managers saw themselves as being more open interpersonally than the British or the Japanese saw themselves as being, and the Americans were seen as even more open by all the other groups.
4. The British global managers were perceived as being more closed interpersonally than they saw themselves as being.
5. The Japanese global managers saw themselves as being only slightly closed interpersonally but were regarded as being very closed by all the other groups except the Singaporeans who worked for them (they thought the Japanese were only slightly closed).

This state of affairs should not surprise anyone, but when it comes to conducting valid performance evaluations, perceptual biases among people from different cultures are no longer a topic of amusement or intellectual curiosity; they can threaten performance and careers. Consider the following "close call" that an American global manager experienced in France:[13]

> In France, women are legally allowed to take six months off for having a baby. They are paid during that time but are not supposed to do any work related to their job[s]. This expatriate had two of three secretaries take maternity leave. . . . The American expatriate asked them to do some work at home, not really understanding the legalities of his request. The French women could be fired from their job[s] for doing work at home. One of the women agreed to do it because she felt sorry for him. When the American's French boss found out [that] one of these two secretaries was working at home, he became very angry and intolerant of the American's actions. As a result, the American felt he was given a lower performance evaluation than he deserved.

Set the scene in your mind. One secretary is in the American's doghouse because she will not do any of her work at home. The other secretary is in the American's good graces but in the French manager's doghouse for breaking the law. The American is in the French manager's doghouse, but he does not know why initially. When he finds out why, he cannot get the French manager to understand his reasoning. The French manager thinks that the American is insensitive and possibly incompetent.

What happened next? The American asked his former boss, another American, to intercede with his French superior. After a while, the French manager came to understand why the American had done what he did, and he modified the performance appraisal to something more reasonable to the American. (What happened to the secretaries is unrecorded.) The point is that the French manager simply believed that the American manager should have been aware of French laws governing maternity leave; this assumption led to problems for everyone involved. Such "war stories" are common to all global managers; they are part of the territory. What becomes important, however, is that if cross-cultural misunderstandings remain unresolved, they can affect performance appraisal negatively.

Resolving Appraisal Dilemmas in the Global Context

Companies can do several things to lessen the likelihood that invalid performance appraisals will be made in their overseas operations. We have charted an approach for appraising global managers that is general enough to be applied across firms and industries, yet specific enough to directly help the people doing evaluations.

What Should Be Evaluated?

Uncovering the key factors of success for an overseas position is not easy; there are no shortcuts. Only careful analysis can reveal these key factors. It is simple to assume that the company wants to achieve profits or ROI, but external conditions may affect these figures, so it is difficult to determine how well the global manager is doing when exchange rates fluctuate wildly, transfer pricing distorts profit pictures, and differences in accounting procedures affect financial reporting. Companies need to define what they consider success to be in Chile, Japan, the People's Republic of China, Great Britain, or Nigeria.

Obviously, business strategy largely dictates what is expected of a global manager in a specific country. It would be foolish to focus heavily on profits as a criterion of success for a global manager in the People's Republic of China, for example. If the company is in that country to make a lot of money in the short term, top management will be frustrated. More than likely, the company entered the country hoping to build a presence there and eventually—over a period of many years—to position itself to tap that country's burgeoning market. Thus, the question becomes: What should a global manager be doing in Beijing to execute the company's strategy? Superimposing what makes sense from a home perspective would be counterproductive. The key to success in China is developing close personal relationships with key government officials, and investing in training Chinese workers over a long period so that when governmental restraints on business dissolve, the company will be positioned for success. An important issue to resolve, then, is whether the firm's strategy in the country makes sense. If it does not, global managers will be between a rock and a hard place, feeling compelled to give the home office what it demands while simultaneously expending energy on what they consider to be the real issues.

Even if the strategy does make sense and the evaluation criteria are clear to everyone, the ways to meet the criteria may need to be different in the assignment country versus those at home. For example, if output of production is an important criterion, the best way to ensure high output in Chile is for the global manager to spend most of his or her time on labor-management relations. In Chile, the primary key to keeping output on target may not be to focus on supply costs and inventories, but simply avoiding strikes and getting people to work on time. In locations where workforce stability cannot be taken for granted, spending time developing personal relationships with union leaders may make the difference between the workers' striking twice instead of twenty-two times during the global manager's tenure.

How can a company fine-tune performance appraisal criteria to specific locations? Time simply must be spent on getting the facts. Executives must travel to the foreign locations to observe, ask a lot of questions, and solicit the current global managers for their insights. At the home office, outside experts from universities, consulting firms, and government agencies, as well as other individuals who have lived and worked in those locations, should be brought in and thoroughly interrogated for information that could help uncover the key factors of success in the foreign locations in question.

Ideally, a manager who has returned to the home office from an overseas site should be a permanent part of the team that updates performance criteria for overseas assignments. Reevaluating the criteria and their prioritization periodically will ensure that the performance evaluation criteria remain current with the reality of the overseas situation.[14] It may make sense to have returned global managers travel to their past location assignments every three to six months. They should see how the current manager is performing and interview him or her to gain insight into the current situation in the country's business climate, the challenges facing the firm in that country, and any changes that are needed from a strategic or an operational perspective. In this manner, the criteria on which the global manager is evaluated can be fluid, changing according to the business climate.

Who Should Do the Evaluating?

Companies vary widely on who appraises global managers. Exhibit 7.2 illustrates the results from the study mentioned at the beginning of this chapter.

On average firms utilized three evaluators for every international assignee. Roughly 12 percent used only one rater; 43 percent used two raters; 20 percent used three raters; 15 percent used four or more raters. Interestingly, in purely domestic situations, these same companies use an average of six raters per employee performance appraisal.

Exhibit 7.2 illustrates that an international assignee who is working in Brussels for a U.S. firm could conceivably be appraised by someone from the home office, someone from regional headquarters, and a human resource executive. One study found that U.S. expatriates are most often evaluated by people from their home offices.[15] In our more re-

Inside Host Country* | **Outside Host Country**

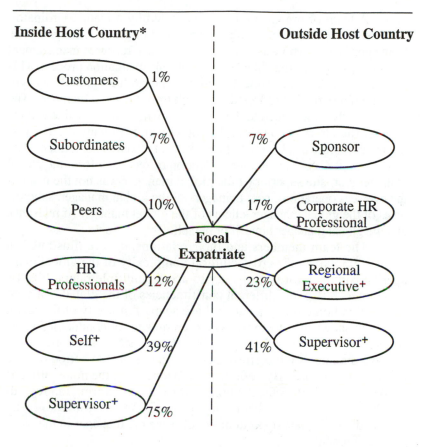

*Inside country raters are local nationals 33% of the time.

+Indicates a positive relationship with appraisal accuracy.

NOTE: Percent (%) is the average percentage in which each type of rate is involved in evaluations across sample firms.

Exhibit 7.2
Raters of Expatriate Performance

cent study, we found that a majority of the raters are inside, not outside the country of assignment. If this is a trend, it is probably a good one.

The leading-edge companies in our study took more of a team approach to performance appraisals. This team approach highly correlated with the perceived effectiveness and fairness of performance appraisals. Although variations occurred, the following description captures this leading-edge approach.

A team of organization members, led by a team coordinator, was assembled for the performance appraisal of global managers. The team coordinator, who was often a senior human resource management executive, served as the "hub" of the multiple evaluation process. This executive's task was to collect, analyze, and draft a "global manager evaluation report" that reflected feedback from the team members. The report was then forwarded to the individual who had direct-line authority over the global manager and to other senior executives, and was filed at corporate headquarters, in the human resource department. The "hub manager" coordinated the collection of feedback from the global manager's on-site superior (if the global manager was not the head of the overseas operation), peer managers of the global manager, subordinates of the global manager, clients of the global manager (if relevant), and the global manager himself or herself.

The team members and their relationships are illustrated in Exhibit 7.3. Given the cross-cultural complexity of the global manager's assignment, it is necessary to access multiple raters. Ideally, those raters reflect the different constituencies of the global manager. Notice that home office personnel are a small minority of the team. Research shows that the most basic prerequisite for conducting a performance evaluation is that the rater had "an adequate opportunity to observe the ratee's job performance over a reasonable period of time (e.g., six months)."[16] By definition, someone from the home office is unlikely to qualify. Thus, the home office needs information regarding the quality of the global manager's performance from those who have had an adequate opportunity to observe the manager in the overseas assignment.

It is dangerous to rely on one rater's evaluation of a global manager, given possible rater bias due to cross-cultural issues. For example, if the global manager's immediate superior is the same nationality, the superior may feel that the manager is doing wonderfully; the reality, however, may be that both individuals are poor performers because of their lack of familiarity with the local culture, the business climate, negotiation norms, and so on. Thus, an unwarranted "halo effect" and a commensurate inflated performance rating may occur. Conversely, as illustrated in the example of the global manager in France, an immediate superior who is a host-country national may be unfairly tough on the global manager because of cross-cultural misunderstandings. Thus, relying solely on the rating of **one** person will not give a clear picture of a global manager's performance. The performance evaluation wheel in Exhibit 7.3 reflects a more comprehensive approach to accessing feedback about global managerial performance.

On-Site Superiors. These individuals are in the best position to report on the relationship between the global manager's job performance and the foreign unit's organizational goals and objectives and to observe the manager's performance on important tasks, projects, and organizational concerns.

Peer Managers. Obtaining feedback from peer managers, of various nationalities if present in the setting, will reflect, to some degree, how well global managers work with others to accomplish the organization's objectives. The responses of these managers will also

Exhibit 7.3
Global Manager Evaluation Wheel

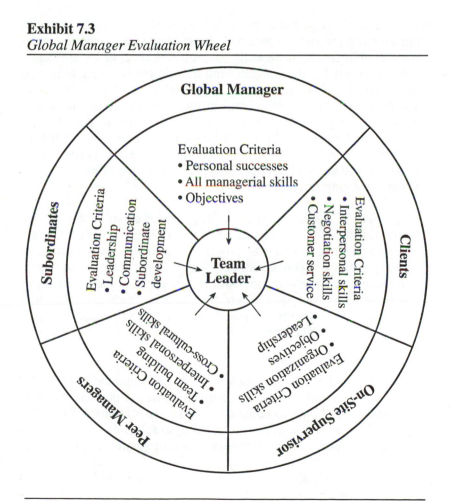

reflect the degree to which global managers possess managerial skills, interpersonal skills, cross-cultural skills, and multicultural team-building skills.

Subordinates. Ratings from global managers' subordinates, especially if they are mostly host-country employees, will counteract "halo effect" ratings by an immediate superior who is of the same nationality as the expatriate. Feedback from subordinates will give some insight into cross-cultural managerial skills, communication skills, leadership abilities, and the degree to which global managers can work effectively among individuals who are different from them.

Clients. A global manager's job description usually includes representing the firm to external institutions to enhance the company's public image, generating business, influencing governmental decisions related to the company and its industry, fostering alliances, and generally gaining favor in the larger community. The only way to ascertain the success of the international assignee in this area is to question a sample of the foreign operation's clients. Clients will not be able to provide insight into in-house managerial skills, but they can provide useful feedback about global managers' expertise in negotiation, "figurehead" duties, interpersonal skills, sales skills, and alliance-building skills.

Self. While the opportunity for rater bias exists in self-ratings, international assignees should be given a chance to express their accomplishments, frustrations, progress, and challenges since the previous appraisal was conducted. Personal points of view are an important piece of the performance puzzle. Since global managers know that their input is only one part of the appraisal "network," they will be motivated to write reports that do not wildly exaggerate their performance in a positive vein.

When Should Appraisals Be Done?

Much research has been conducted on this issue, and the results seem fairly clear. According to Casio, "Research over the past twenty years has indicated that once or twice a year is far too infrequent. Considerable difficulties face a rater who is asked to remember what several employees did over the previous six to twelve months. . . . People often forget the details of what they have observed and they reconstruct the details on the basis of their existing mental categories."[17] Managers tend to evaluate a six-month period by what happened in the last six weeks rather than across the entire time period.

The dilemma is that for the sake of timely and consistent performance appraisals, effort is drained from managers who could be focusing their energies on activities that enhance profits—after all, organizations do not exist so that elaborate performance appraisals can take place. A balance should be achieved between the need for timely evaluation and the need to use organizational time for more task-oriented activities.

The team leader should prepare a report on the global manager every six months. That does not necessarily mean, however, that all the input should be gathered only twice a year from the various team members. For global managers, performance appraisals should be conducted in the following time frames, from the following performance sources.

On-Site Superiors. Global managers should be appraised not by chronological time periods but after the completion of significant projects, tasks, or other organizational milestones. This method allows the superior to focus his or her evaluation within a specific task context, rather than in a fuzzy "gestalt" context. These periodic reviews are then forwarded to the team leader and are filed for later use when the team leader formally writes the "global manager evaluation report."

Peer Managers. Peer managers should be asked to evaluate global managers once every six months. By nature, their interactions with the global managers will be sporadic—sometimes heavy and sometimes light—so six-month intervals are necessary for them to build up a mental database on which they can report when asked to do so.

Subordinates. Subordinates can be asked to evaluate the global manager's activities in concert with the on-site superior's evaluations—that is, after major projects are completed. This approach will prompt subordinates to respond to direct task-oriented issues, rather than to their own general attitudes about the global manager.

Clients. This source should be accessed once a year. Clients are busy people who do not want to be bothered to fill out forms every three months. What is the proper way to approach clients and ask them to be part of an evaluation process? The global manager, the on-site superior, the regional superior, or executives at corporate head-quarters could be asked to generate lists of clients who could be contacted. Feedback from these clients could be gathered formally (phone interviews and surveys) or informally (over dinner)—whatever makes sense in terms of the clients' personalities and cultural preferences. External observers could even be used to evaluate the global manager's dealings with the firm's clients if the act of contacting clients personally is seen as too intrusive. These observers could be in-house managers, university professors, or consultants.

Linking Patterns of Globalization and Strategy Orientation to Appraisal

Again, we would like to emphasize that a firm must seek a fit among its stage of globalization, competitive strategy, and its people-management practices. In addition, the five people-management functions must support and reinforce one another if each function is to be successful. For example, little long-term benefit is derived from carefully organizing an elaborate performance appraisal system for global managers and then, at the completion of the assignment, placing these individuals in positions that do not make use of the skills they have developed. The appraising function allows good management development and career planning to take place; it is an important link among functions in the people-management process.

Throughout this chapter, we have focused on ideas that will enhance the effectiveness of an appraisal system for global managers. All companies have different strategies, however, and are at different stages in the globalization process. Therefore, we would like to discuss the appraisal function briefly in this light. In terms of performance appraisal, the following general principles apply:

1. *The more a company's competitive strategy moves toward differentiation, the more comprehensive and complex the performance appraisal system needs to be.* Even at the export stage of globalization, if a firm has a differentiation strategic orientation, global managers require above-average cross-cultural skills to be effective. They need to understand the foreign culture well, since products or services are designed to be culturally compatible with the consumers' preferences.

2. *The more a company's stage of globalization moves away from export and toward more integrated stages (MNC and global), the more comprehensive and complex the performance appraisal system needs to be.* As companies become more globally integrated, global managers find themselves not only responsible for "hard" organizational performance objectives (e.g., profits, ROI, market share, and so on), but also for "soft" organizational performance objectives (e.g., socializing foreign managers into the firm's corporate culture, coordinating and balancing the home office's and the subsidiary's concerns, representing the firm to external stakeholders, and so on). Thus, the criteria for the success of global managers increase in number and magnitude, and the team approach to performance appraisal is necessary.

Summary

No matter how many global managers a firm has overseas, they have to be evaluated in a way that makes sense in the context of each one's overseas situation, the firm's strategy for that overseas unit, and the stage of globalization the firm is in. The overarching principle to remember is that no matter what the context, the global manager should be evaluated on criteria that are truly important for success overseas, and not on criteria that are ancillary to success. This hurdle is difficult to overcome in international performance appraisal, but tackling it will yield more effective and successful global managers.

Notes

1. Gregersen, Black, and Hite, "Expatriate Performance Appraisal: Principles, Practices, and Challenges"; Gregersen, Hite, and Black, "Expatriate Performance Appraisal in U.S. Multinational Firms."
2. Casio, *Managing Human Resources.*
3. Beer, "Performance Appraisal: Dilemmas and Possibilities"; Casio, *Managing Human Resources.*
4. Casio, *Managing Human Resources.*
5. Beer, "Performance Appraisal," pp. 25–26.
6. Robinson, *International Business Management: A Guide to Decision Making.*
7. Oddou and Mendenhall, "Expatriate Performance Appraisal: Problems and Solutions."
8. Gregersen, Black, and Hite, "Expatriate Performance Appraisal: Principles, Practices, and Challenges"; Tung, "Career Issues in International Assignments."

9. Oddou and Mendenhall, "Expatriate Performance Appraisal."
10. Korn-Ferry International, *A Study of the Repatriation of the American International Executive.*
11. Gregersen, Black, and Hite, "Expatriate Performance Appraisal: Principles, Practices, and Challenges."
12. Stening, Everett, and Longton, "Mutual Perception of Managerial Performance and Style in Multinational Subsidiaries."
13. Oddou and Mendenhall, "Expatriate Performance Appraisal."
14. Ibid.
15. Stening, Everett, and Longton, "Mutual Perception of Managerial Performance and Style."
16. Casio, *Managing Human Resources.*
17. Op cit, pp. 302–303.

8

Rewarding: Recognizing People When They Do Things Right

Many businessmen and businesswomen expect the rewards for good performance to translate into $, ¥, £, or some other equivalent symbol. Regardless of the symbol, if it represents money, it can and will get counted by both the firm and the manager being transferred globally. We have yet to run into an international assignee who felt he or she was paid too much or a firm that felt it paid too little. Compensation and benefits for internationally transferred employees traditionally receive a significant amount of corporate attention. These topics receive the bulk of space in this chapter as well, but will be placed in the context of broader objectives. While compensation is important, the overall structure of compensation systems as well as other forms of rewards for global assignments helps to encourage the right things that people do. Consequently, this chapter first outlines the basics of existing reward systems and then proposes a more comprehensive and integrated reward system for employees on global assignments.

The Problem of Rewarding *A* While Hoping for *B*

One of the common problems of international assignment compensation is that various allowances (more on this later in the chapter) create what is commonly referred to as "rewarding *A* while hoping for *B*."[1] Essentially, this phrase captures the problem of rewarding one behavior while hoping that the person will actually exhibit another. For example, professors hope that students learn the material and expand their understanding, but they often only reward students' ability to regurgitate memorized facts and figures. In business, employees are often quick to point out that although their bosses hope they will show initiative and solve problems, they often reward employees for simply following orders and adhering to "standard operating procedures." Because this problem is so commonplace, examples abound. Two reasons for this pervasive problem are that (1) objectives often are not clear or are not clearly understood, and (2) even when objectives are clearly understood at the outset, the means of achieving them eventually supplants the original objectives and becomes an objective itself. International assignment reward systems are just as vulnerable to this phenomenon as to any other.

To avoid the trap of rewarding *A* while hoping for *B,* it is important to consider two critical objectives of global assignment reward systems and the special issues involved when people are moved around the world.

Attracting and Retaining Quality People

One of the first objectives of reward systems is to attract and retain quality people for global assignments. Although there are positive and appealing aspects of living in a different country and culture, there are also numerous uncertainties and negative consequences. Leaving family, friends, familiar and comfortable living conditions, education and healthcare facilities, entertainment and recreational opportunities, favored foods and shopping areas, and so on, are not things most people want to do. Therefore, money is often used as a means of "buying off" the loss of the things left behind or as a means of simply buying them while abroad, or paying for them to be brought along. As one manager in Jakarta pointed out, "the normal grocery store here doesn't carry Wheaties, but with enough money, I can get my Wheaties."

Although firms may hope that quality people are attracted to international assignments and that these individuals will adjust effectively to the foreign cultures, many of the financial rewards of accepting a foreign assignment often encourage the expatriate and family to transport or purchase a lifestyle similar to the one they had at home and to make little effort to adjust to the foreign culture and country. This practice is rewarding *A* while hoping for *B*.

Enhancing Feelings of Equity

International reward systems are designed to enhance feelings of *equity,* which should not be confused with feelings of *equality.* Most organizations are *not* built on the principle of equality; firms have levels of hierarchy, and financial compensation almost always increases as the person moves up the hierarchy. Equity involves comparisons of the *ratio* between what is contributed and what is received. People at different levels in the organization do not expect identical financial rewards. However, employees at the same organizational level, performing at virtually the same level of performance, do expect similar rewards.

In the international context, this principle means that significant differences in pay should be avoided between expatriates originating from different countries but assigned to the same location and performing equally well at similar jobs, or between expatriates performing equally well at the same job in different locations. For example, any seasoned HR manager knows that placing an international assignee from the UK and one from Germany of roughly the same "rank" in a third country (say, Japan) will create significant headaches. Brits and Germans of the same rank in the same organization often receive very different salaries in their home countries. As long as they are working "at home" they don't pay much attention to the differentials. However, these differentials come into clear focus when international assignees work side by side in a third country. A country manager in Japan heading up the local office for a large U.S. multinational commented, "I have a German expatriate working two levels below me, with a compensation package equal to mine. The German's is also twice as large as a British expatriate's one level above him."

Financial incentives that are used to attract quality people to international assignments often create a strong sense of *inequity*. Host-country nationals just one level below expatriates frequently see large gaps between what *they* contribute and receive and what expatriates contribute and receive. Many of the rewards that expatriates receive are lost if not used, encouraging expatriates to use them or lose them, which adds to feelings of inequity between local nationals and expatriate managers. Firms may hope for equity, but many of their reward systems encourage the maximum inequity. Consider the following comment from the spouse of an American expatriate:

> I feel this firm does not really care about its people and their families as well as it should. Everything is done "on the cheap," which makes adjusting to the new country so much harder, which in turn makes their employees even more stressed out. Comparing this assignment to those of other major New York banks' employees, our benefits were extremely below standard and embarrassing! For example, the

housing allowances of many people we met were 25 percent higher than ours. Home-leave airfares were only economy in our company, while other firms were business class. Significantly higher bonuses were given by other firms. Our bank has lost and will continue to lose a great many excellent people should they continue to deal in this way. By the way, my husband left the bank for these reasons since our repatriation.

Basic Compensation Approaches

As long as expatriate employees exist, they will make both internal and external comparisons of compensation packages. These packages consist of more than the individual allowances, however. They are a composite of monetary and nonmonetary reward systems. As a final preliminary step before we discuss both aspects of effective reward systems, we will examine the basic approaches for fitting individual allowances into a general monetary reward system.

Balance Sheet

The balance sheet arguably represents the dominant approach in the United States. The basic objective of this approach is to ensure that employees maintain a standard of living in the country of assignment similar to what they enjoy in their home country. This system lessens the shock from changes in standard of living throughout the entire international assignment cycle. Exhibit 8.1 provides a rough illustration of how this approach is designed.

This approach works well when the conditions are right. Because the objective is to keep the standard of living constant before, during, and after the international assignment, the balance sheet assumes that individuals return to their home country after completion of the assignment. This condition is true in many firms, but others have systems in which a cadre of career international managers move from one international assignment to another. In this case, it becomes difficult to determine both the home country of employees and the rationale for making their living standard abroad equal to that of an arbitrary home country.

Balance sheets work better when most of the firm's expatriates originate from the same country. If expatriates originate from different countries with different standards of living and yet work together in the same country of assignment, the balance sheet highlights the imbalanced or unequal standards of living that these individuals enjoy (or suffer). Consequently, expatriates of equal responsibility may find it difficult to accept unequal compensation packages due primarily to accidents of birth.

This method is most effective if reliable, detailed figures for calculating and comparing standards of living are available. Take the case of a biotechnical firm with headquarters in Salt Lake City and regional headquarters in Geneva, Switzerland. The firm recently transferred one of its leading managers, married with two small children, to Switzerland from Los Angeles. The company's director of corporate personnel inquired how much the annual rental would be in Geneva for a three-bedroom house or apartment. The estimate came back that annual rentals in Geneva would be approximately $25,000 per year. The director knew that annual homeowner costs in Salt Lake City for a three-bedroom house were about $13,500. This translated to an $11,500 housing adjustment to be made in favor of the employee. Instead of using these figures, however, the director could

Exhibit 8.1
Balance Sheet

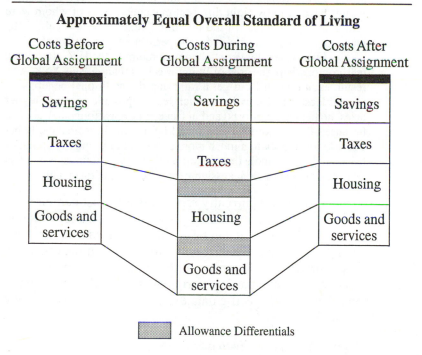

Approximately Equal Overall Standard of Living

| Costs Before Global Assignment | Costs During Global Assignment | Costs After Global Assignment |

Allowance Differentials

easily have relied on national averages for Switzerland and the United States in making an assessment of the housing allowance needed to bring about a balance. Standards of living (and the expenses associated with them) vary, not just by country but also by region, city, and even neighborhood. This particular expatriate's annual housing costs were $16,500 per year for his three-bedroom house in Los Angeles. The average annual rental for a three-bedroom apartment in Switzerland in general was $21,000, or $4,000 less than in Geneva. Thus, the figures that are available, how they are calculated, and which ones are used can make a significant difference in the amount that is needed to "balance" living standards.

Unfortunately, firms utilizing the balance sheet tend to create situations in which employees experience significant changes in compensation upon returning home. Consider the following comments from American expatriates:

> When I returned, my base salary was reduced 16.7 percent versus the stated policy of a maximum of 10 percent. In the last twelve years, I have received consistently outstanding performance reviews. These ratings have been by eight different managers, three of whom were senior vice presidents. In the last three years, I have received the maximum bonus available under the performance incentive plan.
>
> I was generally very unhappy to return to the U.S. after living in Toronto, where the cost of living was less than in New York. As a result, even though I did get a raise and the additional benefit of a second lease car, I now have much less disposable income (higher taxes, higher housing costs) and in fact can't even afford *one* lease car, because I can't afford parking for it! I am being hurt financially because I moved back to a much more expensive city, and my company has no policy to handle that. It hurt particularly in contrast to the fact that I felt my international assignment benefited me financially.

The balance sheet currently represents the most common approach. Most employees considering global assignments see it as reasonable and fair; therefore, it can be an effective means of attracting quality people to these assignments. It works best, however, when employees return to their home countries upon completing their assignments, when most expatriates originate from the same country, and when accurate and specific data exist on the standards of living for both locations.

Parent-Country Equivalency

This approach is in many ways quite simple and straightforward. Compensation of all expatriate employees (or all expatriate employees above a certain level) is based on market rates in the country of the parent firm. For example, a U.S. chemical MNC provides all expatriates, regardless of country of origin, the same salary and benefits as for employees in the U.S. This compensation plan reduces the inequality that expatriates from different countries of origin who are working in the same location often experience with other approaches.

The effectiveness of this approach is also subject to several important conditions. It works well when the home country of the parent firm has relatively high wages and a fairly high standard of living, because it is easier to convince individuals to accept pay scales and standards of living that are greater than (but not less than) what they would otherwise have. This approach also works well when the expatriate managers in global assignments are career internationalists who move from one foreign assignment to another. This situation reduces the negative impact that the loss of cost-of-living adjustments creates when individuals return home to countries with lower pay scales and lower living standards.

Parent-country equivalency works best with a relatively small number of managers (fifty or fewer) on international assignment, or with a cadre of career international expatriates. Paying parent-country wages and ensuring parent-country living standards, especially when they are high relative to world standards, can become very costly for a large group of expatriate managers. Moreover, large groups of managers trotting around the globe enjoying relatively high wages and standards of living can intensify the inequity that host-country managers and employees feel and can hurt an expatriate manager's ability to work effectively with local staff people.

Regional or Composite Markets

Some companies are attracted to an approach based on *regional* or *composite markets*. This approach involves calculating an average salary and standard-of-living index for a set of countries. The term *regional market* generally refers to a set of countries related by geographic proximity (e.g., Central America, the Middle East, Scandinavia, and so on). The term *composite market* refers to a set of countries grouped by some other criterion, such as market importance to the firm. This approach is often less costly than the parent-country approach, because it allows the firm the opportunity to arbitrage the difference in wages and cost of living between the parent country and other countries.

This system works well when expatriate managers come from and stay within regional or market boundaries. The more employees move between regions or markets, the greater the chance that feelings of inequity will emerge. This approach also works best when regional or market boundaries are drawn around countries that have wage and living-standard levels that are more similar than different. For example, drawing a boundary around Canada, the United States, and Mexico as the North American region would create feelings of inequity because of the significant wage and living-standard differences between Mexico and the other two countries.

Local Markets

The fourth major approach to expatriate compensation starts from the premise that being sent on an international assignment is not highly unusual, so no special compensation or benefits should be expected or paid. Accordingly, all employees, whether they are working in their home country or not, are paid according to local market rates. A slightly less absolute version of this approach provides some allowances for the first year or two and then drops them to treat the transferred employee as a host-country national. A slight variation involves a "one-time premium" paid at the beginning of the assignment (or sometimes at the beginning and at the end). The obvious implication of this basic approach is that quality employees will accept global assignments to countries in which wage structures and standards of living are higher than those of the country of origin. It is quite difficult to entice employees to make the opposite move, however.

This approach can work under some restrictive conditions. First, if the firm generally takes a multidomestic strategic approach to business and desires little transfer of information into or out of countries, then its need for expatriate managers will be relatively low. Second, if the firm is expanding into countries that are more developed than the country of the parent firm or the country of origin of the most desirable expatriate employees, then this approach can work because employees will be receiving higher wages than they had before. To some extent, however, this increase may be offset by high cost-of-living expenses in the developed country.

Allowances

With these general approaches to expatriate compensation in mind, we can now review the long list of allowances that are often granted to expatriate managers. The number and variations of allowances offered to expatriate managers are nearly as large and varied as the firms providing them. Several are quite common, however, and it is helpful to examine them and the trends among companies.

Foreign Service Premiums

A foreign service premium is money paid in recognition of the employee's and family's willingness and sacrifice in accepting a global assignment. This compensation is given in exchange for the inconvenience of living in a foreign land, with alien customs, food, weather, transportation systems, education, shopping, and healthcare facilities, and for leaving family, friends, and familiar surroundings back home. A 1990 survey by Organization Resources Counselors (ORC) of more than 250 U.S. multinational firms found that 78 percent pay a foreign service premium.[2] The policy of most firms paying this premium is to pay a percentage of the base salary. This figure is generally between 10 and 25 percent of base pay. Some firms set a maximum for this premium—say, $50,000. However, over the last ten years, this percentage has dropped dramatically. Once organizations push toward and then above 50 percent of sales being "international," most discontinue paying any foreign service premiums.

Hardship or Site Allowances

A hardship allowance is paid in addition to a foreign service premium (if the latter is paid) in recognition of particularly difficult aspects of the specific country or site of a global assignment. Hardships may include physical isolation, climatic extremes, political instability and risk, and poor living conditions due to inadequate housing, education, health care, or food. The survey by ORC found that 68 percent of MNCs pay hardship allowances for expatriates, depending on the country of assignment. Although this percentage has remained fairly constant, the number of countries to which hardship allowances are applied has dropped dramatically. In most companies, countries such as Japan, Singapore, and Spain have been eliminated from the "hardship" list.

It is difficult to identify and evaluate hardships and then determine a fair compensation value. Most firms take a two-fold approach. The first test is an external market test. Firms look at the competitive practices of similar firms with expatriate managers serving in the countries or locations in question. About 50 percent of firms use outside experts to make this assessment. The second test is an internal market test. In this test firms simply assess the compensation that is necessary to attract quality individuals to a country or site. Correlation between external and internal market tests can range from high to low.

Several dynamics influence firms to choose the most expensive of the two market rates. Generally, firms know that not long after arrival, their employees will compare their hardship allowances with those of employees of other firms. Consequently, even if internal market rates are lower than external market rates, firms often choose to go by the external market rates to avoid feelings of inequity and complaints among their employees. Firms may also choose internal market rates over the lower external market rates to entice quality employees to accept hardship assignments. Regardless of the method or methods utilized, a strong majority of firms do not phase out hardship allowances over the duration of a global assignment.

Cost-of-Living Allowances

Cost-of-living allowances (COLAs) are utilized in recognition that the costs of equivalent standards of living vary by country. Over 90 percent of multinational firms pay COLAs. Essentially, firms or their consultants compare the cost of a "basket of goods" in the country of assignment to the cost of the same "basket" in another country (usually the country of origin). If the country of assignment is more expensive than the comparison country, a cost-of-living adjustment is made. If the cost of living in the country of assignment is less than that of the comparison country, there is no adjustment; very few firms make negative adjustments.

The general method of making positive COLA calculations can be illustrated with the following example. Janet McWilliams, a senior manager with a large accounting firm, is being transferred from Boston to Tokyo. The accounting firm contacts a consulting firm specializing in overseas COLA calculations. The consulting firm determines that it costs a single individual, without a family, 65 percent more to live in Tokyo than in Boston. Next, the consulting firm estimates that 60 percent of Janet's $100,000 salary is spendable income (i.e., goods, services, and housing) and that the remaining 40 percent is disposable income (i.e., taxes, savings, and so on). Accordingly, it determines the COLA for Janet McWilliams in Tokyo to be $39,000. It figures that, of Janet's $100,000 salary, $60,000 is spendable income. Because living in Tokyo is estimated to be 65 percent more expensive than living in Boston, Janet will need slightly over $99,000 of spendable income in Tokyo, an adjustment of $39,000. This adjustment is generally given "tax free." Most COLAs are also subject to review to compare cost-of-living changes between the two countries, due primarily to differences in inflation and exchange rates.

The timing of the inflation review and the rate of inflation can be particularly important. For example, if the annual inflation rate is 120 percent in Indonesia, then the frequency and timing of COLA calculations can have a significant impact. Suppose that company A evaluates inflation every three months, while company B evaluates it every month. Every three months, employees of both firms will have approximately 30 percent more rupiah added to their COLAs. The purchasing power of employees in company B will have been much better protected, however. If an employee from each firm receives 100 million rupiah in January, both employees will receive approximately 130 million rupiah in April. While the employee in firm A will have received 100 million rupiah in both February and March, however, the employee in firm B will have received 110 million in February and 120 million in March, or a total of 30 million more rupiah over the three months than the employee in firm A.

COLAs are also subject to changes in exchange rates. Foreign exchange rates can fluctuate considerably. For example, in the early 1980s, the dollar appreciated over 30 percent in real terms relative to the yen and then depreciated by over 35 percent in the late 1980s. In the late 1990s, it once again appreciated against the yen and several other Asian currencies. In Korea, for example, it appreciated nearly 100 percent. To illustrate the importance of exchange-rate fluctuations, let us continue the example of Janet McWilliams. Suppose that at the time of Janet's transfer to Tokyo the Japanese yen-to-dollar exchange rate is ¥150 to $1. The total COLA for Janet in yen will be ¥5,850,000. Suppose that six months after she arrives in Japan the yen-to-dollar exchange rate changes to ¥130 to $1. Now $39,000 exchanges into only ¥5,070,000. This fluctuation is a loss to Janet of ¥780,000, which at the 130-to-1 exchange rate will require an additional $6,000.

Official exchange rates are not always accurate reflections of unofficial or real exchange rates. Especially in developing countries, whose national currency is not freely traded on world exchange-rate markets, governments have a tendency to overvalue their currencies. Thus, while the dollar may officially buy only 10 yuan in China, it may unofficially buy 20 yuan. In particular, the combination of high rates of inflation and slow adjustments in official exchange rates can have significant and negative impacts on the true purchasing power of expatriates. Failure by firms to recognize these issues can often lead to dissatisfied employees and families and to costly early returns from global assignments. This situation was highlighted in the late 1990s with the "Asian Debt Crisis," in which currencies such as the Indonesian rupiah depreciated by 80 percent over a six-month period.

Housing Allowances

In many parts of the world, housing allowances have become the single most expensive item in expatriate compensation packages. For example, apartments in Hong Kong and Tokyo can easily cost $5,000 to $10,000 per month. Firms use three major methods to determine housing allowances.

The first method involves a flat allowance. In this case, the employee is given a fixed amount, which often depends on family size and organizational rank, to spend on housing. If the employee finds something suitable for less than the allowance, he or she can keep the difference. If suitable housing costs more than the allowance, the employee pays the difference. The firm must have accurate, up-to-date data to avoid either paying too much in housing allowances or creating dissatisfied employees because it is paying too little.

The second method is to determine the housing costs of the employee in the country of origin and the cost of housing in the country of assignment. If the housing costs in the country of assignment are higher, an allowance equal to that difference is paid. About a quarter of U.S. firms handle housing allowances in this manner.

The third method is to provide housing in the country of assignment either rent-free or at the same cost as in the employee's country of origin. Most firms that provide housing rather than housing allowances charge employees rent comparable to what they would pay in the country of origin.

Utility Allowances

There are two general approaches to how utility allowances are handled. The first approach provides a utility allowance to the employee. As with set housing allowances, the firm must have an accurate knowledge of utility rates and reasonable usage in the country of assignment. The costs of overpaying for utilities or of not allowing enough to run an air conditioner in a tropical climate can be equally high. The second approach assesses the cost differentials between the countries of assignment and origin and provides a utility allowance equal to the difference if utility costs are higher in the country of assignment. In general, however, these special utility allowances are increasingly rare and are usually factored into the COLAs.

Furnishing Allowances

There are three major ways in which firms handle furnishing allowances. The first approach involves shipping the employee's furnishings to the new location. There is usually a maximum weight limit, such as 15,000 pounds, set on what can be shipped. The benefit of this approach is that employees and their families have their own home furnishings. This approach can become expensive, however, and both damage and delays can lead to dissatisfied or angry employees.

A second approach is for firms to purchase or (more often) lease household furnishings and then provide them free to international managers. This approach is often accompanied by a shipment of less than 1,000 pounds of personal belongings. Firms often pay for storage of furniture during an assignment. This task may seem simple, but if it is poorly done, employees can become dissatisfied. One American expatriate declared: "Almost all of our personal effects were ruined while in storage. It was difficult and extremely stressful to straighten the mess out. The company didn't really offer much help—we were on our own."

The third approach provides the employee with a fixed sum of money ($8,000–$10,000) with which furnishings can be purchased. If the desired furnishings cost less than this amount, the employee keeps the difference. If they cost more, the employee must pay the extra yen, pounds, rupiah, or lire.

Education Allowances

Children's education is a critical issue in the minds of most parents who are asked to transfer to a foreign country. Most firms' internal markets are such that the firms would find very few quality people willing to accept global assignments if the children were forced to attend local schools in the countries of assignment. Consequently, most firms provide an education allowance that covers the normal costs (i.e., tuition, books, supplies) of attending local "international" schools. If adequate educational facilities are not available in the country of assignment, many firms provide assistance that covers part of the cost of boarding schools in the country of origin. More comprehensive education allowances also include one or two round-trip tickets for the children to visit the parents. More limited allowances only provide air fare, without boarding school support or assistance.

Home-Leave Allowances

Most companies provide executive employees and their families business-class air fare between the countries of assignment and origin once a year. Employees strongly favor being given the equivalent sum in cash, to use as they please. This arrangement allows them to purchase less expensive economy-class tickets and keep the difference, to take their home leave away from home by visiting some other place or country, or to select an inexpensive plan that allows them to do both. Most U.S. firms do not require employees to take home leave in their home country.

Relocation Allowances

The relocation allowance is provided to recognize that a variety of expenses cannot be predicted accurately, and that they vary by individual. These miscellaneous expenses associated with moving are typically covered by a fixed allowance equal to one month's salary or $5,000, whichever is less. Nearly half of U.S. firms pay a flat sum, most often at the beginning and at the end of an assignment.

Rest-and-Relaxation (R&R) Allowances

Rest-and-relaxation allowances are most often associated with hardship assignments. Generally, these R&R allowances are provided for the employee and the family to get away and recover from the hardships of the country of assignment. These trips are often necessary for the employee and family to purchase goods or receive medical care not available in the country. Many firms have a "use-it-or-lose-it" policy with R&R allowances, because they do not want employees or their families to trade physical or emotional health for the allowance money. Typically, R&R allowances are only granted for the most challenging locales.

Medical Allowances

Firms cannot afford to put the health of employees and their families at risk, so they pay for all medical expenses (often excluding optical and dental). Some firms even pay for any medical expenses in excess of those covered by insurance. In developing countries, firms may have to pay for employees or members of their families to receive adequate medical care in countries other than the country of assignment.

Car-and-Driver Allowances

If a company provides a car allowance, except for senior executives, it is based on the differential between owning and operating a car in the country of assignment and in the country of origin. Increasingly, companies are eliminating car allowances. External market pressures seem to be the biggest determinants of whether a car or a car and driver are provided to senior executives. Less than a quarter of U.S. firms provide a company car for all expatriates from headquarters, while two-thirds provide company cars when they are essential. In Pacific Rim countries, external market pressures prevail so that American executives are often provided cars and drivers to which they would not be entitled even in similar-level positions in the United States.

Club Membership Allowances

In many countries, club memberships are the only (or often the least expensive) means that employees and families have to gain access to normal recreational facilities, such as tennis courts, swimming pools, exercise rooms, and so on. In other locations, club memberships are essential for gaining access to the informal but important contexts of business decisions and political and business contacts. Most companies pay for club memberships for expatriates on a case-by-case basis, and safety and rank are the two dominating factors in the decision.

Taxes

Taxes are a complex issue in the case of managers working in global assignments; the details and specifics are best handled by experienced professionals. Understanding a couple of important issues, however, will enable firms or individual managers to be better consumers of expatriate tax-consulting or tax-preparation services.

There are two major approaches to tax policies and global assignments. The first approach is commonly referred to as *tax protection.* Under this policy, firms reimburse employees for taxes paid in excess of what they would have paid if they had remained in the country of origin. Many of the benefits and allowances previously described add to the employees' taxable income, making it greater than it would have been if they had remained at home. The extra money reimbursed to compensate for these additional taxes is also taxable income, generating additional taxes and creating the need to provide even more reimbursement. Carried to the extreme, this method can become a never-ending cycle of compensation and tax-reimbursement escalation. Consequently, the firm must decide whether to limit this cycle to one or two rounds. Another major issue is that employees transferring from higher-tax home countries to lower-tax assignment countries may actually owe less in taxes than they would have if they had stayed home. In this case, the firm must decide if it will allow employees to keep the benefit or reimburse the firm for the difference. Most firms in this situation find it difficult to require employees to reimburse the difference.

The second major approach is commonly termed *tax equalization*. The objective of a tax-equalization policy is to ensure that employees pay no more and no less than they would have paid in the home country. Under a tax-equalization policy, the tax that the employee would have paid is subtracted from the salary. The firm then pays all actual taxes in the home and the host country that employees owe. The tax-equalization approach has several advantages. First, subtracting the hypothetical home-country tax from the total salary reduces actual taxable income. ORC found differences in how this hypothetical tax was computed. Roughly 25 percent of U.S. firms estimate it on base salary alone, 54 percent estimate it on base salary plus bonus, and 8 percent estimate it on base salary, bonus, and all premiums. The benefit to the firm of tax equalization can be quite substantial, especially with respect to employees originating from high-tax countries. This potential benefit is probably why nearly nine in ten U.S. firms take this approach.

Another advantage to this approach is that it reduces problems upon repatriation. For example, if an employee from the United States were sent to Saudi Arabia (which has virtually no personal income tax) and were allowed to keep the tax windfall, the employee would experience a significant shock upon repatriating. The person could easily experience a drop in disposable income of 30–50 percent. Yet another advantage is that making adjustments for different tax policies in different countries through tax equalization makes it easier to motivate employees from low-tax countries, such as Saudi Arabia, to go to high-tax countries, such as Sweden. One last advantage is that if the majority of the firm's employees sent on global assignments originate from relatively high-tax countries, the firm often receives a net benefit (or cost reduction) due to differential tax rates.

An Integrated Solution

What sense can be made of these basic approaches, allowances, and fists full of money? Many multinational firms have decided that it is all too costly and too complicated and are taking drastic measures to reduce the number of expatriate managers; however, these firms may be ridding themselves of the good with the bad. After reviewing the strengths and follies of some cost-reduction and simplification approaches, we will outline an approach that can be both less costly and more effective for a wide variety of multinational firms.

Anorexic Versus "Lean and Mean"

As is clear from all the common allowances that most firms provide to internationally transferred employees, these assignments can be expensive. One multinational U.S. firm with 500 employees in global assignments estimated that the incremental cost for these employees was $80 million. Consequently, most firms direct their cost-cutting activities at slashing the number of expatriates to reduce total expatriate costs. The fastest way for a firm to cut $40 million from a $80 million total in incremental costs is to cut the number of expatriates from 500 to 250, as one West Coast bank did recently. This step may be appropriate, but a few things should be considered to determine whether the firm is spending its money wisely.

If future key leaders of the organization need international experience to be prepared to lead the firm in a global environment, then cutting the number of global assignments to reduce costs may be a short-term sacrifice of the firm's long-term future in a global marketplace (see Chapter 1 and the discussion of strategic roles of expatriates).

In addition to the strategic roles of succession planning and knowledge transfer, the coordination and control function should also be carefully considered before the total number of managers on global assignment is cut. Many authors have recently talked about the role that corporate culture can have in reducing coordination and control costs.[3] The shared values of a strong corporate culture are often referred to as *second-order control mechanisms.* This notion suggests that the costs of directly monitoring, reporting, and evaluating (first-order controls) the behavior of employees worldwide is more costly than having employees internalize a set of values that then guide their decisions and behavior (second-order controls). Although the content of cultures and values differs the world over, one common element is that people are socialized by other people to accept certain values. Therefore, if the organization wants to establish or maintain a strong corporate culture, it will need people who accept the desired values and can socialize other people to them. Effective socialization generally requires significant and direct periods of contact. Therefore, *if the firm wants a strong worldwide organizational culture, it will need to move managers throughout its worldwide operations.*

Expatriates are expensive; international assignments are costly. No one will debate these two statements, but executives and policy makers should carefully consider succession planning, knowledge transfer, and coordination and control before launching programs to significantly cut the number of expatriates. Reducing programs should leave the organization "lean and mean" but not anorexic.

Leaping Ahead to the Past

Everyone agrees that expatriates can be expensive and that expatriate compensation systems can be complex. As a result, many firms are trying to simplify the process by setting a percentage premium and leaving it at that. Increasingly, policy makers are saying, "Give these managers an extra 20 percent, and send them." These changes in expatriate compensation actually represent a return to the past. In the early days of expatriate compensation—in the 1950s—most managers were given a little extra, and off they went.

However emotionally appealing this simplification may be to frustrated personnel directors and other executives, the results are likely to be disappointing because the approach does not solve a number of problems. It will not solve the problem of attracting quality people to take international assignments. It will not solve the problem of the significant effect that exchange-rate fluctuations can have on real purchasing power in another country. It will not solve the problem of lowered standards of living due to high inflation rates in the country of assignment. It will not eliminate the sense of inequity that employees feel when they compare themselves to other expatriates at similar organizational levels in other firms.

Expatriate compensation systems are expensive and complex, but the focus should be first on the entire reward system and then on the effectiveness of the compensation system. From a strategic perspective, simply cutting the number of employees in global assignments may do nothing positive and may actually have negative consequences for organizational and individual effectiveness. Likewise, merely simplifying the compensation system may increase efficiency at the expense of effectiveness. Many people and systems are expensive and complex, but that is not the issue. The real issue is how to ensure that costly and complex assets are worth the trouble and expense.

A Broader Perspective

One way to take a broader view of the issue is to answer a seemingly narrow question: Why do we have to pay so much extra to get people to accept overseas assignments? The simple answer is that, human motivation being what it is, the anticipated benefits must be greater than the anticipated costs before someone can be enticed to do something. To the extent that the firm is perceived by employees as taking an out-of-sight, out-of-mind approach to international assignments, the career costs can be substantial. We surveyed 174 American managers recently returned from overseas assignments to over twenty-six different countries and found that 80 percent felt that their international experience was not valued by their firms, and that only 11 percent had been promoted upon returning.[4] In another survey, while 65 percent of HR professionals thought an international assignment had a positive career impact, 77 percent of expatriates felt that an international assignment had a negative career impact.[5] Facts such as these, and horror stories about someone being caught in a holding pattern for six months after returning from overseas, raise the career costs in people's minds of accepting a global assignment. Some people are willing to accept these career costs for extra compensation. The greater the career potential of the individual, the greater the costs, and the greater the compensation that firms must provide to encourage the individual to accept the assignment.

There are, however, many benefits of accepting an international assignment, independent of the monetary compensation. Most employees expect—and actually experience—greater job autonomy and responsibility while abroad.[6] They develop market knowledge, language skills, contacts, and global perspectives. Certainly, these factors are positive in the cost-benefit analysis; for most employees, they would be. It seems unlikely, however, that these expected short-term benefits could simply eliminate the long-term anticipated career costs, especially if these acquired skills and experiences were unlikely to be utilized by the firm in the future. Money may be the second-best means of balancing the equation.

The point is not to try to examine all the potential costs or benefits that might go into employees' decisions to accept or reject global assignments; rather, the point is that employees do make these judgments, and both monetary *and* nonmonetary factors are included in the decisions. This is why focusing on money is a formula for rewarding *A* (maximization of short-term monetary benefits over costs to the individual) while hoping for *B* (inclusion of both long-term monetary and nonmonetary factors in the decision and performance). One simple means of reducing, but not necessarily eliminating, the escalating costs per individual manager sent abroad is to increase rewards for successful completion of a global assignment. In Chapters 9 and 10, on repatriation, we specifically discuss how to redesign repatriation policies to maximize their positive influence on employees' perceptions of potential rewards. We argue that at least some of the extra monetary rewards could be replaced by nonmonetary rewards such as better expatriation policies, career systems, and repatriation procedures. If employees thought that expatriation policies would enhance their ability to perform well during overseas assignments, and if they believed that their performance abroad would be rewarded upon repatriation, then they would be motivated to accept global assignments with lower levels of immediate monetary incentives. Notice that we say they would accept *lower* levels, not that they would be willing to forgo all monetary compensation. These ideas are illustrated in Exhibit 8.2 with the framework of a well-known theory of motivation: expectancy theory.

A firm's reward system will be most successful if the efficiency and effectiveness of both monetary and nonmonetary elements are consistent with the goals and objectives of the firm, as well as with its circumstances. Most of the previous chapters of this book have outlined specific steps that can be taken to enhance the efficiency and effectiveness of expatriation policies. These policies can also serve the dual purpose of enhancing employees' beliefs that their efforts will result in good performance during a global assignment. Later chapters provide more detail on how to enhance the repatriation and career development systems, thereby enhancing the reward system and further motivating international managers. Even with these important additions to the reward system, there are still several ways to increase the cost-effectiveness of monetary compensation structures and policies.

Basics of a Three-Step Approach

Although effective compensation policies must attract quality people and enhance feelings of equity, these policies must also cut unnecessary costs. What we outline here provides both a general strategic approach and specific tactical tips for designing international compensation systems. Our proposal is not totally new, nor is it a panacea.

Exhibit 8.2
Expectancy Theory and Global Assignments

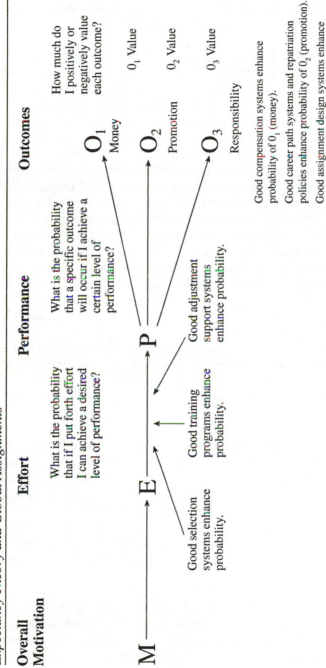

Overall Motivation	Effort	Performance	Outcomes

Overall Motivation

Effort

What is the probability that if I put forth effort I can achieve a desired level of performance?

Performance

What is the probability that a specific outcome will occur if I achieve a certain level of performance?

Outcomes

How much do I positively or negatively value each outcome?

M —— E —— P

O_1 Money $\quad O_1$ Value

O_2 Promotion $\quad O_2$ Value

O_3 Responsibility $\quad O_3$ Value

Good selection systems enhance probability.

Good training programs enhance probability.

Good adjustment support systems enhance probability.

Good compensation systems enhance probability of O_1 (money).

Good career path systems and repatriation policies enhance probability of O_2 (promotion).

Good assignment design systems enhance the probability of O_3 (responsibility).

Still, it suggests some interesting issues to consider in the design of compensation systems for global assignments.

Step 1. This general approach assumes that most people will not be willing to move to a foreign country if they must experience a significant decrease in their standard of living. Consequently, as in the "balance sheet" approach, the first step requires estimating what it takes to maintain a standard of living in the country of assignment, reasonably similar to that in the country of origin. Firms must be careful to make accurate calculations for individuals. For example, comparisons can be made between living in the United States and living in Japan, or between living in Boston and living in Tokyo. In many cases, the difference between general and specific comparisons is substantial. We have already seen that the differential between average U.S. housing costs and average Japanese and Swiss housing costs was much larger (and therefore more costly to the firm) than specific housing differentials between Boston and Tokyo and between Los Angeles and Geneva. Although detailed comparisons are not always available, they are clearly the most accurate. Therefore, if outside consultants are utilized, two important issues are how they compute living costs (especially housing) and the level of detail they can provide. This first step also requires that each individual be assigned a country of origin. For most employees, this will simply be the home country. For career internationalists, however, there may not be an easily defined "home country." In this case, they need to be assigned "career" home countries.

Step 2. Once the cost of living for the individual in the country of origin and in the country of assignment has been computed, the country-of-origin cost of living should be subtracted from the individual's normal base salary. This cost-of-living figure usually involves the costs of housing, utilities, food, clothing, transportation, medical care, entertainment, education, and taxes. The remainder is the individual's disposable income. This disposable income is paid to the employee through the normal system and in the currency of the country of origin.

Step 3. The estimated cost of living in the country of assignment is paid to the employee in the currency of the country of assignment. This system significantly reduces the exchange-rate adjustments and risks that currently frustrate many international compensation managers. Employees are paid, in the foreign currency, only what they are estimated to need for living costs in the assignment country, but they are free to transfer money from a home-country bank account to the assignment country and to individually bear the risk (or enjoy the rewards) of transferring the money.

Benefits and Conditions of the Three-Step Approach

This three-step approach, especially in the context of well-designed nonmonetary rewards, ensures in principle that people will not experience significant drops in standard of living. The risks and rewards of increasing their standard of living by transferring money into the country of assignment is their decision. This basic approach also reduces the inequity between expatriates and host-country nationals, or among expatriates of different countries of origin, because international managers will receive, in local currency, amounts pegged to the costs of living in the country of assignment. The differentials that certainly will exist in disposable income among expatriates from different countries of origin (or even from different regions in a single country) will generally be "out of sight" in home-country bank accounts during the international assignment. At the same time, the firm is likely to reduce its overall expenses.

In our discussion of other basic approaches to compensation, we examined the conditions under which the specific approaches would be more or less effective. These general conditions involve (1) having many or few expatriates, (2) having expatriates who return to the home country or move from one international post to another, (3) having expatriates come from the same or from similar countries of origin, and (4) having detailed figures for cost-of-living differentials. Accordingly, it is fair to examine the extent to which this three-step approach is dependent on or independent of these conditions.

The first condition on which this approach depends is the availability of accurate and detailed cost-of-living information. The three-step approach can be used even in the absence of detailed information, but its effectiveness will be a function of how well the general cost-of-living information matches the specific situations of the employees involved. This approach is relatively independent of the other three major conditions, however. Although the total savings of this approach will generally be larger the more expatriates a firm has, it can be used independently of the total number of expatriate managers. This approach can also be used independently of whether expatriates return home or are career internationalists; the only thing required in the case of career internationalists is that they be assigned "career" home countries. One large U.S. firm selects the "career" home country on the basis of the country in which the individual believes he or she is most likely to retire. Finally, because what expatriates receive is only estimated "spendable income" during their global assignments, whether expatriates in a given country come from different home countries with different wage structures or standards of living is not a critical factor. (As mentioned earlier, disposable income differentials remain "out of sight" in the individual's home-country bank account.) Thus, even though the other basic approaches discussed can be effective under certain conditions, this approach is much more general.

One implication of utilizing this three-step approach is that a tax-equalization policy is required. Under a tax-equalization policy, the individual's hypothetical home-country tax is subtracted from the base salary, reducing the total taxable income, and then the firm pays all taxes due. Under the three-step approach, in addition to the individual's hypothetical tax, the individual's hypothetical home-country cost of living is subtracted from the base salary, which significantly reduces taxable income. This substantial savings accrues to the firm, at no cost to the individual.

Another important implication of this approach is that expenses for similar quality of education for children are paid by the firm. In many cases, the education costs deducted from the country-of-origin base salary will be less than the expenses paid in the country of assignment. Our experience and belief is that it will be hard to entice quality people to accept international assignments if they must pay the increased cost differential of similar-quality education for their children, or if children will experience a drop in educational quality.

The final implication of this approach is that inflation in the country of assignment must be monitored and factored into COLAs. Although splitting the spendable and disposable income of internationally assigned employees nearly eliminates the risk and the complex adjustments entailed in exchange-rate fluctuations, it does nothing to eliminate the need to monitor the impact of inflation on purchasing power. Each firm should carefully consider the frequency with which COLA changes are made, but some general rules apply. If the rate of inflation in the country of assignment is greater than 15 percent per year, employees are likely to feel significant losses of purchasing power and some disappointment with the firm if semiannual adjustments are not made. Inflation rates of 30 percent or more should be accompanied by at least quarterly adjustments. Cost-of-living adjustments should be made monthly if the inflation rate is 80 percent or more. Inflation rates of 350 percent are likely to require weekly adjustments. If the inflation rate is greater than 1,000 percent, expatriate employees will need almost daily adjustments.

Allowances

Even if this three-step approach is adopted, several decisions about allowances must be made. The basic objective of this discussion is to point out areas where allowances can be reduced without hurting the effectiveness of compensation systems.

Hardship Allowances. Unless the firm has a strong internal market, it is unlikely that hardship allowances can be totally eliminated. Nevertheless, there are many cities for which external markets pay hardship allowances that could be eliminated without severe costs to the effectiveness of international assignment compensation systems. For example, many firms in the Pacific Rim still provide hardship allowances of $1,000 to $5,000 for cities such as Hong Kong, Seoul, Singapore, Taipei, and Tokyo. Although arguments concerning issues of safety, health, and pollution can be made for such allowances in Bangkok, Manila, or Mexico City, these arguments are much harder to make for clean, safe cities like Tokyo.

Housing and Utility Allowances. Under the three-step approach, an allowance for similar housing and utilities in the assignment country must be provided. In cities such as Tokyo and Hong Kong, this expense can sometimes be greater than the individual's base salary. Where patterns and numbers of expatriates are somewhat predictable and consistent, firms may save considerable sums of money by purchasing houses and apartments rather than by providing rental cash. In many cases, providing housing can also reduce the tax burden for the firm. Finally, firms should generally discourage employees from purchasing houses in the country of assignment or selling their houses in the home country, especially during high-inflation periods. Many American managers sent overseas in the 1970s sold their houses, only to find when they returned that inflation had priced them out of the U.S. housing market. Many U.S. firms discourage their employees from selling their houses when they leave for an overseas assignment. The firms usually cannot afford to buy and sell employees' homes, but they may be able to facilitate their rental during assignments.

Furnishing Allowances. In moves of any significant distance, providing a lump sum for furnishings and an allowance for shipping less than 1,000 pounds of personal items is generally cheaper than shipping the individual's belongings and furniture. Although care should be taken in determining this lump sum, it is generally between $7,000 and $10,000 and people are free to buy or rent what they choose and keep or pay the difference. If expatriates are to stay three to five years, as opposed to one to two years, paying a lump sum at the beginning is usually much cheaper than providing a rental allowance for furnishings over the entire duration of the assignment.

Home-Leave Allowances. Expatriates generally prefer to receive a lump sum equal to round-trip business-class flights and hotel expenses when they travel between the assignment country and the home country. Expatriates and their families should be required to revisit their home country if they are planning to return after the current international assignment. We would not recommend that firms take a parental attitude of providing actual plane tickets; however, reporting requirements should call for expatriates to return home at least once a year.

Relocation Allowances. We have interviewed many American expatriates who consistently pointed out unexpected expenses associated with the move to and from a global assignment. Very few consistently pointed out unanticipated "moving" expenses during the assignment, however, so if firms provide an annual relocation allowance they are probably overpaying. Firms may be unable to attract quality people if no relocation allowance is provided at all, but providing a lump sum at the beginning and at the end of the assignment is probably all that is needed for cost-effectiveness.

Summary

Sending people on global assignments is costly, and the reward systems are complex. The critical issue, however, is the cost-effectiveness of global assignments and their associated reward systems. The overemphasis on monetary rewards has been partly responsible for problems of "rewarding *A* while hoping for *B*"—of rewarding maximization of monetary incentives while hoping for recognition of nonmonetary incentives. We have argued that good selection, training, adjustment, and repatriation policies can enhance the probability of effective performance during and after the global assignment, and it can be effective in promoting a focus on the nonmonetary rewards of a global assignment and increasing an individual's motivation to accept and do well in an assignment. A good reward system must contain monetary and nonmonetary rewards, however. Although many firms want to reduce total expatriate costs, we have argued that they should be concerned first with the cost-effectiveness of individual expatriates. We have proposed a three-step approach to expatriate compensation that is much more situation-independent than other basic approaches and that has the potential for substantial savings per expatriate. The number of globe-trotting expatriates may indeed be too high and should be reduced. Nevertheless, reductions, as well as the selection of expatriates in the future, must be considered in light of the strategic roles that these employees can play in the firm's global competitiveness.

Notes

1. Kerr, "On the Folly of Rewarding *A* While Hoping for *B*."
2. Organization Resources Counselors, *1990 Survey of International Personnel and Compensation Practices.*
3. Edstrom and Galbraith, "Transfer of Managers as a Coordination and Control Strategy in Multinational Organizations"; Ouchi, "A Conceptual Framework for the Design of Organizational Control Mechanisms"; Ouchi, "Markets, Bureaucracies, and Clans"; Ouchi, "The Relationship Between Organizational Structure and Organizational Control."
4. Black and Gregersen, "When Yankee Comes Home: Factors Related to Expatriate and Spouse Repatriation Adjustment."
5. Gregersen, Black, and Hite, "Expatriate Performance Appraisal: Principles, Practices and Challenges."
6. Gregersen and Black, "Global Executive Development: Keeping High Performers After International Assignments."

9

Repatriating: Helping People Readjust and Perform

Many expatriates and their families expect a hero's welcome after returning home from a successful global assignment,[1] but most are lucky to receive any welcome at all.[2] As the spouse of one American expatriate put it:

> If you look at repatriation as a "homecoming," you're setting yourself up for failure. My husband's company left him dangling in the wind, so to speak. I think that is wrong. He took a real demotion when we came home. No one in the company volunteered anything. He had to initiate everything. He fell through the cracks in the system . . . if indeed there was a repatriation system in this company. Why can't companies deal more efficiently and compassionately with employees returning from overseas assignments?

We interviewed one American expatriate who actually lost his "identity" during repatriation. Apparently, he did not exist on company records for up to three months after his return; he found out about the problem through a credit agency when he was denied two critical loans (house and car) because he was unemployed. While this case may seem atypical, our research and consulting have taught us quite the opposite. In fact, most expatriates returning home are functionally unemployed once the plane lands. They might be on their employers' records, but they do not have permanent positions in their firms.[3] In our research, we have found this situation to be the case for American, European, and Asian expatriates when they return home. Indeed, we have found that expatriates and families from many countries face significant challenges when returning home. A small sample of these challenges is captured in the following comments:

> Be mentally prepared for enormous change when coming home. Expect repatriation culture shock to surpass the culture shock you might have experienced when you went overseas.
>
> —*Expatriate returning from seven-year assignment in Indonesia*

Coming back home was more difficult than going abroad because you expect changes when going overseas. It was real culture shock during repatriation. I was an alien in my home country. My own attitudes had changed, so that it was difficult to understand my own old customs. Old friends had moved, had children, or just vanished. Others were interested in our experiences, but only sort of. They simply couldn't understand our experiences overseas, or they just envied our way of life.

> —*Expatriate spouse returning from three-year assignment in Vietnam*

Treat coming home as a "foreign assignment" and spend time getting the "lay of the land." Don't expect any special treatment—you're basically a "new hire." Look out for yourself, because no one else will. After being home for nine months, and after giving thirty-three years of my life to this company, I still have no office to work in—just a "bullpen" with a temporary assignment.

> —*Expatriate returning from one-year assignment in England*

Now that I'm home, it seems like my overseas assignment is a punishment, a real "ball and chain," in terms of my career.

> —*Expatriate with fourteen years of international experience*

To some top executives and line managers (especially those without international experience), these comments may seem a bit overstated, but our research on repatriations found that 60 percent of American, 80 percent of Japanese, and 71 percent of Finnish expatriates experienced some degree of culture shock during repatriation (see Exhibit 9.1). Our results are similar to those found in Nancy Adler's decade-old study of American expatriates, in which the culture shock of coming home was usually more difficult than the culture shock of going overseas.[4]

Unfortunately, most executives have little sympathy for repatriation problems. In fact, the home-office response often goes like this: "Culture shock coming home? What's the big deal? After all, they're coming **home**." The problem with this perspective is that it contains elements of both fact and fiction. Although expatriates are returning home, the degree and types of changes that returning expatriates face are significant. These changes may include contending

Exhibit 9.1
Repatriation Culture Shock

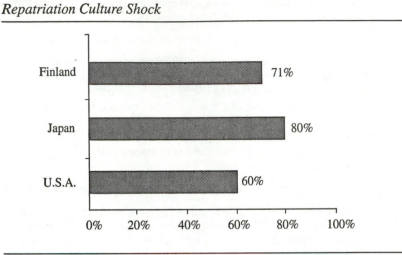

Note: This chart shows the percentage of managers who found repatriation adjustment more difficult than the original adjustment overseas.

with new political systems, transportation systems, social groups, eating habits, languages, and so on. Also neither the expatriates themselves nor their homes are the same after an international assignment of three to five years.

The Repatriation Process

Without a doubt, expatriates and home countries change throughout the duration of an international assignment. Some major components of these changes are outlined in Exhibit 9.2. Before an international assignment, expatriates have consciously and unconsciously acquired the mental maps and behavioral routines that work effectively for them in the home country. Furthermore, when expatriates embark on a global assignment, relatively few have previous work experience in the country of assignment, and even fewer receive any cross-cultural preparation or training.[5] Thus, they enter the new country with little prior knowledge of what to say and how to act in a foreign country. After living in a foreign country for several years, most expatriates acquire new mental maps and behavioral routines for how to act and what to say in the new familiar "foreign" culture.

As expatriates adjust and change overseas, many objective aspects of the home country simultaneously change. For example,

Exhibit 9.2
Components of Change

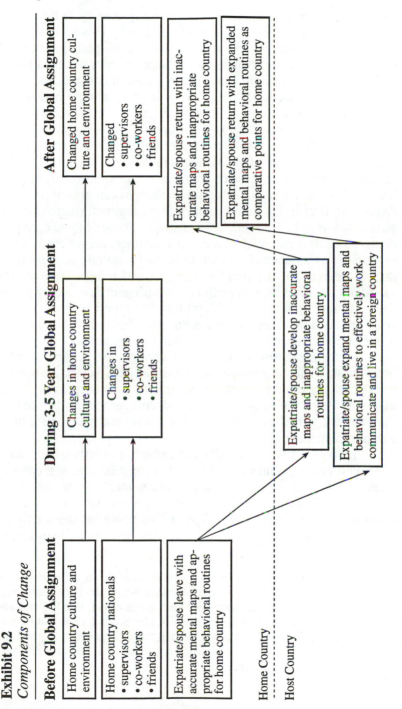

consider the economic cycles that occur in any country, or the sweeping political changes of the late 1980s and early 1990s. Besides the potentially dramatic changes at home, there are—perhaps more important—endless little changes in the home country during a global assignment. These changes can occur in a host of contexts, for example, previous home country neighborhoods (people move in and out), friendships (old friends get new friends), and schools (funding levels may shift, or teachers change). Accordingly, some expatriates advise repatriates to "treat repatriation as another foreign assignment. Returned managers rapidly feel like aliens in their native land. They also should not expect their home country to stay the same as they remembered it." Finally, dramatic and simple changes can also occur at the employing firm in the home country (e.g., restructurings, strategic shifts, managerial advancements, and so on). Some of these corporate changes and their potential impacts on adjustment are reflected in this expatriate's experience after working in the parent company for more than 18 years: "The division I worked for was reorganized, and the subsidiary I worked for was placed under stringent cost-cutting guidelines. My reentry was very cold, with little support in finding a job, since previous management had been fired. Instead of placement, I had strong feelings of displacement when coming home."

At the same time that objective changes are occurring in the home country and the parent company, expatriates' subjective perceptions of what used to be in the home country and company and what may still be in the home country and company can also change throughout a global assignment. There are several reasons for these changes in mental maps.

Individuals have difficulty remembering exactly what used to be in their home country, and if they do remember, these memories often tend to focus on the ideal aspects of home. This process could be called the **Dorothy Syndrome**, after Dorothy who lived in the land of Oz and felt that there was "no place like home" as she fondly recalled her life in Kansas. Reflecting on this perceptual distortion of the past, one spouse commented:

> All of the years that I lived overseas (largely in underdeveloped countries), I always thought that the U.S. was really better, more efficient, and so on, than anywhere else in the world. For 26 years and four global assignments, I carried this idea around. Now that I am finally back home, I am finding out that things in general are just as inefficient in the U.S. as in other countries. This has been a very difficult reality to accept.

Most expatriates work and live in foreign countries and cultures with different languages, attitudes, and behaviors for three to five years. If they have successfully integrated themselves into the foreign environment, they have undoubtedly changed in both attitude and behavior. For example, many American and European families find it uncomfortable to leave their shoes on whenever they go into someone else's home after assignments in the Pacific Rim. Other changes during global assignments are much more challenging. For example, Japanese men often gain a new sense of family, with stronger bonds to their wives and children, during global assignments, but these relationships are often lost when they return to Japan. Many Japanese expatriates become quite bitter and resentful toward their firms for "stealing" away their newfound roles of husband and father. Yet another Japanese example of change is reflected in the experience of one Japanese spouse we interviewed. She cried every day for six months after returning to Japan, and begged her husband to get transferred back overseas. During her husband's assignment in Britain, her social role as the wife of a vice president had given her the opportunity to interact, entertain, express opinions, and discuss world events. These activities were not accepted when she returned to Japan.

In addition to changes at home, changes occur in the workplace. For example, most expatriates find it difficult to unlearn the autonomy they had in their global assignments and to relearn the nuances of corporate bureaucracies.[6] One Japanese expatriate said, "When I first went overseas, I was scared to make decisions without a big group around me. Now that I'm back home, I've not only forgotten how to effectively manage consensus decision making, I'm not sure I even like it."

Another example of the influence of changed perspectives is captured quite well in one American expatriate's experience: "It is still difficult to deal with the attitude of American people at work: managers, clerks, sales people, and so on. I never realized the apathy that exists in our society until I lived and worked in Japan for three years." Indeed, the new reference points gained through global assignments often cause more negative than positive evaluations of the home country. For example, a Finnish manager returning home from Germany stated, "I became quite critical of my home country after having the opportunity to compare our way of living to the continental European way. People seem very materialistic, even though things are so terribly expensive in Finland."

When expatriates and families return home after three to five years abroad, their supervisors, co-workers, and friends have also changed but often incorrectly assume that the expatriates and their family members have not. One spouse returning to Finland after a six-year assignment described this dynamic well when she said, "Family and friends didn't want to admit that I had 'grown up' during the years in a foreign country." An American expatriate expressed similar sentiments: "Previous friends expected me to return unchanged and resume life *as if I had not left.*"

The changes in home countries and in individuals (expatriates overseas and friends and co-workers at home) over the course of a global assignment produce many of the same dynamics of cross-cultural adjustment that were discussed in Chapters 2 and 5—even though people are coming home. Specifically, people often return home from global assignments with incorrect mental maps of what to do, learned inabilities regarding how to do it, and uncertainties about what the results of their actions will be in the now "foreign" home country.

Repatriation Adjustment and the Bottom Line: Performance

In our work with multinational firms around the world, executives frequently ask, "Why should multinational firms pay attention to the adjustment of expatriates and their families during repatriation?" Our response, based on research and experience, is that failure to pay attention to repatriation adjustment can have a negative impact on the bottom line—in other words, reduced executive and managerial performance. Specifically, we found that when expatriates adjust effectively during repatriation, they are better performers.[7] Furthermore, when the family of an expatriate adjusts during repatriation, a positive "spillover" effect occurs in which the productive home situation spills over to work and increases an expatriate's effectiveness.[8] Spouses' repatriation adjustment to interaction and the general culture were significantly related to repatriates' work performance.[9] The realities of adjustment spillover and performance failure were emphasized in this American expatriate's experience: "My spouse has had a very difficult time coming home from Europe and living in the suburbs of America. She hates it. Her adjustment difficulty has made my life less than wonderful and my work performance less than excellent."

Dimensions of Repatriation Adjustment

To parallel cross-cultural adjustment during international assignments, we have identified three basic areas that expatriates and their families adjust to when returning home.[10] First, expatriates need to adjust to new jobs and work environments. Even though most expatriates have almost fifteen years of experience in a parent company, they still make comments such as, "Be prepared for corporate culture shock when you come home!" One expatriate with twelve years of experience in the parent company commented: "Our organizational culture was turned upside down. We now have a different strategic focus, different 'tools' to get the job done, and different buzz words to make it happen. I had to learn a whole new corporate 'language.'" Interestingly, work-related adjustment challenges during repatriation were one of the most frequently mentioned problems by expatriates.[11]

Second, expatriates and their families need to adjust to communicating with home-country co-workers and friends. After a global assignment, home-country people often seem more like foreigners. For example, Americans are well known for making small talk at the beginning of a conversation, while people from other cultures may find this mode of conversation insincere. After a Finn spends several years in America and learns small talk, he or she returns home to fellow Finns who react quite negatively to such "trivial" talk. Another common challenge of communicating with home-country people during repatriation is their general lack of interest in repatriates' international experiences. Finally, children of expatriates often encounter significant language difficulties during repatriation. This situation is especially true for younger children born during global assignments, who failed to learn the complexities of their home-country language, and for teenagers, who are very aware and self-conscious of their differences in terms of non-native accents, outdated knowledge of slang, and some loss of correct syntax and intonation. Communicating effectively with home-country people during repatriation is a challenge for expatriates, spouses, and children. Some of these difficulties are reflected in the following comment:

> After coming home, my daughter felt neither British nor American from a cultural standpoint. She went from being president of the school overseas to being a new face at home. Nine months after our return, she still feels quite "different" from the other students.

> —*Expatriate returning from fourth global assignment in nine years*

Third, expatriates and their families face the problem of readjusting to the general living environment (e.g., food, weather, housing, transportation, schools, and so on), even though they have usually lived in their home country for most of their lives. These adjustments to the general culture are often the most challenging. A majority of expatriates from America, Japan, and Europe experience significant general culture shock during repatriation.[12] The following comments describe some of the specific dilemmas of coming home:

> It was challenging to return home and find housing, locate stores, and make friends. Even though I'd lived in the same metropolitan area and country before, this was like moving into a new world, and I had to start from scratch. I never realized that in returning home I would not be *instantly* home.
>
> *—American spouse after six years in Europe*
>
> I was totally unprepared for the long, harsh, cold winters . . . even though I had grown up in Finland.
>
> *—Finnish expatriate after three years in Australia*
>
> I never realized how difficult and exhausting simply commuting to and from work is in Japan until now. I hate it.
>
> *—Japanese expatriate after five years in America*

Factors Influencing Repatriation Adjustment

Repatriation adjustment is a significant challenge for most expatriates and their families. Adjustments fall into three general categories: work, communicating with home-country co-workers and friends, and the general culture of the home country. Research on these aspects of adjustment has found that certain factors either facilitate or inhibit one or more aspects of repatriation adjustment. Exhibit 9.3 summarizes those factors that affect repatriation adjustment before individuals return home and those factors that influence adjustment after they return home. Furthermore, these factors are categorized into several groups, including important sources of information about changes in the home country and the parent company, and individual, job, organization, and nonwork factors that affect cross-cultural adjustment after returning home. We will discuss each of these factors and how they influence the adjustment of expatriates and their families during repatriation.

Exhibit 9.3
Balance Sheet

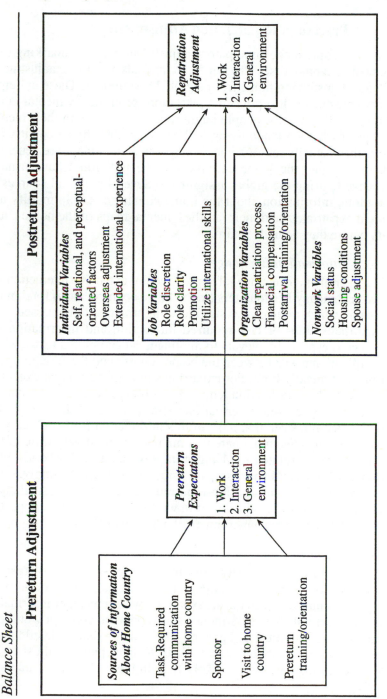

Prereturn Repatriation Adjustment

Just as people make anticipatory adjustment before embarking on a global assignment (see Chapter 5), individuals also make adjustments before transferring home from a global assignment. These anticipatory adjustments just prior to repatriation are primarily mental in nature. In other words, people begin to make changes in their mental maps of what work and living will be like in their home country *before* they actually return home. Changes in mental maps are generally helpful, since the home country and the individual have usually changed during the global assignment. Several potential sources of accurate information about the home country can help modify and mold expatriates' and their families' mental maps of the home country before they actually return.

Information Exchange

Managerial and executive jobs often require extensive interaction between company headquarters (in the home country) and a foreign operation, which often causes significant information to be passed on to expatriates. Job- or task-required interaction and information exchange is especially relevant to multinational and global firms, where coordination needs between the home country and the foreign operation are typically high. For expatriates in managerial and executive positions, the coordination requirements of a job may cause a reasonable level of accurate information to be passed on. It is important to remember, however, that most of this information is undoubtedly focused on changes in the parent company, and relatively little of this information is related to changes in previous neighborhoods, children's schools, and friendships outside of work. Accordingly, information acquired through job-required interaction is most likely to facilitate expatriates' adjustment to work but will have less impact on interaction or general environmental adjustment.[13]

Sponsors

Another source of primarily work-related information is an organization sponsor, mentor, or "godparent."[14] A formally or informally assigned mentor can provide an expatriate with important information about structural changes, strategic shifts, political coups at work, promotion opportunities, and general job- and company-related knowledge. This information is not likely to help people adjust to the general culture; it is more likely to help them effectively adjust to work and to communicating with home-country people during repatriation.[15] Without an effective sponsor during and after a global assignment, an expatriate can be caught in a dilemma like this one: "After spending nine years in Venezuela, fitting in is difficult if you have no ongoing contacts. There is tremendous insecurity, since no one knows you or cares, and you can easily get caught in the next job-reduction plan. Some reward for all the sacrifice of going abroad!" In this repatriate's case, an effective sponsor might have reduced some of the apparent problems encountered during repatriation. Even though sponsors can provide important adjustment-related information during global assignments and helpful support during repatriation, relatively few expatriates actually have designated sponsors throughout an assignment. In fact, our research found that only 22 percent of American, 22 percent of Japanese, and 51 percent of Finnish expatriates had sponsors while on foreign assignments.[16] This low occurrence is unfortunate because individuals with sponsors generally adjusted better at work than those without them.[17]

Home Leave

Still another important source of information about the home country and company is periodic visits to the home country during an international assignment.[18] Visits provide expatriates and families the opportunity to stay in touch with changes at work, among friends, and in the home country. Conversely, visits also allow co-workers and friends to observe changes in the expatriate. While 65 percent of the U.S. expatriates we studied received paid home leave for themselves and their families throughout the international assignment,[19] a study of approximately 250 American and Canadian multinational firms found that only 35 percent of expatriates and families are required to take their "home" leave at home.[20] As a result, the informational and relational benefits of home leaves are often not realized as expatriates use home-leave money for trips to more exotic places.

Repatriation Orientation

Prereturn training and orientation provided by the firm is another source of information.[21] In earlier chapters on training and overseas adjustment, we discussed the potential effectiveness of training and the range of approaches that firms can take to cross-cultural training (see Chapter 4). The same principles can apply to the repatriation process when people recross cultural boundaries and reenter their home country, which often feels quite foreign. Repatriates of various nationalities have emphasized the importance of such training. In fact, except for help in locating an appropriate job after a global assignment, training during repatriation was what expatriates most frequently wanted from multinational firms.[22] Training can facilitate adjustment not only at work but also in communicating with home-country people and in living in the new environment.

Given the importance of prereturn training and the research support for the use of such training, it is somewhat surprising that relatively few multinational firms provide training or orientation during repatriation. In fact, our studies found that 64 percent of American, 92 percent of Japanese, and 77 percent of Finnish expatriates received no training before returning to their home countries. Furthermore, approximately 90 percent of all spouses received no repatriation training.[23] After returning home, one spouse suggested that "a repatriation meeting should be provided to families, like the orientation meeting before going overseas, since many changes occur at home in three to five years." Without training, many expatriates and spouses inefficiently search for (and often do not find) accurate information about their home country during repatriation.

Postreturn Repatriation Adjustment

After expatriates return home, several factors can facilitate or inhibit their adjustment to work, to communicating, and to the general culture. These factors are grouped into individual, job, organizational, and nonwork categories.

Individual Factors

Many of the important individual factors relevant to effective cross-cultural adjustment were outlined in Chapters 3 and 5. These factors apply equally well to the repatriation adjustment process. Specifically, the self-oriented factors, relational-oriented factors, and perceptual-oriented factors have a positive impact on all facets of repatriation adjustment.

Ironically, successful overseas adjustment can ultimately result in more significant adjustment challenges during repatriation.[24] This scenario is especially true for expatriates and families who have completed assignments in cultures very different from the home country and who have stayed overseas for extended periods, either through sequential global assignments or unusually long stays in individual assignments. Essentially, the more people acquire the maps and rules of an overseas culture, the more difficult it is to revert back to the maps and rules relevant to the home country. One American expatriate with extensive international work experience found that "twenty-one years overseas was terribly hard to 'shake' after coming home." In many ways, the challenges of multiple global assignments or long global assignments result in feelings of being an "alien" in one's native country. Extensive international experience also makes it more difficult for expatriates and spouses to adjust to all aspects of the home country during repatriation.[25]

Job Factors

For expatriates, one of the most pivotal components of successful repatriation is the selection of a return job assignment.[26] Unfortunately, only 4.3 percent of North American multinational firms give more than six months' notice to expatriates of their return home; 30 percent received approximately three months' notice, and 64 percent received random notification, reflecting little planning for repatriation.[27] This relatively short-term return horizon is also reflected in the significantly negative job experiences of repatriates whom we studied:

> After being home three months, I am still waiting for a permanent office. All this after thirty years of experience in the company and three international assignments!
>
> *—American expatriate*

> My job description did not even exist when I came home. I felt as though I had no status in the company. In fact, everybody was saying, "Hey, what are you doing here?" It seemed like I was just a temporary "extra" for at least nine months.
>
> *—Expatriate with nine years of experience in the parent company*

> No one accepted responsibility for placing me back in the organization. I ended up without a job, when I was expecting a promotion! My wife also gave up her job with the same company to go overseas (she had twelve years of experience). We were promised a job for her upon our return. Again, no one has helped us find one.
>
> *—American expatriate with fifteen years of experience in the parent company*

Ill-planned Return Job. From these accounts, it is clear that the first step in effective adjustment at work is having a job. Nevertheless, approximately two-thirds of expatriates, regardless of nationality, do not even know what their assignments will be before they return.[28] Because return assignments were so infrequently planned, expatriates often referred to "holding pattern" return assignments, which resembled airplane holding patterns over congested airports when no runways are available. It should come as no surprise that when expatriates did get jobs after returning home, these positions were rarely optimal. In fact, they were frequently ill-defined, low-impact "make work" positions intended to keep the expatriates occupied and out of the way.

Reduced Job Autonomy.   When permanent positions are located, they often have reduced autonomy and authority in comparison to the positions expatriates held during their most recent overseas assignments.[29] Nearly half of all repatriate managers had less autonomy and authority at home,[30] as illustrated by these comments:

> When I was overseas, I felt I had an impact on the business. In the U.S., I felt as though the impact—if any—was minimal. When I came home, I was assigned to a newly created, undefined staff job, where I had no friends, no contacts, and no access to management. Firms need to realize that expatriates have developed independent decision-making skills, have become accustomed to having final authority, and are conditioned to having their business judgment given a lot of credibility by top management. In my new job, my business judgment is much less valued than when I was overseas. Until firms change, expatriates should expect the worst when coming home to avoid disappointment.

> The overall importance of providing repatriates with high-discretion jobs to positively influence repatriation adjustment cannot be overemphasized.[31]

Unclear Job Expectations.   Providing repatriates with clear job descriptions or high **role clarity** facilitates repatriation adjustment at work.[32] Undoubtedly, the first step in clarifying jobs for repatriates is finding them something better than "holding pattern" positions. Otherwise, temporary positions are guaranteed to be highly ambiguous, since they will be essentially "make work" assignments.

Promotion Disappointments.   Many expatriates took their global assignments hoping for promotion after successfully working overseas. Unfortunately, this romanticized myth of global assignments does not usually match the reality of repatriation. As one European expatriate with twenty years of international experience in eight assignments said, "When you go overseas, your firm absolutely forgets you in terms of promotions. In fact, my overseas assignment seems more like a punishment, in terms of my career." For Americans, the picture is not much brighter; "I went on my foreign assignment to the U.K. as a favor for the department. In return, I received nothing special for the ten months I spent away from my family and the hardship I put them through. I really expected a promotion after coming back home and did not receive it." In reality, only about one in ten American and Japanese expatriates receive a promotion over the position they held overseas, while the rate for Finnish expatriates is nearly three times as high.[33]

Demotion Surprises. To some extent, these low levels of promotion may reflect the significant restructuring and downsizing many multinational organizations have gone through. It is unlikely, however, that the high level of demotion for repatriates was matched in the managerial cohort at home. Specifically, upon repatriation, 77 percent of American, 43 percent of Japanese, and 54 percent of Finnish managers were demoted to lower-level positions than they had held overseas.[34]

Poor Skill Utilization. Expatriates often gain unique country knowledge, language proficiency, and international management skills during global assignments. In fact, one of the strategic purposes of overseas assignments is to develop these skills and knowledge in the executive and managerial ranks of a firm. After expatriates return, however, their skills are utilized inconsistently.[35] Less than half of returning managers reported that they have the opportunity to utilize international experience after repatriation. After making million-dollar investments to send, support, and bring home each expatriate, it is surprising that firms are willing to obtain such minimal returns on so many of those investments. Expatriates feel similarly, as these comments suggest:

> Firms must value international expertise . . . not only appreciate it but actually put it to good use. Don't let a corporate headquarter's environment destroy the lessons, "business savvy," negotiation skills, and foreign-language proficiencies that expatriates learned from the real world . . . a global marketplace.
>
> *—American expatriate*

> This company places little value on my international skills. In fact, I am now fluent in Japanese, but the company has shown no interest in placing me in a position to use my recently acquired language skills. What a waste!
>
> *—American expatriate*

I hope I will be able to use my knowledge about Europe in my company in the future, but now I don't feel as if this knowledge is appreciated.

—*Japanese expatriate*

Organizational Factors

The parent company's overall approach to the repatriation process and its provision of adequate financial compensation can have a significant impact on adjustment after expatriates return home.[36] Unfortunately, only a minority of firms pay systematic attention to clarifying the entire repatriation process.

Unclear Repatriation Process.   Most expatriates feel that their companies communicated a very unclear picture of the repatriation process.[37] In general, many expatriates in each country were uncertain and concerned about return positions, career progression, compensation equity, taxation assistance, and so on. This overall sense of uncertainty is reflected in this American expatriate's comment: "What was it like coming home? No clear direction in my job, no clear direction in my career, and no assistance during the return. You are on your own around here!" Undoubtedly, the overall ambiguity of the repatriation process within firms is largely a reflection of a nonstrategic approach to global assignments.

Financial Shock.   In addition to clarifying the repatriation process, firms need to pay special attention to financial compensation packages when expatriates return home. Because nonmonetary rewards received during repatriation are generally quite low (temporary job, demotion, and so on), repatriates pay particular attention to monetary rewards and to potential shifts in living standards after global assignments. Some of these financial dynamics are captured in the following remarks:

> The cost of everything—from housing to the basic necessities—was so much higher in New York that it was literally shocking, even though we expected it. Everything is so expensive in New York City. In Mexico and, before that, Brazil, my family and I lived quite well. After returning to the states, it was back to reality—purchases had to be budgeted, something we hadn't done in years.
>
> —*American expatriate*

When you are overseas, you receive many benefits, such as maybe a free car, or free gas, or a nicer home than you had back in your home country. You become accustomed to these benefits. Then when you return to your home country, things return to normal, and lots of these benefits you were accustomed to disappear. **It's like being Cinderella, and midnight has struck.**

—*American spouse*

For these two families, the balance sheet for expatriate compensation (see Chapter 8) is clearly out of balance. Apparently, they received many of the allowances available to expatriates during an international assignment, but these allowances are generally unavailable after the assignment. Much like drug addicts, expatriates and their families often experience financial "withdrawal" during repatriation. Roughly three-fourths of all expatriates, regardless of nationality, have to cope with significant decreases in standard of living after returning home.[38]

No Repatriation Training. Since many international firms do not pay systematic attention to repatriation compensation and fail to clarify the repatriation process, it is no surprise that very little training and orientation is provided to expatriates after they return home. The overall lack of company-provided training and orientation is well reflected in this American spouse's comment: "Give more information about the home country, and about all the things the company is willing to help with—no matter how small. Only one or two of the wives I know received any formal information about the company. Most of what we found out had to be dug up and passed on by work of mouth, from one to another. As a consequence, much of the information we received was too late to do most of us any good." Training and orientation after a global assignment can enhance repatriation adjustment.[39]

Nonwork Factors

Two primary nonwork factors influence repatriation adjustment: shifts in social status, and changes in housing conditions.[40]

Drop in Social Status. After coming home, expatriates and their families lose the formal status of being foreigners. In one repatriation study, 54 percent of American, 47 percent of Japanese, and 27 percent of Finnish expatriates and spouses experienced a significant drop in social status, while fewer than four percent of the expatriates in all three countries experienced an increase in social status relative to their status during the overseas assignment.[41] These statistics indicate that repatriated expatriates and spouses are less likely to be treated as guests of honor at social and recreational functions (dinners, receptions, and so on) or as "guests" in their neighborhoods, with other families and children interested in their language, culture, and country. As one spouse said, "The biggest surprise of coming home was that I simply didn't realize how specially we were being treated in all aspects of life during our international assignment."

During an overseas assignment, expatriates typically feel like big fish in a little pond. After coming home, they are little fish in a big pond. The demotion, loss of financial perquisites, and absorption into corporate headquarters that typically accompany repatriation can easily increase the sense of lowered social status. According to one American expatriate returning from a nine-year executive position in the United Kingdom, **"If you have been the orchestra conductor overseas, it is very difficult to accept a position as second fiddle when coming home."** In general, net losses in social status have a negative impact on all facets of repatriation adjustment.[42]

Housing Conditions. In addition to shifts in social status, changes in housing conditions can significantly influence repatriation adjustment for expatriates and their families. Specifically, appropriate housing was positively related to all three facets of expatriates' adjustment and to the general adjustment of spouses during repatriation to America.[43] Three major issues influenced perceptions of repatriation housing. First, if expatriates had rented their home-country house during the global assignment, they usually returned home to live in a hotel for two to 15 weeks to repair destruction caused by renters. For some, these costs were over $15,000 for repairs (after only two-year assignments), and relatively few firms compensate repatriates for these losses. Second, if repatriates sold their homes before global assignment, company policies and/or the challenges of living in hotels often led them to find suitable housing as soon as possible after repatriation. In some cases, firms forced expatriates out of the "expense" column by cutting off hotel allowances before housing loans had ever been approved. In other cases, the sheer hassle of hotel accommodations for an entire family led expatriates to make less-than-optimal housing purchases. Third, if repatriates had sold their home before the assignment, and housing prices had generally risen in their home country, but no house-purchase allowance was provided during repatriation (60 percent of North American multinational firms provide no such allowance), repatriates found housing to be a major challenge.[44]

Our research found that Japanese expatriates were most likely to experience a significant decline in housing conditions.[45] In fact, almost 70 percent of Japanese expatriates stated that their housing conditions were less than satisfactory during repatriation. (The Japanese face a somewhat unusual challenge in that their home-country housing is generally much smaller than overseas housing.)

Unique Aspects of Spouses' Repatriation Adjustment

Many of the predeparture and postarrival factors that we have discussed were relevant to expatriates and spouses alike during repatriation. However, some important and unique aspects of a spouse's repatriation are a function of the spouse's career before, during, and after the global assignment.

Spouse Career Challenges

Our repatriation study found that 55 percent of American spouses worked before, 12 percent worked during, and 30 percent worked after a global assignment. In the case of Finnish spouses, 72 percent worked before, 20 percent worked during, and 75 percent worked after a global assignment.[46] Collectively, these data suggest that many spouses make significant career sacrifices to go on global assignments, but many still seek employment afterward.

> The biggest challenge of coming home was going back to work again. Years without training and schooling resulted in a big career loss . . . not to mention the pension loss.
>
> —*Finnish spouse returning from three-year assignment in Saudi Arabia*

> My contacts and visits with work colleagues in the home country were very occasional during the international assignment, and the reestablishment of those contacts and my return to professional life have demanded even more effort than was required during expatriation.
>
> —*American spouse returning from four-year assignment in France*

In many situations, spouses have difficulty finding work immediately after global assignments. Sometimes these challenges are related to the loss of professional skills or political contacts. Other spouses are challenged in the job-finding process when potential employers wonder whether they will go on other global assignments in the near future. Still others struggle with establishing the home and helping children adjust, which leaves little time for the job search.

Given the potential difficulty of finding appropriate work after repatriation, it is unfortunate that very few multinational firms offer any job-finding assistance to spouses after the spouses have made significant career sacrifices to complete global assignments. More specifically, while 15 percent of repatriated spouses received job-finding assistance in Finland, only 2 percent received assistance from U.S. firms.[47]

Unique Challenges for Japanese Spouses

In contrast to the significant career-related challenges many American and European spouses face during repatriation, Japanese spouses (almost all women) face equally difficult but somewhat different circumstances when they return home. Before, during, and after international assignments, Japanese wives generally have three major roles: household manager, mother/educator, and neighborhood member.[48] The role of household manager is important to most Japanese spouses, who handle all financial matters (including investments). During repatriation, 54 percent of the problems described to us by Japanese spouses focused on the role of household manager.[49] These problems range from moving and family finances to housing and living conditions. Generally, Japanese spouses' repatriation adjustment problems stemmed from the difficulty of running a house back in Japan, because many things were better overseas.

The mother/educator role is probably the most important role for Japanese spouses. In Japanese society, the direction of much of one's adult life is a function of one's education. Because the government and major corporations offer lifetime employment primarily to the graduates of Japan's elite universities, much of grammar school, middle school, and high school is geared to doing well on college entrance exams. In fact, nearly all successful applicants to the country's top university have also spent several years attending after-school "cram" courses, called juku. The primary contact with schools and teachers, as well as the main motivator and coach at home, is the mother. The popular phrase in Japanese is kyoiku mamma, or "education mother." Because the educational system in Japan is so rigid, the problems that schoolchildren had upon returning to Japan had a significant impact on the Japanese spouses' adjustment. These challenges usually resulted in the wives making tremendous efforts upon repatriation to hasten their children's assimilation and learning, so that the children would not be permanently stigmatized as foreigners and evaluated as educationally impaired.[50]

The role of neighborhood member includes a Japanese spouse's membership in various social groups, not just the immediate neighborhood. Fundamentally, Japanese spouses gain much of their self-identity through the groups to which they belong and through their ability to belong. In Japan, such groups may include mothers who take their preschool children to the neighborhood park each day, local flower-arranging clubs, and so on. Overseas, the Japanese spouse usually experienced an entirely new set of roles and situations, such as accompanying their husbands to company dinners and events, hosting dinner parties in their homes, or attending dinner parties in the homes of their husbands' business associates. In Japan, wives are not involved in these business and social activities, even if they have been involved in them overseas. The sudden withdrawal from these roles is often frustrating and difficult, since many Japanese wives learn to enjoy these activities and gain a new sense of identity and self-esteem during overseas assignments.

The Impact of Spouse Adjustment

Most firms do little to support spouses during repatriation. Some executives may feel that firms should not intrude into the family lives of employees, but the reality is that the families were asked to accompany the expatriates, and the families face significant challenges after international assignments. Perhaps most importantly, our research shows that spouses' repatriation adjustment has a positive impact on employee repatriation adjustment at work. This transition is important because employee repatriation adjustment has a positive impact on overall performance.[51]

Steps Toward Successful Repatriation

Our discussion of repatriation adjustment has focused primarily on the multitude of challenges and dilemmas that firms face in bringing expatriates and their families back from international assignments. These challenges often leave repatriates and their families with the sense that firms do not care about their success as they "dangle in the wind" at work and at home. We now want to shift our focus to what firms can do to facilitate repatriation.

Define the Strategic Functions of Repatriation

The first step toward effective repatriation is an analysis of the strategic functions that expatriates can accomplish after they return home. Before the assignment, the firm should have defined one or more of the three primary purposes for sending a particular expatriate abroad:

executive development, coordination and control, and transfer of information and technology. If the strategic purpose of the international assignment was executive development, the return assignment should be a critical next step in the development of additional executive skills and knowledge. If the strategic purpose of the international assignment was coordination and control, the return assignment could utilize the expatriate's overseas contacts to continue effective coordination and control between headquarters and foreign operations now that more effective relationships have been established. If the strategic purpose of the international assignment was the transfer of information and technology, the firm should seriously consider what home-country units of the company would benefit most by receiving the information and technology from the repatriate. Unfortunately, corporate headquarters often underestimates what home-country units can learn from overseas operations, limiting the probability that effective information and technology transfer will occur.

Without a planned purpose of repatriation, the investment of more than one million dollars to send the expatriate overseas is likely to be completely squandered. Furthermore, without a strategic purpose for the return, there are few compelling reasons for the firm to pay significant and systematic attention to the multitude of problems the repatriate and the family face.

Establish a Repatriation Team

After a clear strategic purpose for the return has been defined, a team should be formed, consisting of a human resource department representative and the expatriate's sponsor. These individuals should initiate preparations for the return at least six months before actual repatriation. If possible, it is helpful for the human resource department representative to have had firsthand experience with expatriation and repatriation. This opinion was expressed by many expatriates:[52]

> It would have helped, at least, to have personnel with *some* understanding of the experience of repatriation. Most of these people have no appreciation of what needs to be done in coming home. Since we have lived internationally and moved back one time before, we knew what to expect and basically had to manage it ourselves.
>
> —*American expatriate*

> Have a human resources department that understands the trauma of repatriation. In the best-case scenario, the human resources department would be made up of former expatriates.
>
> —*Finnish expatriate*

Most people in the personnel department have not had any international experience. Consequently, they cannot understand the process. This is a big mistake.

—Japanese expatriate

The supervisor or the sponsor will play an important role on the repatriation team by becoming primarily responsible for locating the appropriate return position for the repatriate. For example, the medical system division of GE requires sponsors to play an active role in the repatriation process; sponsors are formally evaluated on the extent to which they effectively perform this function.

Target High-Risk Repatriates

Once the strategic purposes for a return assignment have been defined and the repatriation team is in place, it is critical to target resources on high-risk repatriation candidates, who are likely to have the most problems coming home. Two characteristics of expatriates (and spouses) place them in the high-risk group.[53] First, expatriates and spouses with extended international experience (either multiple assignments or long individual assignments) are likely to have the most difficult repatriation process. Second, expatriates and spouses who return from an international assignment in a country very different from their home country (for example, a German returning from China) will have a difficult adjustment process as well. These expatriates are most likely to have inaccurate perceptions of the home country and the home company because of their extended time overseas or their experiences in very different environments.

Manage Expectations with Accurate Information

Since the expatriate, the parent company, and the home country have all probably changed during the global assignment, numerous aspects of the expatriate's perceptions of home may be inaccurate. Therefore, firms must manage and mold expectations before individuals arrive home, so that expatriates will be more likely to have their expectations fulfilled and to adjust effectively to work and nonwork issues after coming home.[54] The relative importance of managing expectations during repatriation is portrayed well in this expatriate's experience:

I am Austrian by birth and lived in Germany until I was eighteen years old. Then I moved to the U.S., and my ties to Austria and Germany have remained strong all these years. When I had the opportunity to work in England and Germany for the last two years, I happily accepted the German part of the assignment. It seemed like going home. When I went back there, I took with me all my expectations about a country that I remembered mostly through holiday visits and through the eyes of my parents and relatives. In contrast, I had no opinion about England before going there—I just went. I went to England first and, much to my surprise, I loved it. I had no real problem adjusting, even though the differences from my life in the U.S. were great. Then came a Germany that I didn't recognize. I found the people very rigid and inflexible. I felt like a foreigner in a country where I had expected to feel very much at home. If I had trouble adjusting, it had nothing to do with the differences between the U.S. and Germany—I expected those. The differences that caused me the most difficulties were the ones between the Germany that I had lived in years ago and the Germany I was returning to.

Establish Home-Country Information Sources

Firms can use several mechanisms to mold the expectations of repatriates before they come home, including sponsors, prereturn training and orientation, home-country visits, and general home-country information.

Designate Sponsors. Throughout the global assignment, and especially just before return, sponsors can provide important information to expatriates. If an expatriate has not had a sponsor during the assignment, it is still important to assign one to make the coming-home process more effective. The information a sponsor provides will generally focus on company-related changes but may also include news concerning changes in the home country. Several spouses in our study suggested that firms consider "family sponsors," who would be in active contact with families of expatriates during and after international assignments. If this relationship were arranged, family sponsors could provide a significant amount of information about general changes in the home country.

Provide Training. Training and orientation can provide essential information about the entire repatriation process to expatriates and their families. As one expatriate said, "Don't just give expatriates a brochure and walk away." Expatriates need information about changes in their jobs, about how to interact with home-country people, and about changes in the general living environment. Job-related information could focus on structural and political changes in the firm, technological innovations, procedural changes, and so on. Communication-related training could focus on the differences in interaction styles between the country the expatriate is currently in and the home country. This training could also include warnings about the general lack of interest that people at home will have in the expatriate's international experiences. This lack of interest will be felt at work and outside of work. These things may seem simple, but they are significant to expatriates who return home expecting others to sit fascinated for hours as they recount their overseas adventures. Finally, training and orientation can be provided about housing, financial compensation changes, tax laws, school systems, price levels, and so on.

It is also important to provide spouses and other family members with information relevant to their return process. One spouse from Finland reinforced the importance of formally provided information. After spending eight years overseas in four different assignments, she stated, "In big companies, it seems so easy to forget that getting through training and orientation is important for the well-being of people when they are overseas *and* when they come home!"

One question that executives often ask us about repatriation training is, "Who will provide the training when expatriates do not return home in groups?" Clearly, it would be expensive and time-consuming to send trainers to all parts of the world to provide custom repatriation-training programs. If groups of expatriates come home from concentrated areas, this strategy might work. For many firms, however, individuals return from global assignments at different times. To cope with this problem, one of our client firms in high technology is developing a video-based training system that can be sent to expatriates and their families before they return home. This video will provide company-specific information, as well as general information relevant to repatriation. In another case, we formed a consortium of noncompeting firms and pooled their repatriates for a one-day repatriation program that was offered at regular intervals throughout the year.

Encourage Home Leave. Along with sponsors and training, visits to the home country throughout the global assignment, and especially just before return, provide expatriates and spouses with opportunities to develop more accurate expectations. As we mentioned earlier, two-thirds of the expatriates we studied received paid home leave from their companies, but only one-third of companies required expatriates to take home leave in the home country. This issue is important, since requiring home leave to be taken at home can benefit firms by providing expatriates and their families the opportunity to acquire information about home during the global assignment.

Provide Access to Newspapers/Magazines.   Another important source of information about the home country is home-country newspapers and magazines. As one spouse from Finland suggested, "When you know you are going back, you should make time to read newspapers and magazines from home. Then you have a much better idea of what is happening." Newspapers and magazines can be expensive, but there are creative ways to use them. Some firms send only Sunday editions of a major home-country newspaper. Others send only weekly or monthly magazines, while others provide single copies to groups of expatriates in the same office (one problem with the latter approach is that the newspapers and magazines are unlikely to make it home for spouses and children to get updates on home-country changes). Regardless of the method, the purpose is to provide information about the home country so expatriates and spouses can develop accurate expectations.

Preparing the Home-Country Job Environment

To avoid many of the problems associated with repatriation, the repatriation team, in consultation with the expatriate, needs to explore the expatriate's career path and options after repatriation. Ideally, the return job will provide the repatriate an opportunity to accomplish one of three strategic objectives for global assignments; otherwise, firms can expect a low return on the investment in people sent abroad and brought home. The return job should also contain some element of challenge, with a reasonable level of autonomy. Most executives or managers want these attributes in their work, but repatriates are especially attuned to them after working overseas in very responsible positions with high levels of autonomy. In addition to creating challenging jobs, with discretion to make things happen, it is important to assess the match between what the employee learned in the global assignment and how those skills can be utilized after the return home. As one returning expatriate suggested, "Expatriate employees who were successful in various worldwide assignments have considerable and varied insight into conducting business. Firms should treat such insight and perspective as an asset, rather than discarding, wasting, and hindering such contributions." We concur with this position, as does our research. When an appropriate skill match occurs, the employee is much more likely to adjust well to the return job. As an excellent example of this process, consider the following executive's experience after returning to Ford: "After coming home, I took a position that gave me the opportunity to use what I learned while working at Mazda in Japan for the last three years. The new job is terrific. Overall, coming home has been easy, since I returned to an area that deals specifically with international activities. In my new group, it is critical to know how Mazda works, and I have that knowledge." In this situation, the job appears to be challenging and utilizes specific skills that the expatriate acquired overseas. More important to the firm, however, the return assignment seems to have accomplished a critical strategic objective—information transfer. Knowledge gained by this Ford expatriate was effectively utilized by the parent company after the global assignment.

In some firms and other industries, it may not be possible to provide expatriates with ideal jobs when they come home, because of downsizing, restructuring, and so on. It is better to communicate the situation to employees clearly and early rather than leaving them in the dark overseas. One expatriate from a large U.S. energy firm described this "mushroom-growing" approach to return assignments: "Why can't firms provide at least some information about the progress, or lack of it, in finding a new assignment while expatriates are waiting to come home? Correspondence I sent home from Jakarta during the last three months of my stay was never answered. Being in the dark for months is very hard when you know you are going to repatriate!" Basically, if expatriates should not expect a good job when they return, they should be told before they return. Otherwise, they come home with inflated, inaccurate expectations that cause adjustment problems.[55]

After an appropriate job is selected, the firm should consider the backgrounds of the repatriate's future supervisor and co-workers. These people often have little or no international experience, and have difficulty understanding and working around someone who is experiencing the challenges of repatriation. In our repatriation study, for example, we found that very few American repatriates (29 percent) had supervisors with any international experience.[56] Generally, supervisors with no previous international experience can be expected to have little understanding of or empathy for the challenges of repatriation. In some cases, supervisors and co-workers have actually inhibited the adjustment process. An American expatriate confided, "When I came home, co-workers were very jealous of my assignment, even though my responsibilities were vastly decreased in comparison to my recent overseas position." In Finland or Sweden, co-workers and supervisors may be less jealous of the assignment but more jealous of the repatriate's new tax-free automobile and previous tax-free earnings, since cars and earnings are heavily taxed in Scandinavia. Taking a different perspective, one American expatriate returning to a firm in the U.S. transportation industry said, "I was shocked at the animosity of co-workers because I had learned to work successfully with the Japanese during my international assignment." After experiences like this, repatriates learn to keep their mouths shut about their international expertise.

Home-country co-workers or supervisors can frustrate the strategic purposes of a global assignment and return position, as happened in this American expatriate's case: "There was a lack of knowledge of and interest in what is happening in the world outside this company. No one really cared what I had done or learned overseas. It seemed like everything had to be 'homegrown' in the U.S.A. or in the parent company." To avoid these potentially significant problems, we would suggest that firms provide training and orientation not only to expatriates before they come home but also to co-workers and supervisors, in order for them to be understanding and supportive of the repatriation process.

Developing Appropriate Compensation

Most expatriates experience a significant decrease in compensation after returning from a global assignment. This decrease often reflects the "rewarding A while hoping for B" approach to compensation throughout the international assignment cycle. During global assignments, firms often reward expatriates with significant benefits and allowances to encourage them to successfully complete the postings. At the same time, this focus on monetary rewards as incentives often sets firms and expatriates up for failure during repatriation, since most expatriates suffer significant financial losses upon returning. While it is easy to justify increased financial support for an expatriate in a faraway land, compensation specialists can more easily gauge financial need when the expatriate returns. Perhaps most importantly, firms often cannot see the need for extra compensation or assistance during a repatriation transition, since coming home is certainly not seen as a hardship worthy of perks.

In this awkward situation, the firm must still pay attention to the compensation of expatriates; otherwise, repatriates will either be less adjusted to work and to home after repatriation or will leave the firm and go to work where they feel that their international expertise is valued. A first step in the development of a repatriation compensation package is to compare the repatriate to cohorts of employees who stayed home and assess potential inequities. Without such comparison, problems can occur, as this American expatriate found out: "During the international assignment, I went through hell getting any recognition for my performance from my direct supervisor stationed back home. After returning to the U.S., my salary, which was not adjusted for the two years I was gone, was terrible. When I got back, I had to work my tail off to regain parity. Now the job is done, and life goes on." To address these types of repatriation problems and other financial dilemmas that may present themselves throughout global assignments, firms should attempt to follow the three-step approach to expatriate compensation outlined in Chapter 8.

Facilitating Adequate Housing

Locating and acquiring adequate housing is a major challenge for many repatriates and has a major impact on spouses' adjustment after coming home. Some repatriates have had positive experiences:

> Coming back to our own home really helped. We had a place to identify with, and friends and neighbors who cared about us. It also helped being in the same school upon return, since we were in contact with teachers during the assignment, and they remembered us.
>
> —*American spouse*

> It is critical to keep your previous flat in your home country, especially when teenage friends and social contacts are so important. It was terrific to have the children return to their own school and neighborhood.
>
> —*Finnish spouse*

As recommended in Chapter 8, the best-case scenario for repatriation would be one of continuity for the expatriate, the spouse, and the children. One challenge for those expatriates who rent their homes is to repair the damage that may have been caused by tenants. Firms need to consider temporary housing, financing, and the time required to make repairs, which may be major.

People who have not kept their homes during global assignments will need assistance in locating, purchasing, and moving into new homes. House-hunting trips during the last few months of a global assignment would be helpful. If the house-selection process must occur after the expatriate returns home, the firm needs to provide adequate time for the expatriate and the spouse to make a sound decision.

Providing Support Groups

In our research, repatriates and spouses often suggested that firms should consider providing informal opportunities to meet and socialize with other repatriates and their families.[57] This enviroment would provide an opportunity to share international experiences; as one spouse said, "Support groups could help us answer the many questions a returning family has. A great many changes occur during the global assignment, and searching for the answers alone can be most frustrating and cause needless tension in the family unit." For a firm, this endeavor is relatively cost-free and may provide important benefits.

Planning for "Downtime"

The challenges of coming home to new work and home routines often require significant amounts of time, but many expatriates, like these Americans, fly home one day and go back to work the next:

> Arrived home on Saturday. Started work at 150 percent on Monday. I have worked constant seventy-hour weeks since.

> I arrived home on Tuesday and started work on Wednesday and have been working ten- to twelve-hour days since. I haven't adjusted yet to much of anything and really feel depressed.

> I worked fourteen-hour days, six days a week. There was little time to look for housing, yet the company still pressured me to move out of a hotel, in order to get me off the "expense" status.

Many European expatriates suggested taking the traditional vacation of three to four weeks upon return, to get things in order. American expatriates recommended two weeks at the most, and some suggested that firms should force repatriates to take time off. Regardless of the amount of time, the important thing is that firms should allow repatriates some time to make the transition.

Appreciating Contributions to the Firm

A final aspect of repatriation adjustment focuses on appreciation. Several of the expatriates, especially spouses, told us how much it would mean to them if firms would appreciate them for the job they have done or show a little more interest in families coming home. One spouse from Finland said, "Why can't companies take a moment to say 'thank you' to the wife and children for the sacrifices they made to uproot, go overseas, and come back home?" We agree.

End with the Beginning in Mind

As the last step in a global assignment, effective repatriation provides positive feedback to the next generation of expatriates. When repatriates' co-workers are offered global assignments, they may say what this Ford expatriate said: "You want to know what some of the difficulties were coming home? Were we supposed to have difficulties? Things went very well!" How had Ford treated this expatriate and his family after the three-year assignment in Japan? Ford provided three hours of general and culture-related training, which was seen as valuable. The company provided a job with clear work expectations and moderate levels of responsibility, as well as an excellent financial package (at least from the expatriate's perspective). The individual returned to his previous work unit (from before the global assignment), with co-workers and supervisors who placed a high value on his global experience. Finally, he had developed accurate expectations about coming home.

The bottom line is that inattention to the difficulties of repatriation hurts employees' performance and corporate performance. By contrast, small and often relatively inexpensive steps can lead to significant returns on investment and enhanced competitive position in a global marketplace.

Notes

1. Oslund, "The Overseas Experience of Expatriate Business People."
2. Black and Gregersen, "When Yankee Comes Home: Factors Related to Expatriate and Spouse Repatriation Adjustment"; Napier and Peterson, "Expatriate Re-entry: What Do Repatriates Have to Say?"; Harvey, "Repatriation of Corporate Executives: An Empirical Study"; Clague and Krupp, "International Personnel: The Repatriation Problem"; Oddou and Mendenhall, "Succession Planning for the 21st Century: How Well Are We Grooming Our Future Business Leaders?"; Gomez-Mejia and Balkin, "The Determinants of Managerial Satisfaction with the Expatriation and Repatriation Process"; Adler, "Re-entry: Managing Cross-Cultural Transitions."
3. Napier and Peterson, "Expatriate Re-entry"; Black and Gregersen, "When Yankee Comes Home."
4. Black and Gregersen, "When Yankee Comes Home"; Black and Gregersen, "O Kaerinasai: Factors Related to Japanese Repatriation Adjustment"; Gregersen, "Coming Home to the Cold: Finnish Repatriation Adjustment"; Adler, "Re-entry"; Adler, *International Dimensions of Organizational Behavior.*
5. Black and Gregersen, "When Yankee Comes Home"; Gregersen, "Commitments to a Parent Company and a Local Work Unit During Repatriation"; Gregersen and Black, "Antecedents to Commitment to a Parent Company and a Foreign Operation"; Black and Gregersen, "Antecedents to Cross-Cultural Adjustment for Expatriates in Pacific Rim Assignments"; Black, "A Tale of Three Countries."

6. Black and Gregersen, "When Yankee Comes Home"; Black, "A Tale of Three Countries"; Oddou and Mendenhall, "Succession Planning for the 21st Century"; Clague and Krupp, "International Personnel"; Adler, "Re-entry."

7. Gregersen and Black "Global Executive Development: Keeping High Performers After International Assignments"; Black and Gregersen, "Functional and Dysfunctional Turnover After International Assignments."

8. Black and Stephens, "Expatriate Adjustment and Intent to Stay in Pacific Rim Overseas Assignments"; De Cieri, Dowling, and Taylor, "The Psychological Impact of Expatriate Relocation on Spouses"; Black and Gregersen, "When Yankee Comes Home"; Black and Gregersen, "The Other Half of the Picture: Antecedents of Spouse Cross-Cultural Adjustment."

9. Black and Gregersen, "When Yankee Comes Home"; Black and Gregersen, "O Kaerinasai: Factors Related to Japanese Repatriation Adjustment"; Gregersen, "Coming Home to the Cold: Finnish Repatriation Adjustment."

10. Black, Gregersen, and Mendenhall, "Toward a Theoretical Framework of Repatriation Adjustment"; Clague and Krupp, "International Personnel"; Adler, "Re-entry."

11. Black, "A Tale of Three Countries."

12. Black, Gregersen, and Mendenhall, "Toward a Theoretical Framework of Repatriation Adjustment"; Boyacigiller, "The Role of Expatriates in the Management of Interdependence, Complexity, and Risk in Multinational Corporations."

13. Black, Gregersen, and Mendenhall, "Toward a Theoretical Framework of Repatriation Adjustment"; Harvey, "Repatriation of Corporate Executives"; Harvey, "The Other Side of Foreign Assignments"; Oddou and Mendenhall, "Succession Planning for the 21st Century."

14. Black, Gregersen, and Mendenhall, "Toward a Theoretical Framework of Repatriation Adjustment."

15. Black, "A Tale of Three Countries."

16. Black, "A Tale of Three Countries."

17. Black, Gregersen, and Mendenhall, "Toward a Theoretical Framework of Repatriation Adjustment."

18. Black and Gregersen, "Antecedents to Cross-Cultural Adjustment."

19. Organization Resources Counselors, 1990 Survey of International Personnel and Compensation Practices.

20. Black, Gregersen, and Mendenhall, "Toward a Theoretical Framework of Repatriation Adjustment"; Black and Mendenhall, "Cross-Cultural Training Effectiveness: A Review and Theoretical Framework for Future Research."

21. Black, "A Tale of Three Countries"; Gregersen and Black, "Antecedents to Commitment to a Parent Company and a Foreign Operation"; Black, Gregersen, and Mendenhall, "Toward a Theoretical Framework of Repatriation Adjustment."

22. Black, "A Tale of Three Countries."

23. Gregersen and Black, "Antecedents to Commitment to a Parent Company and a Foreign Operation."

24. Black and Gregersen, "When Yankee Comes Home."

25. Black and Gregersen, "When Yankee Comes Home"; Black and Gregersen, "O Kaerinasai"; Gregersen, "Coming Home to the Cold"; Black, "A Tale of Three Countries"; Oddou and Mendenhall, "Succession Planning for the 21st Century."

26. Organization Resources Counselors, 1990 Survey of International Personnel and Compensation Practices.

27. Black, "A Tale of Three Countries."

28. Black and Gregersen, "When Yankee Comes Home"; Clague and Krupp, "International Personnel"; Oddou and Mendenhall, "Succession Planning for the 21st

Century"; Adler, "Re-entry"; Black, Gregersen, and Mendenhall, "Toward a Theoretical Framework of Repatriation Adjustment."

29. Black, "A Tale of Three Countries"; Oddou and Mendenhall, "Succession Planning for the 21st Century."

30. Black and Gregersen, "When Yankee Comes Home"; Black and Gregersen, "O Kaerinasai"; Gregersen, "Coming Home to the Cold."

31. Black and Gregersen, "When Yankee Comes Home"; Gregersen, "Coming Home to the Cold."

32. Black, "A Tale of Three Countries."

33. Black, "A Tale of Three Countries."

34. Black and Gregersen, "When Yankee Comes Home"; Clague and Krupp, "International Personnel"; Gomez-Mejia and Balkin, "The Determinants of Managerial Satisfaction"; Black, "A Tale of Three Countries."

35. Black, "A Tale of Three Countries"; Clague and Krupp, "International Personnel"; Oddou and Mendenhall, "Succession Planning for the 21st Century"; Adler, "Re-entry."

36. Black, "A Tale of Three Countries."

37. Black, "A Tale of Three Countries."

38. Black and Gregersen, "When Yankee Comes Home"; Black and Gregersen, "O Kaerinasai"; Gregersen, "Coming Home to the Cold."

39. Black, "Coming Home: The Relationship of Expatriate Expectations with Repatriation Adjustment and Job Performance"; Black, Gregersen and Mendenhall, "Toward a Theoretical Framework of Repatriation Adjustment"; Black, "The role of expectations during repatriation for Japanese managers"; Black, "O Kaerinasai: Factors Related to Japanese Repatriation Adjustment"; Gregersen and Black, "Global Executive Development: Keeping High Performers After International Assignments."

40. Black, "A Tale of Three Countries."

41. Black and Gregersen, "When Yankee Comes Home"; Black and Gregersen, "O Kaerinasai."

42. Black and Gregersen, "When Yankee Comes Home."

43. Organization Resources Counselors, 1990 Survey of International Personnel and Compensation Practices.

44. Black, "A Tale of Three Countries."

45. Black, "A Tale of Three Countries."

46. Black, "A Tale of Three Countries."

47. Black, "The Other Side of the Picture on the Other Side of the World: Repatriation Problems of Japanese Expatriate Spouses"; Nakane, Japanese Society.

48. Black, "The Other Side of the Picture on the Other Side of the World."

49. White, *The Japanese Overseas.*

50. Black and Gregersen, "When Yankee Comes Home"; Black and Gregersen, "Functional and Dysfunctional Turnover."

51. Black, "A Tale of Three Countries."

52. Black and Gregersen, "When Yankee Comes Home."

53. Black, "Coming Home: The Relationship of Expatriate Expectations with Repatriation Adjustment and Job Performance."

54. Black, "Coming Home."

55. Black, "A Tale of Three Countries."

56. Black, "A Tale of Three Countries."

57. Black, "A Tale of Three Countries."

10

Retaining: Utilizing the Experienced Global Manager

Consider this account from a high-performing expatriate with seven years of international experience in two assignments, and 16 years of experience with his former employer:

> After coming home, I was an "outsider" in my colleagues' eyes. The salary was lousy—a 6 percent increase after four years overseas—and they never found a "suitable" job for me. When they did locate a job, five months after I had come home, I informed them that I was leaving the firm to take a position with a 55-percent salary increase as a technical consultant in a smaller company. After making the jump, I have used my technical skills, language skills (I learned Arabic on an earlier assignment in Saudi Arabia), and negotiation skills to benefit a competitor of my former employer. What a waste of resources!

In Chapter 9, we discussed in detail the dynamics of adjustment and the factors that affect different aspects of adjustment for expatriates and spouses from several areas of the world. We also outlined many ways in which firms can greatly facilitate repatriation adjustment and, in turn, increase job performance after global assignments. In this chapter, we shift our focus to the dynamics of organizational commitment and the various factors that can affect commitment during repatriation. Organizational commitment is critical to keeping high-performing repatriates in the firm after global assignments.[1]

Keeping the Best Global Managers as Strategic Assets

If a multinational firm had invested between $2 million and $4 million in a piece of critical production equipment over the past three years, it would be hard to imagine the production manager not taking serious action if the equipment were headed out the door to a competitor's production facility; yet each year, executive and managerial "assets" (in whom firms have invested literally millions of dollars) walk out the company door after returning home from global assignments. In one of our studies of American repatriates, for example, we found that 42 percent had seriously thought of leaving their firms since returning home, 74 percent did not expect to be working for the same company one year hence, and 79 percent felt that the demand for their international skills was high and that they could find good jobs in other firms. Moreover, 26 percent of the American repatriates had been actively looking for alternate employment after coming home.[2] More specifically, we have worked with some American and European multinationals that lost between 40 and 55 percent of their repatriates through voluntary turnover.

Even if repatriates stay in their parent firms after coming home, most feel their market knowledge, technical skills, foreign-language ability, and so on are underutilized (see Chapter 9). These sobering realities have pushed leading multinational firms to consider some strategic human resources management questions:

- Are we receiving an adequate return on our investment after bringing expatriates home from expensive global assignments?
- Are we retaining the best global managers and utilizing their unique skills after repatriation?

If the answer to these questions is no, then valuable investments are being wasted as repatriates either go to work for competitors or stay in the company but perform below their potential.

We have found that four general patterns of repatriate behavior, which may or may not benefit the strategic objectives of the firm, occur during the repatriation process.[3] These patterns are shown in Exhibit 10.1. Ideally, multinational firms want repatriates to be in quadrant 1 after returning home. Essentially, *functional retention* occurs when repatriates are high performers and when they stay in the firm. Two primary factors are associated with functional retention: 1) high repatriation adjustment and 2) high commitment, or loyalty, to the parent company. As discussed in Chapter 9, high repatriation adjustment leads to high job performance. Furthermore, high commitment to the organization after repatriation leads to high intentions to stay with the firm.

Organizational Commitment

	High	*Low*
High	**Functional Retention** High performance High intent to stay	**Dysfunctional Turnover** High performance Low intent to stay
Low	**Dysfunctional Retention** Low performance High intent to stay	**Functional Turnover** Low performance Low intent to stay

Repatriation Adjustment (row label spanning High/Low)

Exhibit 10.1
Repatriation Outcomes

Functional Retention

Firms want to achieve "functional retention" for very strategic reasons. For example, if expatriates went overseas to develop an international perspective and to bring it back to headquarters, this strategic function can by accomplished only by keeping the "best." As we have pointed out in several different places throughout this book, our research shows that international assignments are the most powerful means of developing future global leaders. Those managers who performed well overseas and are doing well upon their return have the highest potential of being global leaders in the future. Unfortunately for many firms, the percentage of managers falling into the functional retention category is far too small.

Dysfunctional Turnover

More unfortunately still, the percentage of managers falling into the dysfunctional turnover category is far too large in many firms. Few firms can afford to have a large percentage of their high performers leave within a short time after repatriation, yet this is often the case. This situation happens when repatriates adjust well to work, to interacting with home-country people, and to the general home-country environment but do not show a strong commitment to the parent company. When high performers leave, firms usually incur a significant loss of resources, including firm-specific experience, global perspectives, international skills, and so on. As one American expatriate told us after returning from a two-year assignment in France, "Firms should be using their international managers as assets to grow and expand, instead of giving them away to competitors."

Firms not only lose their investment when high-performing repatriates quit, but they also lose the chance to accomplish the strategic objectives of a global assignment. For example, an American expatriate may have been sent to a Japanese subsidiary to acquire important market information and technology innovations, but this information and technology cannot be transferred if the expatriate quits after coming home.

Functional Turnover

Losing a manager after an international assignment is not always bad. *Functional turnover* can actually benefit a firm, since these repatriates fail to adjust and perform well after coming home; they exhibit low commitment to the firm and leave. Since it is impossible to be 100 percent correct in selecting managers for international assignments, some turnover by low performers after the assignment is likely and would be fine. If a large portion of repatriates falls into this category, serious corrective action is needed at the front end of the cycle, probably in the selection process and decision. High functional turnover is a clear sign that the wrong people are being sent.

Dysfunctional Retention

Dysfunctional retention, the retention of repatriates who are low performers but stay with the firm, is also not desirable for a firm. These repatriates generally have high loyalty to the parent company but fail to adjust effectively to the new work, social, and general environments after returning home. This pattern can occur when 1) the wrong people are sent on assignment, 2) they are not properly trained and perform poorly, and 3) they have no other job prospects upon repatriation. If most of a firm's returning managers fall into this category, serious intervention is needed before international operations get a reputation as where the "has beens" or "never will bes" get dumped.

Factors That Affect Organizational Commitment During Repatriation

For firms to get the best of both worlds—repatriates who exhibit high performance and *stay* with the parent company (functional retention)—they must attend to two critical processes: repatriation adjustment and organizational commitment. Let's first take a look at the factors that affect organizational commitment after repatriation.

The first step toward sustaining a sufficient level of expatriate commitment during repatriation is monitoring commitment patterns *during* global assignments, *before* expatriates return home.[4] In Chapter 6, we discussed how expatriates can become committed not only to a parent company (which sent them out on a global assignment) but also to a foreign operation during the assignment. In addition, we presented some of the specific factors that could help a firm develop and sustain commitment throughout a global assignment. For example, expatriates with several years of experience in the parent firm, and who had clearly defined but fairly autonomous jobs overseas were more committed during global assignments. When expatriates return, firms need to either redevelop or sustain repatriates' overall commitment to the organization.[5] The specific factors that influence this critical commitment to the parent firm are somewhat different from those that played an important role in expatriate loyalty during the global assignment. We have identified four general categories of factors that increase or decrease an expatriate's level of commitment during repatriation: individual, job, organizational, and nonwork factors, and displayed them in Exhibit 10.2.

Individual Factors

In one sense, the company may not be able to control individual factors, but being aware of their impact allows for better planning and anticipation of which managers might have more difficulty or ease in adjusting during repatriation and which ones might have higher or lower loyalty to the company and intent to stay after repatriation.

Tenure in the Parent Company. Average expatriates have significant experience in the parent firm when they embark on global assignments. Most of the hundreds of managers we studied had at least 12 years of experience in the parent company.[6] This significant investment of time and energy in a particular company helps bind the expatriate to the firm. Accordingly, high levels of tenure in an organi-

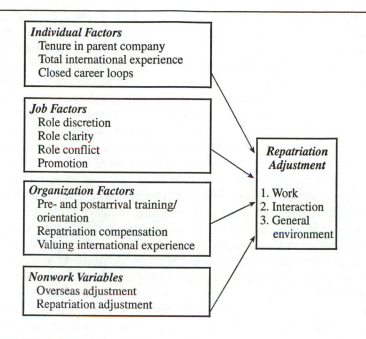

Exhibit 10.2
Basic Framework of Organizational Commitment During Repatriation

zation are generally associated with high levels of commitment to an organization.[7] During global assignments, high tenure was related to higher commitment to the parent company. During repatriation, we found that tenure in the parent company was also an important factor in sustaining American managers' commitment to the parent company.[8] In the case of Japanese and Finnish expatriates returning home, however, tenure in the parent company was unrelated to loyalty.[9] The insignificant impact of tenure on commitment for Japanese or Finnish expatriates may be partly a result of the comparatively low job mobility across companies in both countries.

  Total International Experience. Another important individual factor relevant to commitment during repatriation is the total amount of time expatriates have worked outside their home country.[10] How much international experience do expatriates have? This question is important because those expatriates with the highest levels of international experience (i.e., career expatriates) have usually made significant investments in their international careers. Because many firms fail to utilize managers' international experience after repatriation, some expatriates capitalize on their international expertise by staying out of the home country and continuing to utilize their international skills and knowledge in foreign assignments. In addition, the investment expatriates make in developing a valuable set of international skills often reflects their relative level of *disinvestment* in their home country. In fact, expatriates with extensive international experience can develop an aversion, almost an "allergic" reaction, to their home country and to socializing with home-country nationals. As one American career expatriate in the banking industry explained, "There is little value placed on international experience within my company. Home nationals tend to think that the U.S. is so different that anything learned overseas is largely irrelevant to the domestic U.S. market." In Japan, career expatriates expressed similar sentiments: "When you come home, no one appreciates your international experience as much as you do, or as much as the people you worked with overseas do. In fact, overseas, the mere reality of it, does not even exist for most 'domestic' employees in this company. My suggestion for international firms? They could at least brief or work with the people at home who have never been overseas and help them to appreciate an international perspective a bit more." Reflecting these types of problem, our research has found that American expatriates with high levels of international work experience are generally less committed to the parent company after returning home. In contrast, Finnish expatriates with high levels of international experience were actually *more* committed to the parent firm.[11] This relationship may result from the newness of international activity for Finnish firms as compared to American multinationals and from the importance Finnish firms place on international experience.

Movement Pattern. A final individual factor that can play an important role in sustaining commitment to the parent company during repatriation is the pattern of assignment before, during, and after an international posting.[12] Some expatriates refer to these patterns as *career loops.* In a closed career loop, expatriates work in the same division of a firm before, during, and after a global assignment. In an open career loop, divisional continuity is broken as expatriates are shifted from one division to the next throughout their global assignments. In our research, between 30 and 40 percent of expatriates from the United States, Japan, and Europe experience closed career loops throughout their international assignments.[13] It is important to create closed career loops because expatriates can more easily identify with the work units and the people who are familiar throughout the assignment. The importance of career loops was reflected in our research, which found them to be important to expatriates' commitment during repatriation. Interestingly, Japanese expatriates are an exception. Closed career loops do not seem to affect the commitment of Japanese expatriates during repatriation.[14] This may be a result of the routine transfers that Japanese managers make across functional and divisional boundaries, a practice that is not as common in the United States or Western Europe.

Job Factors

The nature of the job a manager has upon repatriation is one of the most powerful factors affecting commitment to organization and resulting intentions to stay or move on to a different firm. More specifically, four job factors have a significant affect on organizational commitment after repatriation.

Expatriates usually become accustomed to significant, visible jobs during global assignments. Moreover, they often develop a strong action-orientation and a feeling of responsibility for making things happen during their overseas assignments in jobs with high autonomy and discretion.[15] After returning home, however, expatriates often encounter temporary low-level "holding pattern" positions that fail to utilize their skills that could be powerful strategic asset in the global expansion of a firm.[16] Unfortunately, when repatriates return to "make work" holding-pattern assignments, they often end up wanting to leave for "real work," as these comments from high-performing repatriates indicate:

> It is very important to know what the assignment will be after returning home. Companies will easily lose their best expatriates if the work is not challenging and interesting enough.
>
> —*American expatriate*

> My current position has very little to do with what I learned overseas. What a waste for this company, to spend all the money to send me overseas and then bring me back and not even utilize what I learned while I was there.
>
> —*Japanese expatriate*

My suggestions for other expatriates coming home? Update their resumes. The experience that you gain overseas is seldom valued and often discounted when you come home. Other companies will pay for what you know and can do for them. I can't understand why expatriates and companies cannot learn to plan ahead and make use of the skills and experience gained overseas. The rule seems to be that return assignments are just "landing places." What's lost is the opportunity to use an expatriate's ability to the fullest benefit of both the company and the employee.

   —*Finnish expatriate*

  Supporting these comments on the importance of the return assignment, our overall research found that when American, Japanese, and Finnish firms provided repatriates with clearly planned jobs, significant levels of discretion, and few conflicting messages about how to do their work, repatriates exhibited higher loyalty to the parent company during repatriation.[17]

Organizational Factors

Several human resources policies and practices can enhance organizational commitment during repatriation. Each of these activities communicates to returning expatriates that the firm cares, is supportive, and—perhaps most importantly—can be counted on when it sends and retrieves expatriates to and from international postings.[18]

  Repatriation Training. Firms can take an initial step toward being dependable and supportive in the repatriation process by providing training and orientation to expatriates and their families before and after the return home. This training not only facilitates cross-cultural adjustment during repatriation but also communicates to expatriates that they have not been completely "out of sight and out of mind" during the global assignment. In Chapter 6, we discussed the positive impacts that training had on commitment to the parent company during a global assignment. Unfortunately, we cannot report a scientific perspective because so few firms provide repatriation training. In fact, 97 percent of American, 94 percent of Finnish, and 98 percent of Japanese expatriates received fewer than four hours of training and orientation upon or before coming home.[19]

  Compensation. In addition to pre- and postreturn training, providing adequate repatriation compensation is another way firms can communicate their support and dependability during repatriation. Many of the challenges of repatriation have already been outlined in

Chapters 8 and 9. The more firms can ease the financial burdens of repatriation, the more likely repatriates are to exhibit commitment to the parent company. From our research, we know that this correlation is especially true for Americans returning home.[20] The most troubling aspect of repatriation compensation is the potential loss of income and the associated drop in living standard. To minimize the financial loss of coming home and to maximize a repatriate's organizational commitment, firms can follow the three-step approach to financial compensation (outlined in Chapter 8), which minimizes the income shifts throughout the global assignment cycle and reduces feelings of financial inequity after the return home.

Value of International Experience. The final and most critical factor contributing to commitment during repatriation was the extent to which a firm communicates throughout the company that it truly values international experience and perspectives.[21] This value is communicated through the job provided after return, the attitudes of immediate supervisors and coworkers, the formal and informal reward systems for international experience, the promotion paths, and so on. All these factors collectively create a perception that firms either do or do not value international experience. The most important factor in sustaining repatriates' commitment to the parent company is developing an organizational culture that values international experience which in turn keeps them from leaving the parent company during repatriation. Unless firms can foster this type of culture, they are likely to create repatriates who feel unappreciated and go elsewhere for the recognition they feel they deserve. Unfortunately, the vast majority of expatriates (between 60 and 80 percent) feel that their firms do **not** genuinely value international experience.[22] This low utilization rate for international experience is reflected in these expatriates' comments:

> Your own perceived increase in "value" after an international experience is just that—perceived. Expatriates should be prepared for the fact that few—precious few—people are interested in their international experience.
>
> —*American expatriate*

> The most challenging part of coming home was the fact that my overseas experience was not valued in my company as I had expected it to be. Keep your expectations very low when coming home. Remember that no one really cares that you spent time overseas.
>
> —*Finnish expatriate*

> Look at your international experience as an extremely valuable asset, but recognize that few others will fully appreciate it.
>
> —*Japanese expatriate*

Leading firms retain committed and loyal expatriates by carefully assessing their culture and reinforcing the value of global experience and perspectives throughout the organization. While this prescription may seem a simple, many firms are trapped in the dilemma of "rewarding *A* while hoping for *B*," from a repatriate's perspective. For example, American executives are well known for touting the value of international experience, as evidenced in a variety of *Wall Street Journal* articles extolling the virtues and necessity of international assignments for CEOs of the next century.[23] The reality, however, is that fewer than 5 percent of *Fortune 500* firms prove that they genuinely care about international experience by considering previous international experience as a critical selection criterion in current executive promotion decisions.[24] These and other incongruities between what firms say about the importance of international experience and how they actually treat it must be examined in order for firms to effectively and consistently communicate that global managers with global experience are indeed valued.

Nonwork Factors

The final category of factors relevant to sustaining commitment during repatriation concerns cross-cultural adjustment during and after the international assignment.[25] Past research on commitment during global assignments found that the more adjusted American expatriates were to the foreign culture, the less committed they were to the parent company.[26] However, this adjustment has no impact (either positive or negative) on commitment during repatriation for American expatriates. In contrast, our research found that Japanese and European expatriates who had adjusted well during the international assignment were actually more committed to the parent company after the international assignment.[27]

This positive impact of overseas adjustment on repatriation commitment may be a function of at least three factors. First, research has found that Japanese and European firms pay more systematic attention to expatriation policies and practices than American firms do.[28] This planning may result in more parent-company support during the global assignment for expatriates, which translates into more effective adjustment and more significant commitment. Second,

Japanese and European expatriates are simply less mobile than their American counterparts after global assignments. As a consequence, Japanese and Finnish expatriates who adjusted well overseas are more likely to offer a positive return on investment of time and energy by staying with the parent company rather than attempting to change firms in relatively immobile managerial labor markets. Third, Japanese and European firms generally place a higher overall value on global experience than do American companies. The global experience counts more, so it pays for expatriates to adjust effectively during global assignments.

After returning home, expatriates face many significant challenges in adjusting to a new but somewhat familiar home-country culture and parent-company environment. Many details of this adjustment process were discussed in Chapter 9. Here, we want to reinforce the importance of effective repatriation adjustment. In particular, we found that effective adjustment to the home country after global assignments positively influenced commitment to the parent company.[29] Essentially, the efforts that individuals and firms make to facilitate the repatriation process not only help repatriates adjust and perform well but also encourage commitment to the parent company because repatriates feel the company can be counted on for support throughout the entire global assignment cycle.

Strategies for Sustaining Commitment During Repatriation

There are three key issues in influencing commitment during the repatriation process. First, firms can increase commitment by creating a culture that genuinely values international experience, perspectives, and skills. Second, firms can keep high-performing repatriates by carefully planning appropriate return assignments. Third, firms can reduce dysfunctional turnover by paying particular attention to high-risk expatriates when they come home from international assignments.

Creating an Organization That Values Global Experience

Creating an organizational culture that communicates the positive value of global experience is the most critical factor that we have identified for developing commitment to the parent company during repatriation. A global assignment demands personal and familial sacrifices. Firms should ensure that those sacrifices are honored. The last thing that international firms need is repatriates like this one, who suggests that future expatriates "must realize that whatever accomplishments were made overseas, they do not count for anything back at headquarters. You have to earn your 'stripes' all over again, so look after yourself, because nobody else will back home." Firms need to pay attention to the many formal and informal activities that collectively create the perception that firms value or do not value international experience.

Expatriates, like most other employees, carefully observe what is and is not rewarded in a multinational firm. In particular, promotions and executive advancement are critical conduits of information about what really counts. Many firms throughout the world tout international experience as essential to global expansion, yet their own boardrooms and executive ranks contain no one with international experience. By including international experience as a central criterion for advancement and promotion, firms can take an essential first step in communicating the value of international experience. The difference in attitude is apparent in companies such as 3M, Citicorp, and Colgate, where more than 75 percent of senior managers have international experience. In these and other leading-edge companies, people know that global business savvy is valued.

Linked to the promotion process, compensation policies are another significant way that expatriates learn whether a firm "puts its money where its mouth is," when it comes to international experience. In other words, if expatriates return home and do not experience significant financial losses, they are likely to sense that the firm values international experience. If the compensation policies outlined in Chapter 8 are used throughout the global assignment cycle, expatriates are less likely to experience feelings of inequity during repatriation. Basically, adequate compensation after coming home is another essential link in creating an international culture.

Company-provided training before and after repatriation not only facilitates adjustment to "reverse culture shock" but also shows repatriates that the firm is aware of and pays attention to the challenges of coming home. When a firm provides no training or orientation during repatriation, the implicit message is that the firm is complacent ("We don't care about your problems") or ignorant ("We aren't aware of any problems"). In both cases, repatriates quickly learn that their international experience has little value to the firm.

An appropriate return job assignment also communicates that the firm genuinely values international experience and perspectives.

If repatriates are assigned to positions that fail to utilize their international skills and knowledge, they quickly learn that their skills and knowledge are unimportant. As one American repatriate put it, "If a firm really wants to go global, it should value international experience by actually using expatriates' skills and experience gained overseas and by putting more effort into planning the reentry position and career progression within the firm."

In addition to formal mechanisms, firms can communicate that they genuinely value global experience in a number of informal ways. These informal mechanisms cannot be easily "legislated" through policy statements (such as repatriation training or compensation). Instead, they often result when internal human resources policy statements are put into practice. For example, Citicorp genuinely values global experience and promotes individuals who have completed global assignments. As a consequence, board meetings, executive discussions, and strategic planning processes are permeated with international rather than just home-country perspectives. Seeing global perspectives regularly raised communicates to repatriates that global experience really does count.

Another example of implicitly valued global experience can be found in the simple observation of how many foreigners are working in the home-country office, as an index of the extent to which foreigners are not really "foreign" to the firm. As company headquarters becomes permanently "globalized," repatriates are more likely to feel that global experience really counts as they return, look around the headquarters, and see a global environment in their home country.

Finally, the "war stories" traded among employees about the benefits and costs of global assignments are powerful indicators of how much individuals think firms truly value global experience. Essentially, as we wander within firms observing the relative attractiveness of global assignments, we discern whether the informal comments are horror stories about so-and-so losing his job, marriage, and career after going overseas or heroic stories about expatriates accomplishing strategic objectives and returning home to a company that valued their accomplishments. These examples are a few of the numerous informal ways in which repatriates are tipped off about the real value of global experience within a firm.

Strategically Planning the Return Position

Carefully planning and selecting the return position for a repatriate communicates that a firm values global experience, by providing repatriates with a strong sense of responsibility for making things happen. Commitment to the parent firm is partly a function of having a job for which one feels a strong sense of responsibility. If the positions to which repatriates return are unclear or trivial compared to what they experienced overseas, repatriates are less likely to feel a sense of commitment to the jobs or to the firms. Consequently, firms should identify strategic purposes that expatriates can accomplish after coming home, such as continued executive development, coordination and control, or transfer of information and technology. The strategic purpose and how the job facilitates its accomplishment must be clearly and personally communicated to the individual.

A repatriation team, consisting of an organizational sponsor and a human resource representative, should examine potential jobs within the firm. The firm should consider the level of autonomy and discretion that an expatriate has had during the international assignment. If possible, the return position should have an equal or greater level of challenge and the job autonomy to meet the challenge. A well-planned and well-selected return position can be critical to a returned manager's sense of responsibility in the job and sense of commitment and allegiance to the firm. If this type of position cannot be created at home, the firm should communicate in advance—before repatriation—that the return assignment may be less than desirable. It is important to remember that accurate expectations are especially critical when individual expectations may not be met. Finally, the firm should attempt to utilize specific international skills that the expatriate has acquired during the assignment, including language, negotiation, and cross-cultural communication skills or essential knowledge of the foreign market.

While most firms assume that a good return job will turn up— almost magically—leading firms assume exactly the opposite. They start with the assumption that *unless both the individual and organization expend extraordinary effort, a good match is **not** likely*. They know that good matches are made; they don't just happen. As a result, they invest significant time and energy into matching the manager to the return job. A great example of this process is found at Monsanto. Finding the right job for the person coming home entails a two-part process—an individual assessment and an organizational assessment.

Roughly three to six months prior to repatriation, the individual expatriate conducts a personal inventory of his or her international assignment experience. This inventory includes four aspects:

1. Expatriates review the developmental objectives of the assignment that they set prior to going overseas.
2. Expatriates write out how career interests have changed and what direction or possible directions they see themselves going.
3. Expatriates examine the new knowledge and skills acquired during the assignment.
4. Finally, expatriates synthesize all this information and envision the type of job and unit in the organization where they feel they could make a contribution and continue to develop toward their maximum potential.

Concurrently, a team composed of the expatriate's line-management sponsor and a human resource department representative should conduct an assessment. One key to this team's effectiveness at Monsanto is that team members generally have completed international assignments themselves. In most companies this experience is rare, with only about 10 percent of line or HR managers having been on international assignments. The seasoned organizational repatriation team at Monsanto conducts a broad review of impending or possible moves and job changes over several months. The second step requires a careful look at the individual's personal assessment and a discussion with that individual about what he or she sees in the future. The third step is the "matchmaking" process: determining where the individual's capabilities and desires best fit organizational opportunities and needs.

Obviously timing is not always perfect, but Monsanto has dramatically reduced its repatriation turnover due to the deliberateness of its process. The Monsanto process produces better matches and satisfaction all the way around *and* it engenders feelings in the repatriating manager of being valued and treated fairly even when ideal matches are not possible.

Identifying and Tracking High-Risk Repatriates

Firms can better manage their repatriation results by profiling and tracking high-risk repatriates. Specifically, repatriates with low tenure in the parent company or high levels of international work experience are least likely to show commitment to the parent company when returning home. Interestingly, the same profiles exist for expatriates during their global assignments.[30] Accordingly, the firm should pay special attention to expatriates with low tenure in the firm during and after global assignments to ensure that investments are not lost through dysfunctional turnover. Furthermore, expatriates with extensive international experience are most likely to detect incongruities between corporate talk and corporate action regarding the importance and relative value of international experience. This point is critical to remember, since these expatriates often have international experience that could strategically benefit either corporate headquarters or a domestic operation with international linkages. Firms also need to pay special attention to selecting appropriate return assignments for high-risk expatriates whose identity and sense of self-worth are connected to their global skills and experience. If these skills are not utilized in their return assignments, these valuable human assets may leave.

Creating Competitive Advantage By Keeping the Best Global Managers

In the best-case scenario, multinational firms send people on global assignments to accomplish strategic objectives such as executive development, coordination and control, or transfer of information and technology. These strategic objectives can be furthered when similar strategic objectives are accomplished by repatriates in their return assignments. Strategic objectives can be accomplished only if repatriates perform well and do not leave the firm after returning home. If functional retention occurs as repatriates effectively adjust and exhibit strong commitment, multinational firms are much more likely to create sustainable competitive advantages through the effective retention and utilization of global managers. A competitive advantage can be gained by all types of firms by keeping the best global managers after repatriation, but the advantage is even more relevant to companies at higher levels of globalization.

At the export stage of globalization, firms send fewer expatriates overseas and thus have fewer returning home. Nevertheless, the large investment made in each expatriate, and the importance of each repatriate to the future international expansion of the firm, suggests that developing effective repatriation policies and practices to retain the best global managers is critical even for export firms with fewer expatriates.

Firms at the multidomestic stage of globalization utilize more expatriates than export firms do. In contrast to multinational and global firms, however, multidomestic firms tend to keep expatriates on longer individual assignments or to send them on multiple assignments in various countries without bringing them back home. Therefore, compared to multinational and global firms, multidomestic firms have lower repatriation needs. When multidomestic firms do repatriate international managers, they must do it effectively to accomplish current strategic functions and, more importantly, to accomplish future international expansion, since a multidomestic firm may develop into a multinational or global enterprise.

Multinational and global firms have the largest numbers of expatriates moving to and from the host and home countries. The issues addressed in this chapter and in Chapter 9 are very relevant to multinational and global firms, since these firms have made the most significant investments in international managers and executive assets. One financial institution we work with invests close to $30 million per year in expatriate salaries and support, with the firm's total annual profit at approximately $150 million. These significant costs reinforce the need for multinational and global firms to strategically and systematically plan repatriation processes that will keep the best managers.

Multinational and global firms need people in global assignments to serve vital strategic functions, but they also need expatriates to return and bring back international perspectives, market knowledge, technology improvements, and so on, to the home country and to the global strategic planning process. If the repatriation process is mismanaged, repatriates will give counterproductive advice to those still out on assignment:

> Advice about coming home? Don't.
>
> —*Japanese expatriate*

> If you like your overseas position and do not have the desire to work in a bureaucratic corporate environment, stay where you are and enjoy it. If I had the choice all over again, I would go right back to Germany and live there as long as possible.
>
> —*American expatriate*

Unfortunately, the result of this advice could be that fewer and fewer expatriates would want to come home, while multinational firms need them to return. Without their return, "global sclerosis" can set in, as the following repatriates described after coming home to parent companies with few repatriates:

> I was shocked at the severe lack of worldwide thinking in the executive suite.
>
> *—American expatriate*

> My co-workers ridiculed me for carrying and reading *Newsweek* at the office after I had spent four years in the United States. They made me feel like a traitor to my company.
>
> *—Japanese expatriate*

> When I returned home, I found that the home organization was totally unaware of how business is really transacted overseas.
>
> *—Finnish expatriate*

Firms at any stage of globalization need to accomplish strategic objectives by effectively sending people overseas and effectively bringing them home. The importance of managing international assignments becomes even more crucial when firms are at higher stages of globalization and need more expatriates to accomplish strategic objectives. Moreover, firms can make more effective transitions between stages of globalization (for example, from an export stage to a more integrated global stage) by having managed previous global assignments well, so that key decision makers have the necessary global perspective and experience, and so that other managers and employees will want to take global assignments. For these strategic reasons, firms need to keep the best international managers during repatriation by paying particular attention to their commitment, both during and after global assignments.

Notes

1. Black and Gregersen, "Functional and Dysfunctional Turnover After International Assignments"; Gregersen and Black, "Global Executive Development: Keeping High Performers After International Assignments."
2. Black, "A Tale of Three Countries."
3. Black and Gregersen, "Functional and Dysfunctional Turnover."
4. Gregersen and Black, "Antecedents to Commitment to a Parent Company and a Foreign Operation."
5. Gregersen, "Commitment to a Parent Company and a Local Commitment During Repatriation: The Japanese and Finnish Experience."
6. Black, "A Tale of Three Countries."
7. Mathieu and Zajac, "A Review and Meta-analysis of the Antecedents, Correlates, and Consequences of Organizational Commitment"; Mowday, Porter, and Steers, *Employee-Organization Linkages: The Psychology of Commitment, Absenteeism, and Turnover.*

8. Gregersen, "Commitments to a Parent Company and a Local Work Unit."
9. Gregersen, "Organizational Commitment During Repatriation."
10. Gregersen, "Commitments to a Parent Company and a Local Work Unit."
11. Gregersen, "Commitments to a Parent Company and a Local Work Unit"; Gregersen, "Organizational Commitment During Repatriation."
12. Gregersen, "Commitments to a Parent Company and a Local Work Unit."
13. Black, "A Tale of Three Countries."
14. Gregersen, "Organizational Commitment During Repatriation."
15. Adler, "Re-entry: Managing Cross-Cultural Transitions"; Adler, *International Dimensions of Organizational Behavior*; Black and Gregersen, "When Yankee Comes Home: Factors Related to Expatriate and Spouse Repatriation Adjustment"; Clague and Krupp, "International Personnel: The Repatriation Problem"; Harvey, "Repatriation of Corporate Executives: An Empirical Study"; Napier and Peterson, "Expatriate Re-entry: What Do Repatriates Have to Say?"; Oddou and Mendenhall, "Succession Planning for the 21st Century: How Well Are We Grooming Our Future Business Leaders?"
16. Clague and Krupp, "International Personnel"; Black, "A Tale of Three Countries."
17. Gregersen, "Commitments to a Parent Company and a Local Work Unit"; Gregersen, "Organizational Commitment During Repatriation."
18. Gregersen, "Commitments to a Parent Company and a Local Work Unit."
19. Black, "A Tale of Three Countries."
20. Gregersen, "Commitments to a Parent Company and a Local Work Unit."
21. Gregersen, "Commitments to a Parent Company and a Local Work Unit"; Gregersen, "Organizational Commitment During Repatriation."
22. Black, "A Tale of Three Countries."
23. Bennett, "The Chief Executives in the Year 2000 Will Be Experienced Abroad."
24. Korn-Ferry study cited in Oddou & Mendenhall, "Succession Planning for the 21st Century."
25. Gregersen and Black, "Antecedents to Commitment to a Parent Company and a Foreign Operation"; Gregersen, "Commitments to a Parent Company and a Local Work Unit."
26. Gregersen and Black, "Antecedents to Commitment to a Parent Company and a Foreign Operation."
27. Gregersen, "Commitments to a Parent Company and a Local Work Unit"; Gregersen, "Organizational Commitment During Repatriation."
28. Tung, "Selection and Training Procedures of U.S., European, and Japanese Multinationals"; Tung, *The New Expatriates: Managing Human Resources Abroad.*
29. Gregersen, "Commitments to a Parent Company and a Local Work Unit."
30. Gregersen, "Commitments to a Parent Company and a Local Work Unit."

11

Managing the Entire Global Assignment Cycle: Establishing Best Practices

Most of us are so hardheaded that it take a real smack on the head before we are willing or able to rearrange our mental maps of the world. Executives do not generally receive in-depth international management training from MBA programs, from in-house executive education programs, or from their work experience within the company.[1] Less than a quarter of CEOs in America have gone on an international assignment.[2] Of the CEOs who had worked internationally, Canada was by far the most common foreign assignment, followed by Great Britain and then Belgium. Most U.S. CEOs gain foreign experience in Canada or Europe; very few have lived and worked in Latin America or the Far East.

If a company must compete with Japanese, South Korean, German, or Taiwanese companies, the best way to gain a comprehensive view of how they operate is to send the best and the brightest to those countries. It is unsettling to think that, of the top 1,000 firms in the United States, few have CEOs who have worked in the Far East.

If executives are to formulate valid global strategies for their firms—both at headquarters and at subsidiaries—they need to have an international perspective. Otherwise, a "garbage in-garbage out" phenomenon occurs in strategy formulation; strategies are only as valid as the ideas, concepts, and knowledge that strategy *formulators* bring to the process. Most executives would agree that global strategy implementation is crucial to the success of multinational or international companies. Strategies do not implement themselves, however. People implement strategies. To carry out a firm's worldwide strategic aims the way top management desires them to be carried out, the right people must be in place throughout the world. However, the "right people" for global assignments are not easy to find, and they do not automatically emerge out of the top twenty MBA programs. Instead, internationally astute people need to be developed.

Expatriate executives are simply too important to the current and future financial health of a firm to relegate them to a low priority on top management's "worry list." As mentioned in Chapter 1, expatriate executives and managers play important strategic roles for a firm: they coordinate between subsidiaries and headquarters, implement strategies, ensure the quality and effectiveness of organizational control systems, manage global information systems, and gain expertise in international and cross-cultural business skills that are critical to ensuring that top executive positions are filled by those with the necessary international experience and perspectives.

Exhibit 11.1

Contrasting Approaches to International Assignments

Strategic-Systematic	Tactical-Reactive
1. Approach international assignments as long-term investments.	1. Approach international assignments as short-term expenses.
2. Develop future executives with essential global perspectives and experiences to formulate and implement competitive strategies.	2. Focus on a quick-fix approach to a short-term problem in a foreign operation.
3. Increase the effectiveness of critical coordination and control functions between and among the home office and foreign operations.	3. Randomly and haphazardly perform some functions of international assignments and focus attention as problems arise.
4. Effectively disseminate information, technology, and corporate values throughout the worldwide organization.	4. Fail to systematically integrate worldwide organization in terms of values, technology, products, or brand.

Clearly, some firms are leading the way on various dimensions of international assignments; but too few firms pay systematic attention to each phase of the global assignment: selection, training, cross-cultural adjustment, dual allegiance, performance appraisal, compensation, and repatriation. By their own admission, most firms approach global assignments from a tactical and reactive perspective, rather than from a strategic and systematic perspective.

As Exhibit 11.2 indicates, there is still a wide gap between the importance expatriates place on various aspects of support from the company and the satisfaction they have with the support they receive. In the following sections, we highlight some companies that are employing a more systematic and strategic approach to international assignments and capturing the rewards of this approach.

Exhibit 11.2
Satisfaction GAP

Support Services Offered	Importance of Service	Satisfaction with Service	Satisfaction GAP
Cultural Orientation	72%	52%	20%
Language Training	57%	69%	12%
Homefinding/Settling-in	93%	64%	29%
Goods/Services Differentials	91%	73%	18%
Health Care	97%	65%	32%
Home Leave	92%	78%	14%
Ongoing Assistance Abroad	80%	53%	27%
Repatriation	91%	66%	25%
Spouse Counseling	71%	29%	42%
Career Planning	86%	27%	59%

Note: Results are based on a 1997 survey conducted by SHRM Institute for International Human Resources.

Selecting: Selecting the Right People

Our first example of excellence comes from a human-relief organization, Worldvision International. This organization understands that its productivity is tied directly to the quality of the people it sends overseas to accomplish strategic objectives on short- and long-term assignments. Its philosophy is that the organization cannot afford to send the wrong people; thus, it spends significant time and energy on finding people who have the technical and cross-cultural attributes necessary for success in an international setting. Fewer than 50 percent of companies have structured selection systems, and less than 10 percent use any form of testing to screen candidates.[3]

Worldvision International's staffing policies, like those of any firm, are in a constant state of change and evolution, yet the one principle that remains constant is that effective expatriates are the key to overseas success. Worldvision International's selection process has been divided into as many as 9 stages, illustrated in Exhibit 11.3.

Stage 1: Identifying the Position

In the first stage, the personnel department works with the hiring manager to identify the position. They develop job descriptions and submit a personnel requisition for approval by the division vice president, hiring manager, human resources director, and personnel director. All these individuals must agree on the nature and objectives of the international assignment before the search process begins.

Stage 2: Determining Candidates' Qualifications

In conjunction with the hiring manager, the personnel department determines the technical and cross-cultural qualifications required of candidates. These qualifications include educational record, previous overseas background and experience, personality characteristics, and other specific qualifications the position requires. Behavioral dimensions are identified, and a list is developed which is used to assess candidates in interviews.

Stage 3: Screening

An initial screening of applicants is conducted by the personnel department, using the criteria established in Stage 2. The best candidate is selected and presented to the hiring manager and the division vice president for a preliminary review. After the preliminary review, if the decision is positive—to proceed with the candidate—the process

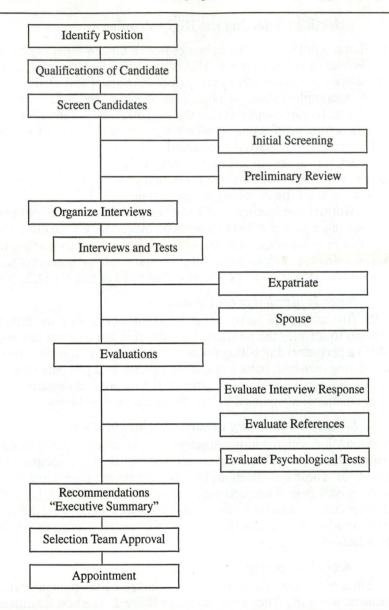

Exhibit 11.3
The Hiring Process at Worldvision International

moves to the next stage. If the preliminary review is negative, the screening process resumes or continues.

Stage 4: Scheduling of Interviews

The personnel staff work with the hiring manager to determine who should interview the candidate. Almost always, multiple interviews are scheduled. Interviews are generally conducted by staff from the personnel department, managers from the hiring department, and any other selected interviewers.

Stage 5: Interviews and Tests

Candidates for global assignments can be evaluated on a variety of dimensions. From the following twenty-eight dimensions, interviewers can select those most critical to a specific overseas assignment.

Impact	Communication skills—written
Oral presentation skills	Problem analysis
Management control	Stress tolerance
Judgment	Negotiation
Energy	Leadership
Listening skills	Organizational sensitivity
Flexibility	Technical translation
Perseverance	Communication skills—verbal
Development of subordinates	Delegation
	Adaptability
Initiative	Planning and organizing
Decisiveness	Sensitivity
Motivation	Political sensitivity
Resource utilization	Independence
Financial analytical ability	

A single interviewer will not cover all the selected dimensions; rather, each interviewer will be assigned to cover specific dimensions in the interview. Dimensions that are not deemed relevant to a particular assignment are ignored. Interviewers have specific questions to ask within each of their dimensions, although they may have latitude to add other questions to the list. Exhibits 11.4 and 11.5 include Examples of such questions.

Interviewers provide written evaluations of their interviews within twenty-four hours. In addition to written observations, interviewers are encouraged to express their evaluations of the candidate via two objective formats on a scale of 1–5: the degree to which each skill dimension was exhibited in the interview itself, and an overall rating of the candidate as excellent, above average, average, below average, or poor.

Stage 6: Evaluations of Interviews and Tests

The personnel department evaluates the written responses of the interviewers, the candidate's references, and the results of any psycho-

Exhibit 11.4
Perseverance

---

1. What big obstacle did you have to overcome to get where you are today? How did you overcome it?
2. Have you ever submitted to your superior a good idea that he or she did not take action on? What did you do?
3. Can you relate an experience in which you believe you persisted too long? How could the situation have been improved?
4. Can you relate an experience in which you believe you gained something because you persisted for a length of time?
5. I see you did not complete —— course or activity. Why didn't you?
6. How long does it take you to complete an average project? What is the longest you have ever taken? Why?
7. How many times do you usually call on an official before you give up?
8. Describe a situation where you gave your all but failed.
9. What is the biggest project you did not successfully conclude? What did you do?
10. What university course gave you the most trouble? What did you do about it?
11. What was the biggest problem you encountered in college? On your last job? How did you handle the problems?

The interviewer should establish the size of problems or barriers in order to gauge the amount of perseverance required to overcome them.

---

logical tests that were administered during the interview process. The candidate's spouse is also interviewed, although less intensively, and given psychological tests to determine adaptability potential.

Stage 7: Personnel's Recommendations

The personnel staff summarizes the results of the interviews, references, and psychological tests and then presents a summary with recommendation to the hiring manager and the division vice president.

Exhibit 11.5
Delegation

---

1. Who is "minding the store" while you are here? How was that person selected? Why? How will you know how well he or she performed? Did you make a formal announcement to your subordinates concerning the responsibilities of the person you left in charge?
2. Explain your biggest mistake in delegating.
3. Explain your biggest mistake in not delegating.
4. What keeps you from delegating more?
5. Describe the type of decision making that you delegate to your subordinates.
6. Describe your criteria for delegating assignments.
7. If the degree of delegation varies among subordinates, explain how and why.
8. When did you have a major problem requiring staff help? What action did you take? Why did you ask particular people to assist you?
9. How much overtime do you put in per week? (Do you need to delegate more?)
10. After being away for several days, how do you familiarize yourself with the current situation in your organization ?
11. Can you cite an example from your own experience where you were faced with delegating authority and/or responsibility? How did it work?

The interviewer should establish the purpose of each delegation mentioned. What did the interviewee want to achieve, and why was the particular person chosen to handle the matter?

Stage 8: Approval

If the recommendation is to offer the position to the candidate, it must be approved by a selection team consisting of the division vice president, hiring manager, human resource director, and personnel director. Personnel discusses the details of compensation and benefits with the hiring manager and then submits a personnel action form for approval by each member of the selection team.

Stage 9: Appointment

The personnel department issues a letter of invitation that includes the job title, starting date, salary, terms of service, specific information related to the movement of household goods, banking arrangements, travel to the field assignment, and any other essential information. While this process can be lengthy and time-consuming, expatriates sent out under this selection process were rated as highly successful by the firm's top management. In Worldvision International's experience, the investment of time and money in effective selection has paid off with significant long-term returns for the organization and the individual.

Worldvision International directly applies many principles that were discussed in Chapter 3. Worldvision International initiated the selection process by involving a team of important "stakeholders," individuals concerned with the future success of the expatriate. The organization then decided what strategic objectives an expatriate could accomplish overseas and developed a comprehensive, focused list of selection criteria that were most relevant to a particular global assignment. Multiple selection methods were used to assess candidates against an array of selection criteria. Finally, Worldvision recognized expatriates' families and involved spouses, as appropriate, in the selection process. The result of this approach is an impressive record of successful overseas assignments. Essentially, Worldvision International uses a strategic-systematic approach to international staffing (versus a tactical-reactive approach). The differences between these approaches are illustrated in Exhibit 11.6. Rather than being victimized by hasty selections based on a subsidiary's immediate need, Worldvision International carefully considers the nature and purpose of an assignment and then locates candidates who can effectively accomplish strategic purposes.

Training: Helping People Do the Right Thing

In Chapter 4, we pointed out that while predeparture training is important, in-country training—especially after two to six months—is

Strategic-Systematic	Tactical-Reactive
Purpose	**Purpose**
• Executive development	• Fix a short-term problem
• Coordination and control	
• Transfer of innovation, technology, culture	
Focus	**Focus**
• Technical skills	• Technical skills
• Cross-cultural skills	
• Family situation	
Process	**Process**
• Multiple selection criteria	• Single selection criterion
• Multiple selection methods	• Single selection method

Exhibit 11.6
Two Approaches to Selecting

critical to expatriate productivity. After the expatriate and spouse have settled in and begun to negotiate the intricacies of the foreign culture, they are more motivated to really understand the host culture. At this time, rigorous training methods can produce long-lasting results. If expatriates are not exposed to the "meat" of the host culture during this period, they may develop mistaken "cognitive maps" that inaccurately explain the host culture. This is often the time period when rigid stereotypes or faulty attributional tendencies are entrenched. Once these misunderstandings are established, expatriates are unlikely to actively seek out new and more accurate knowledge about the host culture.

To help avoid these problems, we have worked with firms such as IBM-Asia Pacific and IBM-Japan, which recently offered in-country training to their senior executives and their spouses transferred to Tokyo. Our intensive, week-long seminar of over sixty hours covered a variety of topics crucial to understanding the Japanese people and Japanese business culture, including ancient, medieval, and modern history; Japanese religions and philosophy; socialization within Japan; psychological and sociological constructs of Japanese society;

organizational behavior in the Japanese workplace, the business history of Japan; Japanese organizational design and structure; the Japanese human resources system; business negotiations in Japan; strategies for learning the Japanese language; and relationships among business groupings, the government, the education system, and the Japanese "Mafia."

The three-step learning process described in Chapter 4 requires expatriate managers to first *attend* to the norms of the new culture, then *retain* and understand the nature of the new norms, and then *practice* new behaviors. By offering training in-country, IBM enhanced this learning process because the executives were able to relate the concepts covered in the seminar to experiences they had just had the week or even the day before. This method also allowed them to practice and validate what they were taught by implementing the knowledge immediately.

Consistent with the principles espoused in Chapter 4, IBM opted for the following instructional methods: lecture, films, books (homework assignments), cases, survival-level language training, role plays, and field trips. Each of these methods was more effective in its delivery because the participants were studying Japan *in* Japan. Consistent with research findings and recommendations, spouses were included in this week-long training.

IBM's approach to training international executives reflects an understanding of the need to invest in training in order to increase performance as well as adjustment, as well as to increase the likelihood that strategic objectives of the global assignment (e.g., executive development, coordination, corporate control, or technology transfer) will be accomplished. IBM's strategic-systematic approach to training is in direct contrast with the tactical-reactive approach outlined in Exhibit 11.7.

Language Training

Language training is a thorny, complex issue for companies. While many language firms claim that adults can learn a foreign language in two months by listening to tapes, the reality is that it takes dedicated effort to learn a foreign language. In fact, spoken fluency in a language generally cannot be attained unless one lives overseas. Nevertheless, expatriates can aquire a minimal survival, or conversational, level before going overseas. With that foundation, progress toward fluency can begin immediately. The danger of waiting to learn a new language until arriving in the foreign country is that fear, doubt, work

Strategic-Systematic	Tactical-Reactive
Investment Perspective	**Cost Perspective**
• Job training	• No post-arrival training
• Organization-business training	
• Culture training	
• Language training	
Results	**Results**
• Executive development	• Lower job performance
• Improved current business results	• Higher expatriate turnover
• Enhanced family adjustment	

Exhibit 11.7
Two Approaches to Training

responsibilities, and an overwhelming sense of difficulty can overwhelm the long, deliberate, day-to-day commitment it takes to learn a new language.

With four to six months of notice before departing on a global assignment, it is quite possible, through classes or self-instruction, to reach the survival level in a foreign language. Language instruction must occur for an hour or two *daily* before departure. How much can be accomplished depends, of course, on the ability of the learner to pick up languages, the techniques used to learn, and the difficulty of the language itself.

In our research and consulting, we have not come across any companies that offer a strategic, rigorous, daily language program for expatriates four to six months before departure—even though language skills may be the key to accomplishing strategic objectives during the global assignment. One of the present authors did put this principle of language preparation to the test on a personal basis, however. He received an assignment to spend a semester (approximately five months) in Switzerland. Not wanting to be a tourist in terms of language ability for this period, he studied German for an hour a day for four months. By departure date, he could speak better than at the survival level but not yet at the conversational level. After five months in Switzerland, he spoke at a conversational level. The ability to converse with the average person on the street increased his family's satisfaction with the overseas assignment, reduced stress, impressed the host nationals (who told him that the Americans they knew made no effort at all to learn German), and generally aided him in accomplishing his assignment there.

Cross-cultural training done in-country, plus language training done before departure and after arrival, are indispensable to the effectiveness of expatriate executives. Each company must conduct such programs as best fit its needs, but the research literature to date shows that most companies are ignoring this very important aspect of international people management.

Appraising: Determining Whether People Are Doing Things Right

Effective performance appraisal is an important component of a successful global assignment. In Chapter 7, we discussed several factors that result in performance-appraisal systems that benefit individuals and organizations. 3M has an exemplary appraisal process that incorporates evaluative and developmental components.

Primarily for evaluation purposes, 3M's performance appraisal system begins with expatriates' direct functional managers (who may or may not be host-country nationals). These managers work with expatriates to define performance expectations for individuals and business units on an annual basis. They also jointly define the set of performance expectations for an expatriate's career development. After business and performance expectations have been defined consensually, these criteria are forwarded for review by the area vice president and the reentry (or repatriation) sponsor in the home country. Each of these individuals reviews the strengths of the expatriate and points out potential problems in selecting performance criteria and career or individual developmental needs. A similar "appraisal team" process occurs in assessing the accomplishment of the predefined performance expectations. Initially, the year's accomplishments are reviewed by the direct functional manager and the expatriate; these evaluations are also examined by the area vice president and the reentry sponsor.

3M has also developed a parallel developmental performance-appraisal process, called the Human Resource Review. On an annual basis, four individuals evaluate performance and career issues during global assignments. These individuals are the executive director of human resources for the international division, the area vice president, the area human resources manager or director, and a representative from the corporate executive resources department. During Human Resource Review meetings, these people assess expatriates along several dimensions. They examine performance during the past year and, more importantly, they consider major developmental issues for each expatriate. For example, an expatriate's career progression within the firm, in terms of current and potential positions, is often a point of discussion in the Human Resource Review meeting. This meeting also provides an established forum for managers to consider specific issues for each expatriate, such as costs associated, assignment length, and upcoming repatriation processes.

3M's performance appraisal takes advantage of many principles discussed in Chapter 7. For example, in both the evaluative and developmental appraisal process, 3M involves more than one person. In fact, in assessing an expatriate's performance and career development, 3M incorporates multiple perspectives by including managers and executives who have a stake in the success of the expatriates they evaluate. Moreover, 3M not only examines performance-related issues, but it also broadens the assessment scope to career-related challenges of expatriates. In other words, 3M's approach to appraisal contains three critical elements for success: 1) it utilizes several individuals to rate performance, 2) it incorporates a variety of assessment criteria, and 3) it focuses on evaluative and developmental aspects of the appraisal process.

Rewarding: Recognizing the Right Things People Do

American Express has a well-conceived compensation program for expatriates, which is, in principle, an "equalization" approach. Specifically, American Express calculates housing and utility allowances by determining the costs of housing and utilities in the host country where the expatriate is to be assigned and by explicitly considering the job, salary level, and family size of the candidate. This housing allowance is provided in the currency of the host country. The amount is adjusted for inflation annually or more frequently, depending on the rate of inflation in the host country. Generally, American Express discourages employees from selling their houses in the home country or buying houses in the host country. The company provides information as well as financial assistance for renting and managing individuals' homes while they are on assignment overseas.

While a housing and utility allowance is being paid to the individual in the host country, an estimate of the housing and utility costs the employee would probably have incurred in the absence of a global assignment is deducted from the individual's home-country salary. Consequently, individuals pay approximately the same amount for housing and utilities as they would have if they had not been sent overseas.

This approach also applies to taxes. An initial calculation of employees' home-country taxes is made at the beginning of the year, and a more detailed recalculation is made at the end of the year. This hypothetical tax is based on earned income, which includes salary and bonus. This earned income is reduced by any before-tax benefits and salary deferrals. Itemized deductions that individuals would probably claim if they were working in their home country are also calculated. This hypothetical tax is deducted from the individual's home-country salary over the course of the year. Any adjustment in the taxes that should be deducted or credited based on the year-end recalculation is made at that time and is generally small. American Express then pays all home-country and host-country taxes actually incurred.

American Express also provides a number of other carefully considered allowances. In recognition of the difficulty of moving overseas and back again, American Express pays part of a "mobility allowance" when individuals go overseas, and the rest when they return. The firm also pays for direct moving costs and provides a moderate sum to cover miscellaneous moving expenses. Additionally, American Express helps with educational expenses for children, home leave, and hardship allowances for selected countries that have extreme and difficult conditions.

This approach allows American Express to avoid "rewarding A while hoping for B"—that is, this approach attracts capable people to global assignments but does not make financial incentives the sole or major reason for considering or accepting a global assignment. Furthermore, paying host-country expenses in local currency while deducting expected home-country expenses reduces two potential problems. First, by paying expected costs in the local currency, the company reduces exchange-rate risks. Second, by deducting expected home-country costs, it reduces the inequity that individuals might experience if all spendable and disposable income, as well as allowance differentials, were paid (and therefore visible) in the local currency. In addition to achieving these two objectives, these practices also reduce the overall compensation and tax costs to the firm.

Repatriating: Helping People Readjust and Perform

Less than one-third of U.S. companies have a systematic repatriation program. The average repatriation turnover rate in companies that have systematic programs is 5 percent, whereas it is roughly 25 percent in companies that do not.[4] Given the lack of a strategic and systematic approach of most companies, it is not surprising that, based on their most recent experience, only about 40 percent of international assignees would be willing to take another assignment.[5]

In Chapter 1, we discussed GE's Medical's "people" failure in a French subsidiary. Since that experience, GE Medical has worked hard to understand the international human resources process and, in turn, has created and implemented some very effective expatriate programs. One area that stands out in GE Medical's efforts is the attention it now pays to repatriates. For example, GE Medical Systems has initiated the Expatriate Sponsorship Program to ensure successful repatriation and to contribute to expatriates' career development.[6] The program is straightforward: any long-term expatriate (one year or longer in an overseas assignment) is eligible for the program. The eligible expatriate is assigned a sponsor who is a manager in the home country, preferably in the function where the expatriate is most likely to return. There are four elements of the Expatriate Sponsorship Program: the expatriate, the sponsor, the host manager, and the Human Resource Network.

The Expatriate

Before going overseas, expatriates are expected to take responsibility for their own professional development. In other words, the company makes clear that it will not coddle expatriates throughout the assignment; expatriates will be required to expend effort to enhance their careers. Expatriates are expected to analyze the job opportunity in terms of its potential for personal career development, assess family readiness to live and work overseas, be clear about career expectations, prepare for the assignment by attending language- and culture-training programs with the family, and discuss future career opportunities with the sponsor upon completion of the assignment.

While expatriates are overseas, they are expected to meet personally with their sponsors at least once a year. In this meeting, they are urged to discuss their own performance, career expectations, and other issues relevant to their situation in the firm. Expatriates are also expected to take advantage of company seminars, business meetings, reports, phone calls, and so on, to build and maintain a network back at the home office. Expatriates are expected to work hard to enhance their management skills. Finally, before returning to the home office, expatriates are expected to reassess their career options objectively, which is easier when a strong sponsor-expatriate relationship exists.

The Sponsor

The primary role of the sponsor is to ensure that successful repatriation occurs with the expatriate. Predeparture responsibilities of the sponsor include the following:

- Participating in the expatriate selection process
- Studying the expatriate candidate's repatriation plan to identify opportunities, roadblocks, and dead ends in terms of the expatriate's career
- Meeting the expatriate personally to discuss the sponsor's views of the overseas assignment
- Formally communicating to the Human Resource Network the repatriation plan for the expatriate

During the assignment, the sponsor is required to monitor the expatriate's performance via phone calls to the host manager and the expatriate and from copies of performance appraisals; to meet annually with the expatriate to discuss the assignment; to complete an evaluation of the expatriate's performance for the Human Resource Network; and to encourage the expatriate's exposure to the home office to maintain a personal network. Before expatriates return, sponsors should be willing and able to act as career advisers and provide references to hiring managers on behalf of the expatriate.

The Host Manager

The host manager plays an important role in the expatriation and repatriation processes. Before the expatriate arrives overseas, the host manager must assess the impact of having an expatriate in the workplace, play a large role in the selection of the expatriate, prepare the organization to receive the expatriate, and assign an in-country mentor to the expatriate. During the expatriate's tenure, the host manager is required to complete an annual performance appraisal and send copies of it to the expatriate's sponsor and to the Human Resource Network. Host managers must spend more time communicating with and providing feedback to expatriates than with other employees. Before repatriating expatriates, host managers must activate the Human Resource Network to begin the repatriation process (this begins no later than six months before the term of the assignment is over). Host managers must also complete a performance appraisal for the overall assignment and send it to the sponsor through the Human Resource Network.

The Human Resource Network

The Human Resource Network of GE Medical Systems is required to perform the following functions before the foreign assignment:

- Organize a foreign-assignment planning review twice a year
- Coordinate expatriate candidate identification and selection
- Manage the sponsorship assignments
- Manage the repatriation plan of the expatriate that is sent by the sponsor
- Act as the focal point for all global staffing and expatriation management
- Manage the contractual aspects of the assignment
- Organize the training programs

During the expatriate's assignment, the network coordinates performance appraisal, salary planning, and reviews of the expatriate's performance. The network also monitors communications among expatriates, sponsors, and host managers; and it manages the terms and conditions of the assignment. Then, no later than six months before repatriation, or upon request of the host manager, the network activates the repatriation process to plan for and find an appropriate position for the repatriate.

Very few companies plan for repatriation in such an organized way as GE Medical Systems does. This company understands the importance of effectively supporting expatriates to maintain a global competitive advantage in the future. GE remembers its expatriates by establishing several links with the home country, such as sponsors, frequent communication, clear repatriation processes, and planning for the return assignment. In contrast, most companies, as reflected in Figure 11.8, adopt an "out of sight, out of mind" approach to expatriates that stems from a tactical-reactive philosophy and results in "orphaned" expatriates during and after global assignments.

Strategic-Systematic	**Tactical-Reactive**
Out of Sight ...With Support	**Out of Sight...Out of Mind**
• Organizational sponsor	• No support
• Communication links	• No planning of repatriation
• Visits home	
• Repatriation training and orientation	
• Systematic planning of return job	
• Proactive individual and organization assessment of return opportunities	

Exhibit 11.8
Two Approaches to Support

Global Assignments: A Key to Executive Success and Global Competitiveness

Throughout this book, we have traced the rationale, logic, and evidence for taking a comprehensive, systematic, strategically oriented approach to international assignments. In addition to the economic arguments for an integrated and well-designed international human resources system, there is another equally important consideration: a company's ethical responsibility to its employees.

One way to understand this responsibility is to consider the preparations that go into a successful military campaign. Before going into battle, the soldiers, pilots, and sailors are well trained in the use of weapons, battle tactics, and strategies of war. In fact, they have probably undergone numerous battle simulations or training, at a very high cost. Events such as Operation Desert Storm provide clear evidence of the value of preparation and training. Why do military and intelligence organizations spend so much time preparing their people? The obvious answer is that, without such training and preparation, performance in the field would suffer—lives would be lost.

It would be unethical to send people into situations where their lives could be put at risk without also providing adequate selection, training, and support. This logic seems clear in war, but not when sending individuals on global assignments for multinational companies. Nevertheless, we have seen firsthand the pain, stress, grief, and other psychological challenges that many expatriates experience in overseas assignments if they receive little support and training from their organizations. The following quote summarizes some of our thoughts on this matter:

> One must wonder if it is ethical to uproot an individual or a family, send them across the Pacific or Atlantic oceans, and expect them to make their way skillfully through an alien business and social culture on their own. Perhaps American executives reason that an extraordinary compensation package makes the exchange fair and ethical. Living and working overseas involves adjustments and stresses of a high magnitude. Placing individuals in such conditions without giving them the tools to manage them seems not only economically costly to the firm and personally costly to the individuals, but simply wrong.[7]

Of course, we recognize that sending people from Chicago to Saudi Arabia for business is not the same as sending them off to war. Managers do not put their lives on the line in the same way soldiers do, but expatriates often put their careers, their psychological health, their marriages, their children's education, and other significant aspects of their work and nonwork lives at risk when they accept overseas assignments. This serious reality begs the question: Is it ethical for a multinational firm to send the wrong people, to train them inadequately, or to fail to understand and support them while they live and work in another culture?

We feel that companies are not only economically wise but, perhaps more importantly, duty-bound to offer sufficient support to expatriate employees throughout the international assignment cycle. Leading-edge firms are taking the whole business of globalization and internationalization seriously and investing heavily in internationalizing senior executive teams and high-potential managers—the next generation of global leaders. These same companies are also providing international assignees with the training, tools and support, to accomplish strategic objectives for firms and to wage victorious campaigns against global competitors.

Multinational firms have strategic objectives that span the globe. To implement those objectives successfully, they rely on human as well as financial assets. Battle-hardened global companies have top executives and senior human resource managers who value and understand the need for a strategic-systematic approach to selecting, training, appraising, compensating, and developing people in international assignments. Exhibit 11.9 illustrates what happens in firms where policies toward global assignments reflect that such assignments are key to competitive advantage and future executive excellence. The figure shows an upward spiral of global competitiveness. Each stage of policy increases the potential for success of the next stage.

Exhibit 11.9
Upward Competitiveness Spiral

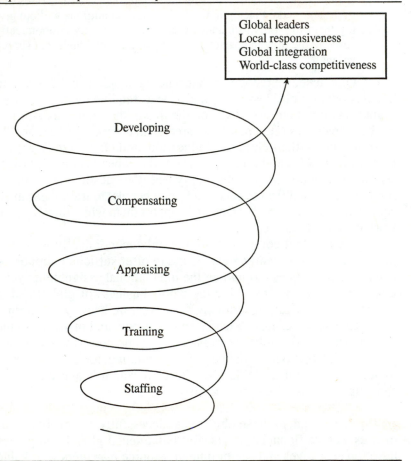

In many ways, this spiral of international human resources policies and practices is similar to the board game "Chutes and Ladders," where one wrong roll of the dice can mean a serious slide downward and loss of the game. In an expatriate's world, one inappropriate policy can result in individual and organizational failure. By contrast, a strategic and systematic approach to global assignments helps ensure that expatriates do not slide down the policy "chutes," but rather that they climb up a "ladder" to accomplish strategic objectives while overseas and after coming home. The result of a strategic-systematic approach is superior job performance overseas, along with higher cross-cultural adjustment, higher levels of performance in foreign subsidiaries, successful repatriation adjustment and performance, and future utilization of critical international experience, skills, and expertise. Successful international assignments, through successful international human resources policies, will be at the heart of successful international firms in the global marketplace of the twenty-first century.

Notes

1. Porter and McKibben, *Management Education and Development: Drift or Thrust into the 21st Century?*
2. Gregersen, Black, and Hite, "Expatriate Performance Appraisal: Principles, Practices and Challenges"; Roman, Mims, and Jespersen, "The Corporate Elite: A Portrait of the Boss."
3. Boles, "How organized is your expatriate program?"
4. Hanse, "Repatriation Programs Work."
5. Frazee, "Research Points to Weaknesses in Expat Policy."
6. Information on this best practice comes from General Electric Medical Systems' *The Expatriate Sponsorship Program.*
7. Black and Mendenhall, "A Practical but Theory-Based Framework for Selecting Cross-Cultural Training Methods," p. 199.

References

Abe, H., and R. L. Wiseman. 1983. "A Cross-Cultural Confirmation of Intercultural Effectiveness." *International Journal of Intercultural Relations 7:*53–68.

Adler, N. J. 1986. "Do MBAs Want International Careers?" *International Journal of Intercultural Relations 10:*277–300.

———. 1984. "Expecting International Success: Female Managers Overseas." *Columbia Journal of World Business 19:*79–85.

———. 1986. *International Dimensions of Organizational Behavior.* Boston: PWS-Kent.

———. 1990. *International Dimensions of Organizational Behavior.* 2d ed. Boston: PWS-Kent.

———. 1987. "Pacific Basin Managers: A Gaijin, Not a Woman." *Human Resource Management 26:*169–92.

———. 1981. "Re-entry: Managing Cross-Cultural Transitions." *Group and Organization Studies 6*(3):34156.

———. 1984. "Women Do Not Want International Careers: And Other Myths About International Management." *Organizational Dynamics 13:*66–79.

———. 1984. "Women in International Management: Where Are They?" *California Management Review 26:*78–89

Adler, N. J., and D. N. Izraeli. 1988. *Women in Management Worldwide.* Armonk, N.Y.: Sharpe.

Arthur, W., and W. Bennet. 1995. "The International Assignee: The Relative Importance of Factors Perceived to Contribute to Success." *Personnel Psychology 48:*99–113.

Aycan, Z. 1997. *Expatriate Management: Theory and Research.* Greenwich: JAI Press.

———. 1997. "Acculturation of Expatriate Managers: A Process Model of Adjustment and Performance." In *Expatriate Management: Theory and Research,* Z. Aycan. Greenwich: JAI Press.

Baird, L., and I. Meshoulam. 1988. "Managing Two Fits of Strategic Human Resource Management." *Academy of Management Review 13:*116–28.

Baker J. C., and J. Ivancevich. 1971. "The Assignment of American Executives Abroad: Systematic, Haphazard, or Chaotic?" *California Management Review 13:*39–44.

Bandura, A. 1983. *Social Foundations of Thought and Action.* Englewood Cliffs, N.J.: Prentice Hall.

———. 1977. *Social Learning Theory.* Englewood Cliffs, N.J.: Prentice Hall.

Bartlett, C., and S. Ghoshal. 1988. "Organizing for Worldwide Effectiveness: The Transnational Solution." *California Management Review 31*(1):54–74.

Beer, M. 1981. "Performance Appraisal: Dilemmas and Possibilities." *Organizational Dynamics 10:*24–36.

Bell, N., and B. Staw. 1989. "People as Sculptors Versus People as Sculpture: The Roles of Personality and Personal Control in Organizations." In *Handbook of Career Theory,* ed. M. B. Arthur, D. T. Hall, and B. Lawrence. Cambridge, England: Cambridge University Press.

Bennett, A. 1989. "The Chief Executives in the Year 2000 Will Be Experienced Abroad." *Wall Street Journal,* 27 Feb., A1–A4.

———. 1989. "Going Global." *Wall Street Journal,* 27 Feb. A1.

Björkman, I., and M. Gertsen. 1992. "Selecting and Training Scandinavian Expatriates: Determinants of Corporate Practice." *Scandinavian Journal of Management.*

Black, J. S. 1992. "Coming Home: The Relationship of Expatriate Expectations with Repatriation Adjustment and Job Performance." *Human Relations 45:*177–92.

———. 1990. "Factors Related to the Adjustment of Japanese Expatriate Managers in America." *Research in Personnel and Human Resource Management 5:*109–25.

———. 1991. "Fred Bailey: An Innocent Abroad." In *Readings and Cases in International Human Resource Management,* ed. M. Mendenhall and G. Oddou. Boston: PWS-Kent.

———. 1990. "Locus of Control, Social Support, Stress, and Adjustment to International Transfers." *Asia Pacific Journal of Management 7*(1):1–29.

————. 1994. "**O Kaerinasai:** Factors Related to Japanese Repatriation Adjustment." *Human Relations 47*:1,489–508.

————. 1991. "The Other Side of the Picture on the Other Side of the World: Repatriation Problems of Japanese Expatriate Spouses." Unpublished paper, Amos Tuck School of Business Administration, Dartmouth College.

————. 1990. "Personal Dimensions and Work Role Transitions: A Study of Japanese Expatriate Managers in America." *Management International Review 30*(2):119–34.

————. 1989. "Repatriation: A Comparison of Japanese and American Practices and Results." In *Proceedings of the Eastern Academy of Management International Conference.* Vol. 1. Hong Kong: Eastern Academy of Management.

————. 1992. "Socializing American Expatriate Managers Overseas: Tactics, Tenure, and Role Innovation." *Group and Organization Management 17*:171–92.

————. 1993. "The Role of Expectations During Repatriation for Japanese Managers." *Research in Personnel and Human Resources Management* (Supplement V.3, *International Human Resource Management*). Greenwich, CT: JAI Press, 339–58.

————. 1991. "A Tale of Three Countries." Paper presented at the annual meeting of the Academy of Management, Miami.

————. 1988. "Work Role Transitions: A Study of American Expatriate Managers in Japan." *Journal of International Business Studies 19*:277–94.

Black, J. S., and H. B. Gregersen. 1991. "Antecedents to Cross-Cultural Adjustment for Expatriates in Pacific Rim Assignments." *Human Relations 44*:497–515.

————. 1992. "Functional and Dysfunctional Turnover After International Assignments." Unpublished paper, Amos Tuck School of Business Administration, Dartmouth College.

————. 1991. "The Other Half of the Picture: Antecedents of Spouse Cross-Cultural Adjustment." *Journal of International Business Studies 22*:461–67.

————. 1991. "When Yankee Comes Home: Factors Related to Expatriate and Spouse Repatriation Adjustment." *Journal of International Business Studies 22*(4):671–95.

Black, J. S., H. B. Gregersen, and M. E. Mendenhall. 1992. "Toward a Theoretical Framework of Repatriation Adjustment." *Journal of International Business Studies 23:*737–60.

Black, J. S., H. B. Gregersen, and E. Wethli. 1990. "Factors Related to Expatriate Spouses' Adjustment in Overseas Assignments." Paper presented at the Western Academy of Management international conference, Shizuoka, Japan.

Black, J. S., and M. E. Mendenhall. 1990. "Cross-Cultural Training Effectiveness: A Review and Theoretical Framework for Future Research." *Academy of Management Review 15:*113–36.

———. 1991. "A Practical but Theory-Based Framework for Selecting Cross-Cultural Training Methods." In *Readings and Cases in International Human Resource Management,* M. Mendenhall and G. Oddou. ed. Boston: PWS-Kent.

———. 1989. "Selecting Cross-Cultural Training Methods: A Practical Yet Theory-Based Model." *Human Resource Management 28*(4): 511–40.

———. 1991. "The U-Curve Hypothesis Revisited: A Review and Theoretical Framework." *Journal of International Business Studies 22:*225–47.

Black, J. S., M. E. Mendenhall, and G. Oddou. 1991. "Toward a Comprehensive Model of International Adjustment: An Integration of Multiple Theoretical Perspectives." *Academy of Management Review 16:*291–317.

Black, J. S., A. Morrison, and H. Gregersen. (In press) *Global Explorers: The Next Generation of Leaders.* New York: Routledge.

Black, J. S., and L. W. Porter. 1991. "Managerial Behaviors and Job Performance: A Successful Manager in Los Angeles May Not Succeed in Hong Kong." *Journal of International Business Studies 22:*99–114.

Black, J. S., and G. Stephens. 1989. "Expatriate Adjustment and Intent to Stay in Pacific Rim Overseas Assignments." *Journal of Management 15:*529–44.

Blake, R., and J. Mouton. 1964. *The Managerial Grid.* Houston: Gulf.

Boles, M. 1997. "How Organized Is Your Expatriate Program?" *Workforce 76*(8):21–2.

Bowman, E. H. 1986. "Concerns of CEOs." *Human Resource Management 25:*267–85.

Boyacigiller, N. 1990. "The Role of Expatriates in the Management of Interdependence, Complexity, and Risk in Multinational Corporations." *Journal of International Business Studies 21:*357–81.

Brein, M., and K. H. David. 1971. "Intercultural Communication and Adjustment of the Sojourner." *Psychology Bulletin 76:*215–30.

Brett and Stroh. 1995. "Willingness to Relocate Internationally." *Human Resource Management Journal.*

Brewster, C. 1991. *The Management of Expatriates.* London: Kogan Page.

Casio, W. F. 1986. *Managing Human Resources.* New York: McGraw-Hill.

Church, A. T. 1982. "Sojourner Adjustment." *Psychological Bulletin 9:*540–72.

Clague, L., and N. Krupp. 1978. "International Personnel: The Repatriation Problem." *Personnel Administrator 23:*29–45.

Chao, G. T., and Y. J. Sun. 1997. "Training Needs for Expatriate Adjustment in the People's Republic of China." In *Expatriate Management: Theory and Research,* ed. Z. Aycan. Greenwich: JAI Press.

Clarke, C., and M. R. Hammer. 1995. "Predictors of Japanese and American Managers Job Success, Personal Adjustment, and Intercultural Interaction Effectiveness." *Management International Review 35:*153–70.

Copeland, L., and G. Louis. 1985. *Going International.* New York: Random House.

Cotton, J. L., D. A. Vollrath, K. L. Froggatt, M. L. Kengnick-Hall, and K. R. Jennings. 1988. "Employee Participation: Diverse Forms and Different Outcomes." *Academy of Management Review 13:*8–22.

De Cieri, H., P. J. Dowling, and K. Taylor. 1989. "The Psychological Impact of Expatriate Relocation on Spouses." Paper presented at the Academy of International Business annual meeting, Singapore.

Deller, J. "Expatriate Selection: Possibilities and Limitations of Using Personality Scales." 1997. In *New Approaches to Employee Management: Expatriate Management: Theory and Research,* ed. Zeynep Aycan. Vol. 4. London: JAI Press, 93–116.

Dennis L. E. and L. K. Stroh. 1993. "Take This Job and . . . A Case Study of International Adjustment." *International Journal of Organizational Analysis 1*(1):85–96.

Devanna, M. A., C. Fombrun, and N. Tichy. 1984. "A Framework for Strategic Human Resource Management." In *Strategic Human Resource Management*, ed. C. Fombrun, M. A. Devanna, and N. Tichy. New York: Wiley.

DeYoung, G. H. 1990. "The Clash of Cultures at Tylan General." *Electronic Business* (10 December), 148–150.

Dowling, P., and R. Schuler. 1990. *International Dimensions of Human Resource Management*. Boston: PWS-Kent.

Dowling, P., R. Schuler, and D. Welch. 1994. *International Dimensions of Human Resource Management*. 2d ed. Wadsworth International Dimensions of Business Series. Belmont, Calif.: Wadsworth Publishing Co.

Dowling, P. J., R. S. Schuler, and D. E. Welch. 1997. *International Dimensions of Human Resource Management*. 3d ed. Belmont: Wadsworth Publishing Co., Calif.

Doz, Y. L., and C. K. Prahalad. 1981. "Headquarters Influence and Strategic Control in MNCs." *Sloan Management Review 7:*15–29.

Earley, P. C. and M. Erez. 1997. *New Perspectives on International Industrial/Organizational Psychology*. San Francisco: The New Lexington Press.

Edstrom, A., and J. Galbraith. 1977. "Transfer of Managers as a Coordination and Control Strategy in Multinational Organizations." *Administrative Science Quarterly 22:*248–63.

Employee Relocation Council. 1997. *International Relocation Issues*. Washington, D.C.

Feldman, D., and H. Tompson. 1993. "Expatriation, Repatriation, and Domestic Geographical Relocation: An Empirical Investigation of Adjustment to New Job Assignments." *Journal of International Business Studies 24:*507–27.

Frazee, V. 1998. "Research Points to Weaknesses in Expat Policy." *Workforce 3*(1):9.

Fuchsberg, G. 1992. "As Costs of Overseas Assignments Climb, Firms Select Expatriates More Carefully." *Wall Street Journal*, 9 January, B1–B4.

Gates, S. 1996. *Managing Expatriates' Return: A Research Report*. The Conference Board.

"GE Culture Turns Sour at French Unit." 1990. *Wall Street Journal*, 31 July, A11.

Gertsen, M. 1989. "Expatriate Training and Selection." In *Proceedings of the European International Business Association Conference*, ed. R. Luostarinen. Helsinki, Finland: European International Business Association.

Ghadar, F., and N. Adler. 1989. "Management Culture and Accelerated Product Life Cycle." *Human Resource Planning 12*(1):37–42.

Gibson, C. B. 1997 "Do You Hear What I Hear? A Framework for Reconciling Intercultural Communication Difficulties Arising from Cognitive Styles and Cultural Values." In *New Perspectives on Industrial/Organizational Psychology*, ed. P. C. Earley and M. Erez, 335–62. San Francisco: The New Lexington Press.

Glissen, C., and M. Durrick. 1988. "Predictors of Job Satisfaction and Organizational Commitment in Human Service Organizations." *Administrative Science Quarterly 33*:61–81.

Gomez-Mejia, L., and D. Balkin. 1987. "Determinants of Managerial Satisfaction with the Expatriation Process." *Journal of Management Development 6:*7–17.

Graen, G. B., C. Hui, M. Wakabayashi, and Zhong-Ming Wang. 1997. Cross-Cultural Research Alliances in Organizational Research: Cross-Cultural Partnership-Making in Action. In *New Perspectives on International Industrial/Organizational Psychology*, ed. P. C. Earley and M. Erez. San Francisco: The New Lexington Press.

Granrose, C. 1994. "Careers of Japanese and Expatriate Chinese Managers in U.S. Multi-National Firms." 10, 4: 59–79.

Greenberger, D., and S. Strasser. 1990. "Development and Application of a Model of Personal Control in Organizations." *Academy of Management Review 11:*164–77.

Gregersen, H. B. 1992. "Coming Home to the Cold: Finnish Repatriation Adjustment." Paper presented at the meeting of the Academy of International Business, Brussels, Belgium.

———. 1992. "Commitments to a Parent Company and a Local Work Unit during Repatriation." *Personnel Psychology 45:*29–54.

———. 1992. "Organizational Commitment During Repatriation: The Japanese and Finnish Experience." Paper presented at the annual meeting of the Academy of Management, Las Vegas.

Gregersen, H. B., and J. S. Black. 1992. "Antecedents to Commitment to a Parent Company and a Foreign Operation." *Academy of Management Journal 35:*65–90.

————. 1995. "Global Executive Development: Keeping High Performers After International Assignments." *Journal of International Management 1:*3–31.

————. 1990. "A Multifaceted Approach to Expatriate Retention in International Assignments." *Group and Organization Studies 15*(4):461–85.

————. 1996. "Multiple Commitments Upon Repatriation: The Japanese Experience." *Journal of Management 22:*209–29.

Gregersen, H. B., J. S. Black, and J. Hite. 1995. "Expatriate Performance Appraisal: Principles, Practices and Challenges. In *Expatriate Management: New Ideas for International Business*, ed. Jan Selmer. Westport, CT: Quorum Books.

Gregersen, H. B., J. Hite, and J. S. Black. 1996. "Expatriate Performance Appraisal in U.S. Multinational Firms." *Journal of International Business Studies 27:*711–38.

Gupta, A., and V. Govindarajan. 1991. "Knowledge Flows and the Structure of Control Within Multinational Corporations." *Academy of Management Review 16*(4):768–92.

Hall, D. 1989. "How Top Management and the Organization Itself Can Block Effective Executive Succession." *Human Resource Management 28:*5–24.

Hall, D. T., and J. G. Goodale. 1986. *Human Resource Management*. Glenview, Ill.: Scott, Foresman.

Hammer, M. R. 1987. "Behavioral Dimensions of Intercultural Effectiveness." *International Journal of Intercultural Relations 11:*65–88.

Hammer, M. R., J. E. Gudykunst, and R. L. Wiseman. 1978. "Dimensions of Intercultural Effectiveness: An Exploratory Study." *International Journal of Intercultural Relations 2:*382–93.

Hansen, F. 1997. "Repatriation Programs Work." *Compensation and Benefits Review 29*(5):14–5.

Harris, P. R., and R. Moran. 1989. *Managing Cultural Differences*. Houston: Gulf.

Harvey, M. 1985. "The Executive Family: An Overlooked Variable in International Assignments." *Columbia Journal of World Business 19:*84–93.

————. 1983. "The Other Side of Foreign Assignments: Dealing with the Repatriation Problem." *Columbia Journal of World Business 17:*53–9.

————. 1989. "Repatriation of Corporate Executives: An Empirical Study." *Journal of International Business Studies 20:*131–44.

Hawes, F., and D. J. Kealey. 1981. "An Empirical Study of Canadian Technical Assistance." *International Journal of Intercultural Relations 5:*239–58.

Hoecklin, L. 1995. *Managing Cultural Differences: Strategies for Competitive Advantage.* Reading, Mass.: Addison–Wesley.

Hofstede, G. 1980. *Culture's Consequences: International Differences in Work-Related Values.* Newbury Park, Calif.: Sage.

House, R. J., N. S. Wright, R. N. Aditya. 1997. "Cross-Cultural Research on Organizational Leadership: A Critical Analysis and a Proposed Theory." In *Perspectives on International Industrial/ Organizational Psychology,* ed. P. C. Earley and M. Erez. San Francisco: The New Lexington Press.

HRM Update. 1996. "Spouses a Concern in International Relocation." *HRMagazine* (May).

Ioannou, L. 1995. Unnatural Selection. *International Business* (July), 54–9.

Jackson, S., and R. Schuler. 1985. "A Meta-analysis and Conceptual Critique of Research on Role Ambiguity and Role Conflict in Work Settings." *Organizational Behavior and Human Decision Processes 36:*16–78.

Jaeger, A. 1982. "Contrasting Control Modes in the Multinational Corporation: Theory, Practice, and Implications." *International Studies of Management and Organization 12*(1):59–82.

Janssens, M. 1995. "Intercultural Interaction: A Burden on International Managers?" *Journal of Organizational Behavior* 16:155–67.

Jelenik, M., and N. J. Adler. 1988. "Women: World-Class Managers for Global Competition." *Academy of Management Executive 2:* 11–9.

Kainulainen, S. 1990. "Selection and Training of Personnel for Foreign Assignments." Unpublished master's thesis, University of Vaasa, Finland.

Katz, J. and D. M. Seifer. 1996. "It's a Different World Out There: Planning for Expatriate Success Through Selection, Pre-Departure Training and On-Site Socialization." *Human Resource Planning,* 32–47.

Kendall, D. W. 1981. "Repatriation: An Ending and a Beginning." *Business Horizons 24:*21–5.

Kerr, S. 1975. "On the Folly of Rewarding *A* While Hoping for *B*." *Academy of Management Journal 18*(4):769–83.

Kobrin, S. 1988. "Expatriate Reduction and Strategic Control in American Multinational Corporations." *Human Resource Management 27:*63–75.

Kopp, R. 1994. International Human Resource Policies and Practices in Japanese, European, and U.S. Multinationals. 33, 4:581–99.

Korn-Ferry International. 1981. *A Study of the Repatriation of the American International Executive.* New York: Korn-Ferry International.

Kroeber, A. L., and C. Kluckhohn. 1952. *Culture: A Critical Review of Concepts and Definitions.* Cambridge, Mass.: Harvard University Press.

Lin, Z. 1997. "Ambiguity with a Purpose: The Shadow of Power in Communication." In *New Perspectives on Industrial/Organizational Psychology,* ed. P. C. Earley and M. Erez, 363–76. San Francisco: The New Lexington Press.

Linton, R. 1995. *The Tree of Culture.* Toronto, Canada: McCleland & Stewart.

Lublin, J. 1989. "Grappling with Expatriate Issues." *Wall Street Journal,* 11 December, B1.

McGregor, D. 1960. *The Human Side of Enterprise.* New York: McGraw-Hill.

Manz, C. C., and H. P. Sims. 1981. "Vicarious Learning: The Influence of Modeling on Organizational Behavior." *Academy of Management Review 6:*105–13.

Mathieu, J. E., and D. M. Zajac. 1990. "A Review and Meta-analysis of the Antecedents, Correlates, and Consequences of Organizational Commitment." *Psychological Bulletin 108:*171–94.

Mendenhall, M., E. Dunbar, and G. Oddou. 1987. "Expatriate Selection, Training, and Career-Pathing." *Human Resource Management 26*(3):331–45.

Mendenhall, M., and G. Oddou. 1986. "Acculturation Profiles of Expatriate Managers: Implications for Cross-Cultural Training Programs." *Columbia Journal of World Business 21:*73–9.

———. 1985. "The Dimensions of Expatriate Acculturation: A Review." *Academy of Management Review 10:*39–47.

Miller, E. 1973. "The International Selection Decision: A Study of Managerial Behavior in the Selection Decision Process." *Academy of Management Journal 16*(2):239–52.

Miller, E., S. Beechler, B. Bhatt, and R. Nath. 1986. "Relationship Between Global Strategic Planning Process and the Human Resource Management Function." *Human Resource Planning 9*(1):9–23.

Misa, K. F., and Fabricatore, J. 1979. "Return on Investment of Overseas Personnel." *Financial Executive 47:*42–6.

Moran, Stahl, and Boyer. 1987. *International Human Resource Management.* Boulder, Colo.: Moran, Stahl, and Boyer.

Mount, M. K., and M. R. Barrick. 1995. "The Big Five Personality Dimensions: Implications for Research and Practice in Human Resources Management." In *Research in Personnel and Human Resource Management,* ed. G. R. Ferris, 13:153–200. Greenwich: JAI Press.

Mowday, R., L. Porter, and R. Steers. 1982. *Employee-Organization Linkages: The Psychology of Commitment, Absenteeism, and Turnover.* San Diego, Calif.: Academic Press.

Murphy, D. W., and L. K. Stroh. 1997. "A Critical Evaluation of Expatriate Selection and the Issue of Fit." Paper presented to the International Conferences on Advances in Management (July), Toronto.

Nakane, C. 1970. *Japanese Society.* Berkeley: University of California Press.

Napier, N. K., and R. B. Peterson. 1990. "Expatriate Re-entry: What Do Repatriates Have to Say?" *Human Resource Planning 14:*19–28.

Negandi, A. R., G. S. Eshghi, and E. C. Yuen. 1985. "The Managerial Practices of Japanese Subsidiaries Overseas." *California Management Review 4:*93–105.

Nemetz, P. L. and S. L. Christensen. 1996. "The Challenge of Cultural Diversity: Harnessing Diversity of Views to Understand Multiculturalism." *The Academy of Management Review 21,* 2:434–62.

Nicholson, N., and I. Ayako. 1993. "The Adjustment of Japanese Expatriates to Living and Working in Japan. *British Journal of Management, 4:*93–105.

Oddou, G., H. B. Gregersen, B. Derr, and J. S. Black. (in press). "Internationalizing Human Resources: Strategy Differences Among European, Japanese, and U.S. Multinationals." *International Journal of Human Resource Management.*

Oddou, G., and M. Mendenhall. 1991. "Expatriate Performance Appraisal: Problems and Solutions." In *Readings and Cases in International Human Resource Management*, ed. M. Mendenhall and G. Oddou. Boston: PWS-Kent.

———. 1984. "Person Perception in Cross-Cultural Settings: A Review of Cross-Cultural and Related Literature." *International Journal of Intercultural Relations 8:*77–96.

———. 1991. "Succession Planning for the 21st Century: How Well Are We Grooming Our Future Business Leaders?" *Business Horizons 34:*2–10.

O'Hara, M., and R. Johansen. 1994. *Global Work: Bridging Distance, Culture & Time*. San Francisco: Jossey-Bass.

Ones, D. S. and C. Viswesvaran. 1997. "Personality Determinants in the Prediction of Aspects of Expatriate Job Success." In *Expatriate Management: Theory and Research*, ed. Zeynep Aycan, 63–92. Vol. 4. London: JAI Press.

O'Reilly, C., and J. Chatman. 1983. "Organizational Commitment and Psychological Attachment: The Effects of Compliance, Identification, and Internalization of Prosocial Behavior." *Journal of Applied Psychology 71:*492–99.

Organization Resources Counselors. 1990. *1990 Survey of International Personnel and Compensation Practices*. New York: Organization Resources Counselors.

Oslund, J. 1991. "The Overseas Experience of Expatriate Businesspeople." Paper presented at the annual meeting of the Academy of Management, Miami.

Osland, J. 1995. "Working Abroad: A Hero's Adventure." *Training and Development* 47–51.

———. 1991. "Working Abroad: A Hero's Adventure." *International Journal of Human Resource Management* 2(3):377–414.

———. 1995. *The Adventure of Working Abroad: Hero Tales from the Global Frontier*. San Francisco: Jossey-Bass.

Ouchi, W. G. 1979. "A Conceptual Framework for the Design of Organizational Control Mechanisms." *Management Science 25:*833–48.

———. 1980. "Markets, Bureaucracies, and Clans," *Administrative Science Quarterly 25:*129–141.

———. 1977. "The Relationship Between Organizational Structure and Organizational Control." *Administrative Science Quarterly 22:*95–113.

Parker, B., and G. McEvoy. 1993. "Initial Examination of a Model of Intercultural Adjustment." *International Journal of Intercultural Relations 17:*355–79.

Pellico, M. T. and L. K. Stroh. 1997. "Spousal Assistance Programs: An Integral Component of the International Assignment." In *Expatriate Management: Theory and Research*, ed. Z. Aycan, 227–44. Vol. 4. London: JAI Press.

Porter, L., and L. McKibben. 1988. *Management Education and Development: Drift or Thrust into the 21st Century?* New York: McGraw-Hill.

Porter, M. 1986. "Changing Patterns of International Competition." *California Management Review 28*(2):9–40.

Robinson, R. 1978. *International Business Management: A Guide to Decision Making*. Chicago: Dryden Press.

Roman, M., R. Mims, and F. Jespersen. 1991. "The Corporate Elite: A Portrait of the Boss." *Business Week*, 25 November, 182.

Ruben, I., and D. J. Kealey. 1979. "Behavioral Assessment of Communication Competency and the Prediction of Cross-Cultural Adaptation." *International Journal of Intercultural Relations 3:*15–7.

Schein, E. 1984. "Coming to a New Awareness of Organizational Culture." *Sloan Management Review 10:*3–16.

Schell, M. and C. Solomon. 1997. *Capitalizing on the Global Workforce: A Strategic Guide to Expatriate Management*. Chicago: Irwin Publishing.

Society for Human Resource Management. 1997. *1996–1997 International Assignee Project*.

Solomon, C. M. 1996. "One Assignment, Two Lives." *Personnel Journal* (May).

Stening, B. 1979. "Problems of Cross-Cultural Contact: A Literature Review." *International Journal of Intercultural Relations 3:*269–313.

Stening, B., J. Everett, and L. Longton. 1981. "Mutual Perception of Managerial Performance and Style in Multinational Subsidiaries." *Journal of Occupational Psychology 54:*255–63.

Stephens, G., and J. S. Black. 1991. "The Impact of the Spouse's Career Orientation on Managers During International Transfers." *Journal of Management Studies 28:*417–28.

Stroh, L. K. 1997. The Family's Role in International Assignments. *Fast Change Magazine* (April).

———. 1995. "Predicting Turnover Among Repatriates: Can Organizations Affect Retention Rates?" *International Journal of Human Resource Management* 6(2):443–56.

Stroh, L. K. and M. A. Lautzenhiser. 1994. "Benchmarking Global Human Resources Practices and Procedures." *Mobility.*

Stroh, L. K., L. E. Dennis, and T. C. Cramer. 1994. "Predictors of Expatriate Adjustment." *International Journal of Organizational Analysis* 2(2):176–92.

Torbiörn, I. 1982. *Living Abroad.* New York: Wiley.

Triandis, H. C., V. Vassilou, and M. Nassiakou. 1968. "Three Cross-Cultural Studies of Subjective Culture. Part Two." *Journal of Personality and Social Psychology* 8(4):1–42.

Triandis, H. C., and D. P. S. Bhawuk, 1997. "Culture Theory and the Meaning of Relatedness." In *New Perspectives on International Industrial/Organizational Psychology,* ed. P.C. Earley and M. Erez. San Francisco: The New Lexington Press.

Trompenaars, F. 1994. *Riding the Waves of Culture.* Burr Ridge, IL: Irwin.

Tung, R. 1988. "Career Issues in International Assignments." *Academy of Management Executive* 2(3):241–44.

———. 1988. *The New Expatriates: Managing Human Resources Abroad.* New York: Ballinger.

———. 1981. "Selecting and Training of Personnel for Overseas Assignments." *Columbia Journal of World Business* 16(1): 68–78.

———. 1982. "Selection and Training Procedures of U.S., European, and Japanese Multinationals." *California Management Review* 25:57–71.

Walker, E. J. 1976. "Till Business Us Do Part?" *Harvard Business Review* 54:94–101.

Ward, C., and A. Kennedy. 1993. "Where's the 'Culture' in Cross-Cultural Transition?" *Journal of Cross-Cultural Psychology* 24: 221–49.

Welch, D. 1994. International Human Resource Management Approaches and Activities: A Suggested Framework. *Journal of Management* 31,2:139–64.

White, M. 1988. *The Japanese Overseas*. New York: Free Press.

Windham International and the National Foreign Trade Council. 1997. *Global Relocation Trends 1995 Survey Report.*

Zeira, Y., and M. Banai. 1985. "Selection of Managers for Foreign Posts." *International Studies of Management and Organization* *15*(1):33–51.

Index

A

Adjustment, anticipatory, 115
  See also Cross-cultural adjustment;
    Repatriation adjustment
Airbus, as multifocal corporation, 24
Allowances, 182–190, 199
  car-and-driver, 188–189
  club membership, 189
  cost-of-living, 184–186
  education, 187
  foreign site premiums, 183
  furnishing, 187, 200
  hardship, 183–184, 199
  home-leave, 188, 200
  housing, 186, 199–200
  medical, 188
  mobility, 270
  relocation, 188, 200
  rest-and-relaxation, 188
  site, 183–184; taxes, 189–190
  utility, 186, 199–200
American Express, compensation program
  of, 269–270
Anticipatory adjustment, 115
Anticipatory expectations, 115
Appointment: of candidate, 264
See also Selection
Appraisal, 18, 20, 156–173
 best practices in, 268–269
See also Performance appraisals
Approval of candidate, 264
See also Selection
Artifacts, 32
Attention in learning process, 90

B

Background data, in selecting international
  candidates, 65

Balance sheet, approach to global compen-
  sation, 178–180
Behavioral control, 108
Belgium, international experience in, 256
Best practices, in managing global assign-
  ment cycle, 256–277
Biographical data in selecting international
  candidates, 65
Bottom line, and repatriation adjustment,
  208
Brownouts, 12–13
Brunswick Corporation, 3

C

Canada, international experience in, 256
Candidates. *See* Global candidates
Car-and-driver allowance, in global com-
  pensation, 188–189
Career loops, as factor in retention, 242–
  243
Castrol, as multidomestic corporation, 22
Chief executive officers (CEOs)
  key concerns and responsibilities of, 2
  need for international experience,
    256–257
Citicorp, value of global experience to, 248,
  249
Clients, in performance appraisals, 170,
  171–172
Club membership allowance, in global compensation, 189
Coca-Cola, as multifocal corporation, 24
Colgate-Palmolive
  in addressing family concerns, 75
  and balancing of dual allegiances, 152
  selection of global candidates by, 4–5
  value of global experience to, 248
Commitment. Organizational commitment

Communication
  and expatriate success, 61
  with home-country people, 209
  with local populace, 95–97, 98–99
  technology in, 5
Compensation: developing appropriate
    in successful repatriation, 230–231
  as factor in retention, 244–245
  See also Allowances; Global compensation; Rewarding
Competitive advantage, by keeping best
    global managers, 252–254
Composite market approach to global compensation, 181–182
Conflict resolution skills and expatriate success, 60
Contributions to the firm, appreciating in
    successful repatriation, 232
Coordination and control, 58
  and global assignments, 5–7
Corporate orientation, linking, to training,
    103–105
Cost-of-living allowance in global compensation, 184–186
Criticality of routines, 47
Cross-cultural adjustment, 32–50, 107–127
  categorization of influential factors in,
    114–121
  dimensions of, 108–114
  factors influencing spouses', 121–122
  fundamental assumptions in, 36–45
  human activity in, 39
  humanity's relationship to environment in, 36, 38
  human nature in, 38
  human relationships in, 38–39
  identifying culture in, 32–36
  job design as factor in, 123, 124–125
  logistical support as factor in, 123, 126
  maximizing chances of successful,
    122–127
  process of, 45–50
  reality and truth, 39–40
  selection as factor in, 122, 123, 124
  social support as factor in, 123,
    126–127
  training as factor in, 123, 124
Cross-cultural training, 103, 268
  designing, 92–98

Cultural diversity, 5–6
Cultural toughness, 94–95, 98
Culture: definition of, 32–36
  matrix of, 35
  process of adapting to new, 88–92
  tangible aspects of, 32
Culture novelty, 120
Culture shock, 47–50
  during repatriation adjustment, 203,
    209

D

Delegation skills, determining, in candidate,
    263
Demotion in postreturn repatriation adjustment, 217
Developing, 19, 20
  See also Retention
Direct moving costs of failed assignments,
    11–12
Dorothy Syndrome, 206
Dow Chemical, as global-strategy multinational corporation, 23
Downtime, planning for, in successful repatriation, 232
Downtime costs of failed assignments, 12
Downward-spiraling vicious cycles, 15
Dual allegiance: balancing, 130–154
  guidelines for effective management
    of, 147–154
Dual citizens, creating, 153–154
Dysfunctional retention, 239
Dysfunctional turnover, 238–239

E

Eastman Chemical, in addressing family
    concerns, 74
Education allowance, in global compensation, 187
Environment, humanity's relationship to,
    36, 37, 38
Ethnocentricity and expatriate success, 62
EuroDisney, 54
Europe, selection practices in, 55–57
Executive capability, gutting, at headquarters, 15–16
Executive performance, and repatriation adjustment, 208

Expatriates
    best practices in dealing with, 271–272
    communication skills of, 61
    compensation for, 177–178
    conflict resolution skills of, 60
    as dual citizens, 141–147
    ethnocentricity of, 62
    expectations of, on repatriation,
        202–203
    flexibility of, 62–63
    as free agents, 132–135
    gender-related factors for, 63–64
    in going native, 135–138
    guidelines for effective management of
        dual allegiance, 147–154
    home allegiance as problem for,
        138–141
    importance of, 257
    in inventorying international assign-
        ment experience, 250–25
    leadership skills on, 60–61
    matching with subsidiaries, 148–150
    professional skills of, 60
    responsibility for professional
        development, 271–272
    satisfaction GAP for, 258
    selection factors predictive of, 59–64
    social skills of, 61–62
    stability of, 63
    strategic roles of, 257
    See also Repatriation
Expatriation, role of host manager in,
    272–273
    Expectations
    of expatriates, 202–203
    managing, with accurate information,
        225–226
Export firms, 21–22
Export stage of globalization, 252
External fit, 25, 103–104

F
Failed assignments, costs of, 11–12
Families
    addressing concerns of, 73–76
    impact of, on selection, 70–71
    interviewing, in selection process, 82
    systems approach to, 71–73
    See also Spouses

Feedback, getting, in repatriation, 233
Feedback instruments, 82
Ferran, David, 6
Financial shock in postreturn repatriation
    adjustment, 218–219
Fit
    external, 25, 103–104
    internal, 25, 103
Flexibility and expatriate success, 62–63
Flour Corporation, 5
Flour Daniel, Inc., 5
Follow-up training, 101
Ford Motor Company
    in balancing dual allegiances, 151,
        152, 153
    referrals of foreign nationals to third
        countries by, 10–11
    value of global experience to, 4, 7
Foreign site premiums in global compensa-
    tion, 183
Foreign subsidiaries: implementor, 8, 149
    innovator, 8, 150
    integrator, 8, 150
    island, 8, 148–149
    matching with expatriates, 148–150
Free agents, expatriates as, 132–135
Functional retention, 237, 238
Functional turnover, 239
Furnishing allowance in global compensa-
    tion, 187, 200
Future needs, assessing, 78

G
G-A-P-S™ *See* Global Assignment Pre-
    paredness Survey
GE Medical Systems
    Expatriate Sponsorship Program at, 271
    Human Resource Network of, 272,
        273
    repatriation team at, 225
Gender-related factors, and expatriate suc-
    cess, 63–64
Générale de Radiologie (CGR), 13–14
General Electric
    and dual allegiance problem, 151, 152
    value of gobal experience to, 1, 4,
        13–14
General Motors, and dual allegiance prob-
    lem, 151, 152

General nonwork environment, cross-cultural adjustment to, 109, 111
Geographic dispersion, 6–7
Gillette, value of global experience to, 4
Global Assignment Preparedness Survey (G-A-P-S™), 66–67, 79, 82
Global assignments
    costs of poorly managed, 11–13
    defining strategic purposes for, 81
    establishing best practices in managing cycle of, 256–277
    framework for people management in, 16–20
    as key to executive success and global competitiveness, 274–277
    and leadership development, 2–5
    rethinking views of, 9–11
    selection factors predictive of success in, 58–59
    selection process for specific, 79–83
    strategic analysis of, 77–83
    strategic roles of, 1–29
    strategic value of, 2–9
    technical approach to, 53–54
    technology, innovation, and information transfers and, 7–9
Global candidates: acceptance/refusal of assignments by, 69–70
    appointment of, 264
    approval of, 264
    defining pool of, 78, 81–82
    determining qualifications of, 259, 262, 263
    evaluation of, 68
    interviewing, 82
    interviews of, 261–262
    making offer to, 82
    personnel's recommendations on, 263
    scheduling of interviews of, 261
    screening of, 259, 261
    testing of, 261–262
    utilizing standardized tests and feedback instruments in evaluating, 65–67, 82, 261–263
Global compensation
    and attracting and retaining quality people, 176
    balance sheet approach to, 178–180
    composite market approach to, 181–182

    in enhancing feelings of equity, 176–178
    integrated solution in, 190–200
    local market approach to, 182
    parent-country equivalency approach to, 180–181
    regional market approach to, 181–182
    three-step approach to, 194–200
    See also Allowances
Global context
    people management in, 21–28
    performance appraisals in, 159–172
Global experience, creating an organization that values, 247–249
Globalization
    export stage of, 252
    linking patterns of, to appraisal, 172–173
    multidomestic stage of, 22–23, 252–253
    patterns of, 21–25
Global Leadership Institute, 1
Global managers
    creating competitive advantage by keeping best, 252–254
    retention of, as strategic asset, 236–239
Global-strategy multinational corporations, 23–24
Going native process, 135–138
    counterbalancing tendency to, 150–152
    negative aspects of, 137–138
    positive aspects of, 138
Great Britain, international experience in, 256
Greiger, Greg, 4

H
Halo effect, 168
Hardship allowance, in global compensation, 183–184, 199
High-rigor training, 92–93
Hired-gun free agents, 132–133
Home country
    changes in, and repatriation, 208
    communication with people in, 209
    establishing information sources in successful repatriation, 226–228

Home-country job environment, preparing, in successful repatriation, 228–230
Home leave
    encouraging, in successful repatriation, 227
    in prereturn repatriation adjustment, 213
Home-leave allowance, 188, 200
Honda, and dual allegiance problem, 130, 151
Host-country nationals
    compensation for, 177–178
    cross-cultural adjustment to interacting with, 109
Host manager, in expatriation and repatriation, 272–273
Housing, facilitating adequate, in successful repatriation, 231
Housing allowances, 186, 199–200
Housing conditions and postreturn repatriation adjustment, 220–221
Human activity, 37, 39
Humanity, relationship to environment, 36, 37, 38
Human nature, 37, 38
Human relationships, 37, 38–39

I
IBM, 64
    training approach of, 265–266
IBM-Asia Pacific, 265–266
IBM-Japan, 265–266
Identity, loss of, during repatriation, 202
Implementor foreign subsidiary, 8, 149
In-country training, 101, 264–266
In-depth culture training, 102
Indirect costs, of failed assignments, 12
Individual factor
    in cross-cultural adjustment, 116, 117–118
    effect of, on organizational commitment during repatriation, 240–243
    in postreturn repatriation adjustment, 214–215
Influential factors, categorization of
    in cross-cultural adjustment, 114–121
Information, managing expectations with accurate, 225–226

Information and technology exchange, 58
Information exchange in prereturn repatriation adjustment, 212
Information transfers, and global assignments, 7–9
Innovation, and global assignments, 7–9
Innovator foreign subsidiary, 8, 150
Integration process, 130–154
Integrator foreign subsidiary, 8, 150
Internal fit, 25, 103
International assignment, contrasting approaches to, 257, 258, 274
International experience
    impact of previous, 116
    value of, in retention, 245–246
International Hotel, 26
International human resources, spiral of, 275–277
Interviews in selecting international candidates, 67–68, 261–263
Island foreign subsidiary, 8, 148–149

J
Japan
    in-country training programs in, 265–266
    selection practices in, 55–57
Japanese expatriates
    and changes in workplace, 207
    commitment of, during repatriation, 243
Japanese spouses, in repatriation adjustment, 222–223
Job autonomy, reduced, 216
Job clarity, 118
Job design, as factor in cross-cultural adjustment, 123, 124–126
Job discretion, 118
Job expectations, unclear, 216
Job factor
    in cross-cultural adjustment, 118
    effect of, on organizational commitment during repatriation, 243–44;
        in postreturn repatriation adjustment, 215–217
    in spouse's repatriation adjustment, 221–223
Job toughness, 97–98
Juku, 222

K

Kentucky Fried Chicken, and dual allegiance problem, 133
Kodak, global assignments at, 10
Korn/Ferry International, 16

L

Language training, 266–268
Leadership development, 58
    and expatriate success, 60–61
    and global assignments, 2–5
Local market approach to global compensation, 182
Logistical support, as factor in cross-cultural adjustment, 123, 126
Lord Corporation, in developing candidate pool, 79
Low-rigor training, 92
Lucent, joint venture with Philips, 9

M

Magnitude of routines, 47
Make work holding-pattern assignments, 243
Managerial performance and repatriation adjustment, 208
McDonald's, routines at, 46
McGregor, Douglas, 38
Medical allowance, in global compensation, 188
Microsoft, 38
Mobility allowance, 270
Monsanto, in addressing family concerns, 75
Motorola, in addressing family concerns, 75–76
Movement patterns as factor in retention, 242–243
Multidomestic corporations (MDCs), 22–23, 252–253
Multifocal corporations, 24
Multinational corporations, global-strategy, 23–24
Multinational firms, strategic objectives of, 275–276

N

Needs, analyzing current, 77–78
Neste Oy, in defining candidate pool, 78

Nestlé, training issues at, 104–105
Newspapers/magazines, providing access to, in successful repatriation, 228
Nike, and geographic dispersion, 6–7
Nonwork factor
    in cross-cultural adjustment, 119–121
    effect of, on organizational commitment during repatriation, 246–247
    in postreturn repatriation adjustment, 219–221

O

Offer, making assignment, 82
On-site superiors in performance appraisals, 169, 171
Operation Desert storm, 274
Organizational commitment
    factors that effect during repatriation, 240–247
    strategies for sustaining, during repatriation, 247–252
Organizational factors
    in cross-cultural adjustment, 116–117, 119
    effect of, on organizational commitment during repatriation, 244–246
    in postreturn repatriation adjustment, 218–219
Orientation in prereturn repatriation adjustment, 213–214
Other-oriented relational factors in cross-cultural adjustment, 118

P

Parent company
    at export stage of globalization, 252
    feelings of repatriates toward staying with, 237
    at multidomestic stage of globalization, 252–253
    in strategically planning return position, 249–251
    tenure in, as factor in retention, 240–241
    value of global experience to, 247–249
Parent-country equivalency approach to global compensation, 180–181

Peer managers, in performance appraisals, 169–170, 171
PENNBANK Malaysia, 40–45
People management
    appraising, 18, 20
    developing in, 19, 20
    in the global context, 21–28
    recruiting/selecting in, 16–17, 19
    rewarding, 18–19, 20
    training, 17–18, 20
Perceptual-oriented factors in cross-cultural adjustment, 118
Performance appraisals, 156–173
    clients in, 170, 171–172
    conflicts in, 157, 158
    criteria in, 165–166
    in the global context, 159–172
    goals of, 157
    invalid criteria, 158, 160–162
    linking patterns of globalization and strategy orientation to, 172–173
    on-site superiors in, 169, 171
    peer mangers in, 169–170, 171
    problematic nature of, 156
    purpose of, 156–158
    rater bias in, 159, 163–164
    rater competence in, 159, 162–163
    responsibility for doing, 166–170
    self in, 170
    subordinates in, 170, 171
    timing of, 170–172
Perseverance, determining, in candidate, 262
Personnel, recommendations on filling foreign assignments, 263
Perspectives, influence of changed, on repatriation, 207
Philip Morris Companies
    and turnover after repatriation, 14–15
    value of global experience to, 4
Philips, joint venture with Lucent, 9
Plateaued-career free agents, 134–135
Position, identification of, 259
Postreturn repatriation adjustment, 211, 214–221
Predeparture training, 88–89, 101, 264
Predictive control, 107
Prereturn repatriation adjustment, 211, 212–214

Professional skills, and expatriate success, 60
Promotion disappointments in postreturn repatriation adjustment, 216–217

Q
Quaker Oats, in addressing family concerns, 74–75
Quaker State, as multidomestic corporation, 22

R
Rater bias, in performance appraisal, 159, 163–164
Rater competence, in performance appraisal, 159, 162–163
Reality and truth, 37, 39–40
Recruiting/selecting, 16–17, 19
Recur Engineering, training program at, 87–88
Regional market approach to global compensation, 181–182
Reichert, Jack, 3
Relocation allowance, in global compensation, 188, 200
Repatriates
    feelings of, toward staying with parent firms, 237
    identifying and tracking high-risk, 251–252
    targeting high-risk, 225
Repatriation, 202–233
    best practices in, 271–274
    and changes in home country, 208
    expectations on, 202–203
    factors that effect organizational commitment during, 240–247
    getting feedback in, 233
    influence of changed perspectives, 207
    loss of identity during, 202
    process of, 204–208
    research on, 203
    role of host manager in, 272–273
    role of sponsor in, 272
    steps toward successful, 223–232
    strategic functions of, 223–224
    strategies for sustaining organizational commitment during, 247–252

Repatriation *(continued)*
    treatment of, as foreign assignment,
        206
    turnover after, 14–15
    unclear process, 218
    See also Expatriates; Retention
Repatriation adjustment, 203–204
    bottom line in, 208
    communicating with home-country
        people, 209
    culture shock during, 203, 209
    dimensions of, 209–210
    factors influencing, 210–211, 237
    postreturn, 211
    prereturn, 211, 212–214
    readjustment to general living
        environment, 210
    by spouse, 221–223
    of spouse, 208
Repatriation team
    establishment of, 224–225
    role of, in retention process, 250
Repatriation training as factor in retention,
    244
Research and development (R&D), 24
Rest-and-relaxation allowance in global
    compensation, 188
Retention, 236–254
    creating competitive advantage in,
        252–254
    dysfunctional, 239
    functional, 237, 238
    of global managers as strategic asset,
        236–239
    in learning process, 90–91
    role of repatriation team in, 250
    See also Repatriation
Return job, ill-planned, 215–216
Return position, strategically planning of,
    249–251
Review pool, 81
Rewarding, 18–19, 20, 175–200
    best practices in, 269–270
    objectives of, 176–178
    problems in, 175–178
    See also Allowances; Compensation;
        Global compensation
Rigor, and length of time spent on training,
    92–93

ROA (Return on Assets), 1
Role conflict, 118
Routines in cross-cultural adjustment,
    46–47

S
Sara Lee, in addressing family concerns, 74
Scandinavia
    selection practices in, 55–57
Scope of routines, 46–47
Second-order control mechanisms, 191
Selection, 52–83
    acceptance/refusal of assignments,
        69–70
    addressing family concerns in, 73–76
    best practices in, 259–264
    candidate evaluation in, 68
    common, 54–55
    comprehensive approach in, 77–83
    evaluating selection factors to increase
        success, 64–65
    as factor in cross-cultural adjustment,
        122, 123, 124
    factors predictive of expatriate
        success, 59–64
    impact of family on, 70–71
    integrating strategy into, 57–58
    in Japan, Europe, and Scandinavia,
        55–57
    as key to future success, 83; methods
        of, 65–68; for specific assign-
        ments, 79–83; systems approach
        to families in, 71–73; technical
        approach to, 53–54
Selection criteria, establishing, 81
Selection team, creating, 79–80
Self, in performance appraisals, 170
Self-oriented factors in cross-cultural ad-
    justment, 117
Site allowance in global compensation,
    183–184
Skill utilization, in postreturn repatriation
    adjustment, 217–218
Social skills, and expatriate success, 61–62
Social status, drop in, and postreturn repa-
    triation adjustment, 219–220
Social support, as factor in cross-cultural
    adjustment, 123, 126–127
Sponsor, role of, in repatriation, 272

Sponsors
    designating, in successful repatriation, 226
    in prereturn repatriation adjustment, 212–213
Spouses
    factors influencing cross-cultural adjustment by, 121–122
    repatriation adjustment by, 208, 221–223
    See also Families
Stability, and expatriate success, 63
Standardized tests, in selecting international candidates, 65–67, 82, 261–263
Strategic analysis of global assignments, 77–83
Strategic asset, retention of global managers as, 236–239
Strategic factors and expatriate success, 59–60
Strategic functions of repatriation, 223–224
Strategic roles of global assignments, 1–29
Strategic-systematic approach
    to international assignments, 257, 258
    to selection, 265
Strategic-systemic approach, to support, 274
Strategic value of global assignments, 2–9
Strategy orientation
    linking patterns of, to appraisal, 172–173
Subordinates in performance appraisals, 170, 171
Subsidiaries. *See* Foreign subsidiaries
Support groups, providing in successful repatriation, 232
Systems approach to families, 70–71

T
Tactical-reactive approach: to international assignment, 257, 258; to selection, 265; to support, 274
Tax allowance in global compensation, 189–190, 270
Tax equalization, 190
Tax protection, 189–190
Technology, and global assignments, 7–9, 53–54

Tenure, in the parent company as factor in retention, 240–241
Tests, in filling foreign assignments, 65–67, 82, 261–263
Theory X, 38
Theory Y, 38
3M: Human Resource Review at, 268–269
    value of global experience to, 248
Total international experience as factor in retention, 241–242
Training, 17–18, 20, 87–105
    and adaptation to new cultures, 88–92
    attention in, 90
    best practices in, 264–268
    and communication toughness, 95–97, 98–99
    cross-cultural, 268
    and cultural toughness, 94–95, 98
    designing cross-cultural, 92–98
    as factor in cross-cultural adjustment, 123, 124
    follow-up, 101
    framework for developing, 100–102
    high-rigor, 92–93
    in-country, 101, 264–266
    in-depth culture, 102
    and job toughness, 97–98, 99
    lack of repatriation, 219
Training *(continued)*
    language, 266–268
    linking corporate orientation to, 103–105
    low-rigor, 92; predeparture, 88–89, 101, 26
    repatriation, 226–227, 244
    retention in, 90–91
    the three-step learning process, 90–92
Transnational firm, 24
Transportation technology, 5
Turnover
    after repatriation, 14–15
    dysfunctional, 238–239
    functional, 239
Tylan Corp., 6
Tylan General, 6

U
Utility allowance in global compensation, 186, 199–200

V

Vacuum General, Inc., 6

W

Walt Disney Company, global selection program at, 54
Welch, Jack, 1, 2
WestCoast Bankcorp., 25–26
Work, cross-cultural adjustment to, 109
Workplace, changes in, for Japanese expatriates, 207

Work samples in selecting international candidates, 67
Worldvision International, staffing policies of, 259, 260, 264

X

Xerox, as global-strategy multinational corporation, 23